Death and the Maiden

Cover Illustration
Robert Sauber
(203) 792-5566
22 Rockwell Rd
BETHEL, CONNECTICUT 06801
rob@robertsauber.com
robertsauber.com

ISBN: 1-4800-4245-5
ISBN-13: 9781480042452

Death and the Maiden:

Living Feminine Transitions Through Fairy Tales

J. N. H. Perkins

2012

For

Sarah

Table of Contents

Also by J. N. H. Perkins

The Sacred Sinner
Life Lessons From the Medieval Legend of Pope Gregory

Rapture Alive
Living the Legend of the Holy Grail

Perceval
King Arthur's Knight of the Holy Grail

Introduction

In this book, we examine some of the traditional folk tales from different cultures of the world to see what they may teach us about the feminine psyche. Rather than imposing a preconceived interpretation on the tales, I discovered after reading them and re-reading them that they revealed an urgent and penetrating message about the state of feminine expression below the surface of our modern-day culture. It wasn't the message I expected, so come join me in exploring the psychological underpinnings of these seven tales, and see if you agree with the startling message and insight that they impart.

I have come to the conclusion that the ancient oral traditions of folklore (not private compositions by individuals) do not reflect the dominant cultural values of any group of people. Rather, such tales express a subculture that emerges from below the threshold of the prevailing civic awareness. For instance, it is possible to view a negative feminine figure, like the witch, in part as the reaction of elemental femininity to the psychological oppression of patriarchy. The characteristic disinterest or absence of the typical fairy tale father figure may be viewed as a compensation to the dictatorial paterfamilias. In other words, folk literature so often reveals what is really going on below the surface of the public consciousness.

Born from and confirmed by the earthy hearts and souls of the common folk, most folk literature is actually quite *opposed* to the reigning status quo. As Joseph Campbell reminded us many years ago, our myths are our public dreams. The purpose of these subversive commentaries is to correct the one-sided bias of collective cultural opinion, inside the psyche of the individual and within the value system of the wider society. In this sense, folk literature is, to a high degree, psychotherapeutic.

Some may think it is dated to speak of these matters nowadays in light of the progressive awakening of women's consciousness that has occurred since the 1960s. Women have come a long way from the stridency of those early days toward appreciating themselves as females who are equal to men but not the *same*. I think many have come to the wise conclusion that although gender and sex are related, they are certainly not the same. In this book, when I speak of femininity or the feminine, I am not addressing the equal rights of women in our common social sphere, but equal rights inside the subjective personality of each female and male human being. Men and women each contain the elements of the opposite sex psychologically, and it is precisely the creative interpenetration of these two gender partners within each person that leads to the wholeness of a fulfilled life. Women are women and men are men, but each has a subjective auxiliary companion that compensates, augments, and extends their dominant sexual identity.

Let us remember that the characters and events in a fairy tale are much more than their literal articulation. Beneath their objective reality are vast psychological truths that emerge when one looks "through a glass darkly" into the interior landscape of the human soul. One must avoid the mistake of assuming that the main character, for instance Snow White in the tale of the same name, is a didactic role model for women's external role in the culture.

She is far too opaque for that, and in addition, she is just a seven-year-old child, not a mature adult. Because this little girl is depicted with virtually no dynamic interiority, she is merely an archetypal component within a much larger system, as are all fairy-tale characters. Snow White is the rich femininity emerging from the unconscious psyche of both men and women, and in that sense, she may be seen to represent a fresh new approach to living as this change of attitude enters and transforms our traditional conforming consciousness. It is possible to appreciate Snow White as the innocence we have lost and that we need to regain in a more coherent form.

As we become familiar with folk literature the world over, we will realize that the typical humanity that the story describes is not captured by the main character at all, nor by any single one of the separate characters in the story. Rather, all of the individual personalities in a folk tale taken together portray the interior subliminal dynamics of the average citizen of the age in which the story itself circulated. All the people and situations in the drama are consequently a cross section of the typical human personality, which the tale expresses through the gestalt pattern of its constituent elements. They are like facets of an X-ray image, showing the various bones and organs in the anatomy of the body, or the atoms that make up that highly complex molecule: the human unconscious mind.

Postmodern critics tend to limit themselves by forcing a *denotational*, or external and literal, sociological truth upon folk literature, whereas I have come to understand these themes from an interior, *connotative* perspective, seeing the events and characters of each story as symbolic metaphors of the interior dynamics of the personality. There is little to be gained and much to be lost from assuming that these story elements address the actual cultural roles played by men or women in our common life. Taking a story literally is just as foolhardy as understanding our nocturnal dreams as if they were objective facts about other people in the surrounding world. In this sense, folk literature is pure metaphor, neither a lie nor a superstition nor an escapist fantasy.

Snow White, the wicked stepmother queen, the absent king, the seven dwarves, and the prince who arrives toward the end are not human beings at all, but together make up the "facts of the mind" of the typical personality of the age. If there is a message, and I believe there is, it is not the protagonist or antagonist alone that reveals it, but rather the story itself—the whole story! All of the characters live inside us. Every woman is as much the vain stepmother, or the kindly woodsman, or the prince in the end, as she is the innocent little girl who is born at the opening of the tale.

Most of our popular folk tales arose from Late Antiquity to the Renaissance periods of our history. But we shall see that they depict a development, anticipate our present dilemma, and offer hints regarding the challenges and possibilities that are in the process of being resolved within our contemporary lives.

On one level, we shall see that the tales point to the competence and wisdom inherent in the intrinsic femininity of womanhood, leaving behind both the notion that men and women are essentially the same, and that the traditional masculine way of assertion and dominance is the favored behavior for both sexes. Women as women are emerging from a condition of ideological inferiority, a secondary status that in some respects did not change all that much in the transition from patriarchy to the earliest efforts toward feminine emancipation. Now women may confidently experience the age-old feminine heritage of warmth, feeling, nurturing, devotion, and emotional intelligence, along with rational cognition and assertive purpose, without being submerged by certain chauvinistic, patriarchal conventions that haunt the chaotic cellars of their minds. A strong woman who is firmly anchored in an active and creative femininity can afford to be authentically receptive, patient, and tactful when she needs to pursue her own personal and professional interests. She may safely relate to and integrate her masculine abilities, which will then bring her to a full realization of her holistic personhood, not only alone, but in deep and genuine relation to others. In this way she will be a powerful force for change in our contemporary world. The emancipation of women is important, but just as imperative is the emancipation of femininity itself!

The primordial feminine underpinnings of life run the gamut from paralyzing castration and treacherous exploitation to magnificent innocence and disarming charm. As Joseph Campbell reminded us long ago, the feminine is from the left-hand side, that of the heart: mothering, seduction, tidal powers of the moon, and the substances of the body, the rhythms of the seasons, gestation, birth, nourishment, fosterage. But the feminine also embodies malice and revenge, irrationality, dark and terrible wrath, black magic, poisons, sorcery, and delusion. And yet, it also embodies fair enchantment, beauty, rapture, and bliss.

Welcome to the feminine! We shall meet all these terrifying and beguiling ladies during the course of our seven stories.

1
Little Snow White

First, let's take the whole tale, *Little Snow White*,[1] through from beginning to end, and then examine its various episodes piece by piece.

Long ago in mid-winter, when feathers of snow were falling from the sky, a queen sat quietly by a window sewing, and the frame of the window was made of ebony. But just as the queen glanced out toward the swirling white flakes, it happened that she pricked her finger with the needle, and three drops of blood stained the snow on the window ledge. The red looked so brilliant on the fresh white snow that the queen thought, *I wish I had a child, as white as snow, as red as blood, and as black as the dark wood of the window frame.*

Several months later the queen gave birth to a little girl. Her skin was as white as snow. Her blushed cheeks were as red as blood. And her hair was as black as ebony wood. And so the queen named her Snow White. But not long after the baby was born, the queen died.

A year later, the king married again. Although the new queen was very beautiful, she was pompous and conceited, and she despised anyone whose beauty surpassed her own. Now this stepmother queen had a miraculous looking glass, and when she stood before it and stared at her reflection and said, "Mirror, Mirror, on the wall, who in this land is the fairest of all?" the looking glass replied in a human voice, "Thou, oh Queen, art the fairest of all!" Then the proud stepmother was satisfied, because she knew that the mirror never, ever told a lie.

But Snow White was growing up. She was becoming more and more beautiful; and when she was seven years old, she was as beautiful as the day itself, and far more beautiful than the proud queen. So when the queen asked her looking glass, "Mirror, Mirror, on the wall, who in this land is the fairest of all?" it replied, "Thou art fairer than all who are here, Lady Queen. But more beautiful still is Snow White, as I ween.[2]" Then the queen turned yellow and green with envy, and whenever she saw Snow White, her heart swelled in her breast with hatred.

As time passed, jealousy and conceit sprouted taller and taller in the queen's heart like an ugly weed, so that she was restless day and night. Finally, the queen called her huntsman and exclaimed, "Take that girl away into the deepest part of the wood. I can't bear to see her any longer! Kill her and bring back her lungs and liver as proof!" The huntsman obeyed the queen and took Snow White away; but when he had pulled out his knife, and was ready to stab Snow White's innocent heart, the little girl cried, "Oh, my dear huntsman, let me keep my life! I'll run further away into the dark wood, and never come back again."

And because she was so beautiful, the huntsman took pity on Snow White and said, "Run away, then, you poor thing." *The wild animals will soon eat you*, he thought, and yet it seemed to him like a stone had been lifted from his heart because he no longer had to kill the girl. Just then, a young boar came rushing past. He stabbed it with his knife, cut out *its* lungs and liver instead, and carried them back to the queen. The cook was told to salt them, and then the wicked queen sat down in her great hall and ate them for dinner, believing that she had eaten the lungs and liver of little Snow White.

The poor child was now all alone in the dark wood, and so frightened that she looked at the leaves on every tree and didn't know where to turn. Then she started running, and she ran over sharp stones and through thickets of thorns, and the wild animals ran by her, but she came to no harm.

Snow White ran as long as her feet would last, until nightfall. Then she saw a little cottage, went up to it, opened the door, and stepped inside to rest. Everything inside the cottage was tiny, but very neat and very clean, with everything in its place. There was a table, and on it was a white cloth, and seven tiny plates, and resting upon each plate was a tiny spoon. There were also seven tiny knives and forks, and seven tiny mugs. Along the wall stood seven tiny beds in a row, and each one was covered by a snow-white quilt.

Little Snow White was so hungry that she ate some of the vegetables and bread from each tiny plate and drank a drop of wine from each tiny mug, since she did not want to eat everything from one place alone. Then, because she was tired, she lay down on one of the little beds, but neither that one nor the next suited her. Each was either too long or too short, but at last she came to the seventh bed and she found that it was just right. So she stayed in it, said her prayers, and then fell fast asleep.

When it was quite dark, the owners of the cottage came back. They were seven dwarves who quarried in the mountains, searching for ore. The dwarves lit their seven candles, and because the cottage was now full of light, they saw that someone had been there, for nothing was in quite the same order as it had been when they had left the cottage that morning.

The first said: "Who has been sitting in my chair?"
The second: "Who has been eating off my plate?"
The third: "Who has been taking some of my bread?"
The fourth: "Who has been eating my vegetables?"
The fifth: "Who has been using my fork?"
The sixth: "Who has been cutting with my knife?"
The seventh: "Who has been drinking out of my mug?"

When the first dwarf looked around and saw that there was a little hollow on his bed, he said, "Who has been getting into my bed?" The other dwarves came up and each cried out, "Somebody has been sleeping in my bed too." But when the seventh dwarf looked at his bed, he spied little Snow White, who was lying in it asleep. He called the other dwarves, who came running over, and they chattered in astonishment and brought their seven little candles and let the light shine on Snow White. "Oh, heavens above! Oh, heavens above!" they cried. "What a lovely child!" Because they were so glad, they did not wake her, but allowed her to sleep soundly in the bed. The seventh dwarf slept with his companions, one hour with each one of them, and so he spent the night.

In the morning, little Snow White woke up and was frightened when she saw the seven dwarves. But they were very friendly and asked her what her name was. "My name is

Snow White," she answered. "How did you find our house?" asked the dwarves. Then she explained that her stepmother had tried to kill her, but that a huntsman had spared her, and that she had then run all day long until she discovered their cottage. The dwarves said, "If you will take care of our cottage, cook, make the beds, do the washing, sew and knit, and if you promise to keep everything neat and clean, you can stay with us, and you will have everything you need." "Yes," said Snow White, "I will with all my heart," and she remained with them. She kept order in the house, and in the mornings the dwarves went out into the mountains and searched for copper and gold. At night, they came back, and by that time their supper had to be ready. The girl was all alone during the long days, so the good dwarves gave her a warning and said, "Beware of your proud stepmother. Before long she will discover that you are here, so make sure you don't let anyone inside."

But the queen, who thought that she had eaten Snow White's lungs and liver, was sure that she was once again the most beautiful of all; and so, she went to her magic looking glass and said, "Mirror, Mirror on the wall, who in this land is the fairest of all?" And the looking glass answered, "Oh, Queen, thou art fairest of all I see, but over the mountains, where the seven dwarves dwell, Snow White is still alive and well, and none is so fair as she." Then the queen was stunned and amazed because the looking glass never, ever lied, and so she knew that the huntsman had disobeyed her, and that little Snow White was still alive.

The queen thought more and more about how she might kill her fair stepdaughter, for as long as the queen was not the most beautiful woman in the whole kingdom, jealousy kept her from even a moment's rest. At last the queen thought of a way to carry out her plan. She made up her face and dressed herself to look like an old peddler woman, so that nobody would know who she really was. In this disguise she traveled over the seven mountains to the seven dwarves' cottage and knocked on their door and shouted, "Pretty things to sell, very cheap, very cheap." Little Snow White looked out the window and cried, "Good day, my good woman, what have you got to sell?" "Good things, pretty things," replied the old woman. "Stay-laces of many colors," and she pulled out one of them which was made of bright-colored silk. *I may let the harmless old woman in*, Snow White thought, and she bought the pretty laces. "Child," said the old woman, "how awful you look; come, I will lace you the right way for once." Snow White didn't suspect anything, but stood in front of the old woman and let herself be laced with the new laces. But the old woman laced so quickly and so tightly that Snow White couldn't breathe, and she fell down and looked dead. "Now I am the most beautiful," murmured the proud queen to herself, and she ran away.

When the dwarves came home and found Snow White lifeless, they examined her carefully, and when they loosened the stay-laces, Snow White began to breathe once more and woke up. The dwarves warned her a second time never to let anyone into the cottage while they were at work in the mountains. But the proud stepmother, after consulting her looking glass, knew that her attempt to kill Snow White had failed yet again, so this time, employing a secret magic craft, she contrived a comb filled with poison and made herself up in a different way and returned as before. After at first hesitating, Snow White let the peddler woman in and allowed her to comb her hair. But as soon as the comb touched her hair, Snow White fell down dead. When the dwarves came home, they found her lying senselessly on the floor. Examining her again and searching thoroughly, they at last saw the comb, and when they removed it, Snow White woke up. This time the dwarves warned her even more strongly not to allow anyone into the cottage while they were away during the day.

After attempting to kill Snow White, first with the stay laces and then with the poisoned comb, the queen again consulted her looking glass. When she was told that Snow White was yet still alive, the queen trembled and shook with rage. Then she went into a very lonely room in a closed-off section of the castle—a place where no one ever went. There, using conjuring and witchcraft, the proud step-mother contrived a poisoned apple, white with a red cheek, that looked so pretty that anyone seeing it would be seized with a great desire to taste it. Afterward, she made herself up to look like a farmer's wife and traveled over the seven mountains to the cottage of the seven dwarves. When she knocked, Snow White put her head out the window and said she was forbidden to let anyone in. Then the queen offered to give her an apple, but Snow White refused. So the queen said, "What? Are you afraid of poison? Look, I shall eat one half myself and you may have the other." She cut the apple in two and said to Snow White, "Here, you may have the red cheek and I shall eat the white." Now the apple was so cleverly constructed that only the red cheek was poisoned. When Snow White saw the old woman eat her half, she could resist no more. She reached out and took the red half. But the second she got a bite of the apple in her mouth, she fell down dead. Then the queen, with a terrible look on her face, crowed with delight, "White as snow, red as blood, black as ebony wood! This time the dwarves will not wake you again." As soon as the queen had reached home, she once more consulted her looking glass and it answered, "Oh, Queen, in this land thou art the fairest of all."

When the dwarves came home in the evening, they found Snow White lying on the ground. She was breathing no more and was dead. They lifted her up, unlaced her, looked to see if they could find anything poisonous, combed her hair, and washed her with water and wine, but it was no use. The poor child was dead and remained dead. They laid her upon a bier, and all seven of them sat around it and wept for her, and they wept for three days.

They were going to bury her, but she looked as if she were living and still had her pretty red cheeks. They said, "We could not bury her in the dark ground," and they had a transparent coffin of glass made, so that she could be seen from all sides, and they laid her in it and wrote her name on it in gold letters, and they added that she was a king's daughter. Then they put the coffin out upon the mountain, and one of them always stayed with it, standing watch. And birds came, too, and wept for Snow White: first an owl, then a raven, and last a dove.

Snow White lay a long, long time in the coffin, and she did not change, but looked as if she were asleep, for she was as white as snow, as red as blood, and her hair was as black as ebony.

It happened, however, that a king's son came into the forest and went to the dwarves' house to spend the night. He saw the coffin on the mountain, and the beautiful Snow White within it, and he read what was written upon the cover in golden letters, that she was a king's daughter. Then he said to the dwarves, "Let me have the coffin; I will give you whatever you want for it." But the dwarves answered, "We will not part with it for all the gold in the world." Then the prince said, "Let me have it as a gift, for I cannot live without seeing Snow White. I will honor and prize her as my dearest possession." Since he spoke in this way, the good dwarves took pity on him and gave him the coffin.

The king's son had his servants carry it away on their shoulders. It happened that they stumbled over a tree stump, and the shock jolted the coffin so much that the poisonous piece of apple came bursting out of Snow White's throat; and before long, she opened her eyes, lifted up the lid of the coffin, sat up, and was once more alive. "Oh, heavens, where am I?" she cried. The king's son, full of joy, said: "You are with me," and he told her what had happened. Then he said, "I love you more than everything in the world. Come with me to my father's palace, and you shall be my wife." And Snow White was willing, and went with him, and their wedding was held with great show and splendor.

Snow White's wicked stepmother was also invited to the marriage feast. After she dressed herself in beautiful clothes, she stood before the looking glass, and said, "Mirror, Mirror, on the wall, who is the fairest of all?" The looking glass answered, "Oh, Queen, of all who are here, the fairest art thou, but the young queen is fairer by far as I trow."

Then the wicked woman uttered a curse and was so wretched, so utterly wretched and frightened, that she knew not what to do. At first, she would not go to the wedding at all, but she had no peace, and could not resist the urge to see the new young queen. And when she entered the great hall of the palace and recognized Snow White, she stood frozen with rage and fear, and could not move. But iron slippers had already been put over the fire, and they were carried in with tongs, and were set before the proud step-mother. Then the royal footmen forced her to put on the red-hot shoes, and made her dance in them until she fell down dead.

1

Long ago in mid-winter, when feathers of snow were falling from the sky, a queen sat quietly by a window sewing, and the frame of the window was made of ebony. But just as the queen glanced out toward the swirling white flakes, it happened that she pricked her finger with the needle, and three drops of blood stained the snow on the window ledge. The red looked so brilliant on the fresh white snow that the queen thought, I wish I had a child, as white as snow, as red as blood, and as black as the dark wood of this window frame.

Several months later the queen gave birth to a little girl. Her skin was as white as snow. Her blushed cheeks were as red as blood. And her hair was as black as ebony wood. And so the queen named her Snow White. But not long after the baby was born, the queen died.

Here we have just the opening scene of this beloved Grimm's tale. The original story was recited with the greatest care by two sisters, Jeanette and Amalie Hassenpflug, in the village of Bokendorf, near Brakel, Germany, in the early part of the nineteenth century. As Jacob and Wilhelm Grimm listened intently and transcribed the tale precisely word for word, they were aware that such storytellers were intelligent folk whose hearts and minds were still swimming in an ancient stream of oral literature, the fountainhead of which had bubbled forth hundreds, or perhaps even thousands, of years before out of subterranean pools. They realized also that they were setting these stories down on paper for the very first time in history.

Although these academic philologists made many subsequent adjustments to their collection of tales—in later editions involving a certain censorship for the sake of what was deemed appropriate for children—it would be a mistake to think that they modified them so pervasively as to lose the essential folkloristic message that had been passed down through such a rich tradition of oral literature. There is more to these tales than patriarchal, cultural indoctrination alone, and if anything, taken as a whole, their "grimm" messages seem quite countercultural. Much can be said for Bruno Bettleheim's views on this subject, even if he was somewhat narrow in his Freudian preoccupation with so-called *Oedipal* issues.

Such occasions of hearing a tale told from vast societal memory, seeming to emerge from somewhere deep within the storytellers themselves, rather than read outwardly from the written page as we do today, must have been mesmerizing. To the little cluster of peasant folk gathered around a fire in a farmhouse kitchen or in a local tavern, listening to a story was not simply an amusing entertainment! It was a deep and poignant meditation that opened a door to yet another layer of reality. The tale's images and plots passed through the audience like bolts of lightning. These powerful currents gripped the souls of the listeners so intensely that they were lifted out of their everyday, matter-of-fact lives and transported to another realm: a golden kingdom seething with treachery and violence, yet also graced with mystery, awe, rapture, and overwhelming beauty. Not

J. N. H. Perkins

unlike their miraculous experience of the Catholic or Lutheran Mass, these enraptured folk were nourished and transformed, as they were carried outside of earthly time and space to another plane of exalted awareness. The uneducated peasant population drank deeply from these refreshing waters, sensing an uncanny yet sublime truth about life, hidden away from the shallowness of ordinary mortal experience.

As the common folk listened intently to the story of Snow White, they were privileged to sit near the queen herself and gaze with her through the same darkly framed window at the gently falling snow. They could join her in watching the endless curtain of white descending silently from the heavens. Intimately familiar with all the typical domestic arts, such as spinning and weaving and sewing, they could intuit that simple repetitive tasks tend to set the imagination free.

The twisting strands of flax or wool stream through the guiding fingers around the spindle. The shuttle clicks back and forth on the loom, to and fro. The needle goes in and out, through and around. It all happens over and over, again and again, like the rosary beads slipping one by one through devoted fingers. Just as the fingers spin the threads or weave or sew the clothing together, the mind is doing another kind of handiwork. Today, one could say that the rhythmic routines of walking, peddling a bicycle, building a fence, digging a trench in the garden, washing dishes, vacuuming the carpets, painting the house, ploughing the field or mowing the lawn, release ideas and thoughts unrelated to the task at hand, as it lets the mind survey the mysterious possibilities of life that exist far beyond commonplace reality.

Gazing out the window at the falling snow, the queen of our present tale falls into a reverie. Seemingly by accident, she pricks her finger with the sewing needle and three drops of blood fall upon the snow. This suggests that the queen has become vulnerable to a certain thread of thought, a spiritual impulse that has struck her sharply and become manifest in the three drops of blood.

Long ago, before modern science, people commonly held the mythic view that the rain or snow falling from heaven was simply the creative insemination of Mother Earth by Father Sky God. This is a very old idea that, in one form or another, pervades most of the cultures of the world. So, we might say that in the queen's meandering daydream, she suddenly encounters an inseminating or creative idea, a kind of spark that comes to her from beyond her normal personal awareness.

Here we see that the beauty of the scarlet red upon the fresh white snow brings on the queen's prayer-wish for a child. And so, with the stream of the imagination comes the poignancy of an urgent idea.

There is such a thing as an impregnation of the mind or the heart. This is a creative or spiritual phenomenon known to certain people. In academia it is commonly termed a "seminal thought," one that leads to a new departure or point of view in one's chosen field of study. We are also familiar with the age-old iconography of romantic love, where Cupid's little arrows strike the hearts of a man and woman, who then become helpless lovers.

A new, life-creating wisdom comes from afar and, entering in, begins something new in the course of our human nature. And here, as Rick Blaine remarks in the emotion-filled climax of the cult film *Casablanca,* "It seems that destiny has taken a hand." For destiny, or providence, as we all know, is not simply what I want or crave to do, but that which is planned or foreseen by the higher powers of life, which are calling into existence things that do not yet exist. And it is only our wildest imagination that can glean even the slightest hint of such matters as these.

With the sight of the fresh blood on the snow, the queen longs for a child with beautiful features matching the colors of the white snow, the red blood, and the black window frame. This child will be an incarnation, or enfleshment, of the queen's contemplation of the natural scene before her, darkly framed by the window. And like the snow, this child, in a sense, will come from the heavens above. Because she is a new life that issues from the beyond—from the unconscious mind of humanity—this girl child is not a product of the standard cultural system, but a new departure, a fresh take on the living of life—one that embodies the voraciousness of "red-blooded" humanity.

And what about the father of this child? It is interesting to note that there is no mention yet of a king, so one could say that the child seems to have no earthly father. Instead, Snow White's "father" seems to reside somewhere in the Kingdom above. The queen, through imagination—through a process of undirected and unapplied thought—received this life from the falling feathers of snow, and put her stamp upon it with her own blood.

Feathers appear in many folk tales, and their symbolism is similar to that in "Snow White." In "Mother Holle" (Grimm's No. 24), a beautiful and decent girl is mistreated and turned into a miserable drudge-servant by her cruel stepmother. Compelled to spin relentlessly, she bloodies her fingers, and in attempting to wash them, she loses the spindle down the well. Forced to retrieve it, she falls head-first into the spring-water and awakens to find herself in an extraordinary new world where she is taken into the house of a kindly old crone named Mother Holle, a strange woman with frighteningly big teeth! In exchange for safe lodging, the girl agrees to do her share of housework. Instructing her, Mother Holle says, " ... dear child ... you must take care to make my bed well, and to shake it thoroughly until the feathers fly, for then there is snow on the earth." Here, it seems that the forlorn little girl has fallen down a well-spring into an underground heaven, an inverse image of the usual cosmic setup.

The opening scene of the film *Forrest Gump* includes a similar theme. Gump, a simple soul, is seated quietly at a bus stop. As the superimposed credits roll up, we see a feather in the sky sailing to and fro on the breeze until it finally descends to the ground at Gump's feet. Gump, initially considered an embarrassing retard, in his very innocence throughout the rest of the film shows that he has an impressive wisdom and heart-warming devotion, of which we sophisticates are sadly incapable. When feathers in the air appear, they generally signify that an astonishing person of good fortune, a heroine or hero, a new attitude of living, is being selected out by the higher powers, who are working invisibly in the background.

2

When little Snow White was born, the queen died. Why did the birth mother die just when her daughter was born? Why was this necessary and what does it mean?

J. N. H. Perkins

The absence of a parent is, for a child, a mixed blessing. In such a circumstance, there is no cultural model for the development and behavior of the growing youngster. A boy without a father has more trouble knowing what it is like to be a man. A girl without a mother is unsure of what womanhood is. This becomes a major challenge in the child's life, even a handicap. As Snow White grows up, she is not guided into the standard patterns and behavior of womanhood, because she has no domestic or cultural model which she can follow. There is a hole in her personality that would normally be filled by the image and example of her mother. And to this we should add that there is something unusual about her actual parentage on the father's side as well. Snow White seems to have been fathered, not by any human being, but by the sky god from whom the snowflakes descended. The queen's husband, the king, is a relative outsider, like Mary's husband Joseph in the Biblical episode when Jesus is born. Snow White's mortal father is mentioned only once: when he chooses a second wife. After that we hear nothing more about him. Like some fathers today, he is absent from the family. But his absence is critical. As in many such tales, the father makes no effort to protect his daughter or ensure her livelihood. Instead, he abandons Snow White to her fate. In the end, however, her father's disinterest is part of a providential plan to set in place the twisting course of Snow White's destiny, a fate that, we shall see later, involves risk and uncertainty. Invariably, it is always a hero or a heroine, usually of royal blood, who is so miraculously engendered. This is because royal persons, as in ancient Egypt and Mesopotamia, were considered to be gods rather than mere humans. Consequently, in a psychological sense they represented emerging truths and new keys to living beyond constructed cultural norms.

The earliest Sumerian kings (3500 BCE in the vicinity of modern southern Iraq) were believed to be the moon gods on earth, while their female consorts were considered earthly incarnations of the planet Venus ("on earth as it is in heaven")—thus the star and crescent icons seen on flags and emblems in the Near East to this very day. Such a notion of divine kingship, if taken literally, is a ridiculous idea in our modern times. But psychologically and spiritually, it conveys a profound symbolic wisdom that opens us to a larger scope of life than that afforded by our common collective mentality. Somewhere deep within the soul of every one of us is a royal and divine person, a king or a queen. That is our prototypical or transpersonal self. It is from this region that our souls hear the poetry and the music of the heavenly spheres, which play a haunting counterpoint to our prosaic existence in the hard-fact secular world.

Snow White also grows up to be incredibly beautiful. It is the clear and innocent beauty of life that is possible when people and cultures and institutions do not imprison it, abuse it, or kill it. We see touches of this in certain young children, who, in their fresh unselfconsciousness, imagination, and spontaneity, and before they are too well programmed by the sophistication of the culture, give us so much delight. In their angel faces[3] one catches a glowing current that runs through us all. It has little to do with actual physical good looks.

Nevertheless, as beauty seems to be one of Snow White's major characteristics, and because beauty itself is the fulcrum for the entire story, we need to understand more fully what this word means. The words "beauty," "fair," and "pretty" have a common root meaning that suggests something different from an alluring face and figure. The

17

English word, for instance, indicates a harmony of form, color, truthfulness or originality. Scientists and mathematicians use the word "beauty" to describe a unique theoretical or conceptual model that is impressively helpful or enlightening. Beauty is associated with the Greek word *cosmos*, from which we get our word "cosmetic." *Cosmos* denotes not lipstick, nail polish, eyeliner, and mascara, but the quality of symmetrical order in contrast to chaos. In the English translation of the Grimm's, the word "fair" is a direct translation of the German word *fegen*, which means literally to clean or sweep, in the sense of tidying or spiffing up, "putting things aright," as the expression goes.

The image of Lady Life that our little girl represents, therefore, is not necessarily restricted to the vanity table or the beauty parlor. There is far more to Snow White than what we normally conceive of as beauty. Snow White's comeliness suggests an order, an innate intelligence, and a clearheadedness of the female mind, rather than outward pulchritude. Snow White refers to life and how it is lived, to beauty in a larger holistic sense, not to the sensual body alone.

A year later, the king married again. Although the new queen was very beautiful, she was pompous and conceited, and she despised anyone whose beauty surpassed her own. Now this stepmother queen had a miraculous looking glass, and when she stood before it and stared at her reflection, and said, "Mirror, Mirror, on the wall, who in this land is the fairest of all?" the looking glass replied in a human voice, "Thou, Oh Queen, art the fairest of all!" Then the proud stepmother was satisfied, because she knew that the mirror never, ever told a lie.

But Snow White was growing up. She was becoming more and more beautiful; and when she was seven years old, she was as beautiful as the day itself, and far more beautiful than the proud queen. So when the queen asked her looking glass, "Mirror, Mirror, on the wall, who in this land is the fairest of all?" it replied, "Thou art fairer than all who are here, Lady Queen. But more beautiful still is Snow White, as I ween.[4]" Then the queen turned yellow and green with envy, and whenever she saw Snow White, her heart swelled in her breast with hatred.

The original queen dies in order to make room for something absolutely new and unique that is not hampered by conventional mother-culture. But before you know it, a stepmother appears, a new paragon of virtue—a narcissistic, self-idolizing egotist. On one level she represents the self-involved and rigid forms of the conventional female culture, which will do anything and everything to stop the emergence of a fresh new vision of life, represented by Snow White.

Stepmothers are ubiquitous in folk literature. The tales examined in this book all have stepmothers or stepmother-type figures who are adversaries to the young heroine. They arrive on the scene as the second wives of fathers, or appear outside the family as malevolent witches, or occasionally as other mean, selfish, or nosy women in the heroine's extended family. Invariably, there is a good mother somewhere in the story who counterbalances the character of the negative feminine figure. In nearly every case, a father or husband is portrayed as absent, distracted, or otherwise oblivious to the plight of the young female protagonist. One may see the absent father as a symbol of the patriarchal values of the contemporary culture that neither understands nor appreciates the worth of such a new development.

We may glean more psychological value from these negative mothers if we can avoid taking the story only in an exterior manner and instead see it from the interior psychology of the child. From a girl's perspective, her natural mother often functions as a stepmother. This does not mean that the birth mother is necessarily a cruel, heartless, or abusive person, although such women certainly do exist. It is just that that there is frequently a glaring difference between what the mother thinks is best for her daughter and the girl's intrinsic character, talents, interests, and abilities. Those who have much experience with children realize that unique, individual traits appear quite early in life, well before the school years.

Many parents wish to create their children in their own image and raise them in accordance with their personal notions of success and fulfillment. This programming is risky and usually counterproductive. Most young people will react to this conflict in one of two ways. They will openly rebel against the parents and swing to the contrary extreme—sometimes absurdly: the daughter of a liberal college professor may choose to join a narrow-minded cult; the daughter of an esteemed surgeon may become a go-go dancer in a strip club. I have actually encountered such defiant young women. On the other hand, the child might succumb to the pressure to conform, adopt the parents' values as her own, and in place of open revolt, fall into painful conflict inside herself. In both instances, however, she will end up submitting to her parents' indoctrination: first, in a negative, reactive manner—doing the opposite; or secondly, in a positive, conforming way by joining the enemy—doing the same. In neither case is justice done to her own unique temperament as a human being. The counselors who talk with teenagers and young adults get their fill of such tensions and complaints.

More enlightened parents refuse to play God to their kids. They progressively encourage them to think for themselves, to start forming their own perspective on life, and to learn to make astute choices. Such nurturing must be tailor-made according to each stage of a child's psychological development, in light of his or her abilities—not too early and not too late. In this manner, young adults will become individuals, developing interests and considering options that agree with their own genuine aptitudes and personality types.

It is the "stepmother" inside the young person that connives against the child's best interests. This usually appears as a bad conscience that gnaws inside like a rat at midnight, instilling relentless doubt, rather than a good conscience that supports independent, creative, and realistic decision-making. The negative mom within whispers, "Mother knows best. Don't follow your own impulses, for this will only hurt both of you. Imitate her and please her. This will make her happy and then she will love you more and think you are a better person." In short, the witchy stepmother is mom's influence *as far as the daughter's own temperament is concerned.*

But what about the positive mom, the real mom inside the child? That is the voice that says, "I love you; I understand you; I honor you; I respect you. I will be your guardian angel on your unique journey. You are in the driver's seat of your own life and I am here to help you with the navigation whenever you need me, but it's up to you."

J. N. H. Perkins

The stepmother represents an arrogance and insecurity within all of us that refuses to change, is threatened by change, loathes and despises change, and will do anything that is necessary to thwart any new development. As one of the pioneering psychiatrists of the last century remarked, "When a new development is in the works, one may be sure that the demons will come from all points of the compass to try to stop it."[5] His lively characterization referred to a patient's resistance to psychotherapy, but the metaphor applies equally to the broader scope of cultural development in our history, including a penchant to cling to the past and what feels safe when a threatening change is on the horizon.

The demon of our present tale, the evil stepmother, was ushered in by the king himself. We could say that this man, in his unrealistic infatuation with the woman who became his second wife, was seduced by the charms of Aphrodite. In the story, he is either completely absent or passive; he does nothing whatsoever to look after the interests of his own daughter after the death of his first wife, as he succumbs to the manipulative beauty and seduction of wife number two.

Wife number two, as we have mentioned before, is a pre-eminent narcissist, just as many parents are today. Parents, when raising a child to fulfill all their own dreams and aspirations, have little understanding or appreciation of the child itself. Instead, the son or daughter is viewed simply as a reflection of the parent. If the child succeeds, this accomplishment is viewed as the parents' own success and they are filled with pride. If the child fails, it is the parents' failure and they are despondent, admonishing the child for being a disappointment because he or she didn't live up to their expectations. Such parents may sincerely think their motivations are for their child's own good, but often, it is really their own self interest which is behind it all. Here, there are no boundaries between parent and child. Neither party has any idea of his own identity and personality apart from the other. Later in life, many psychological difficulties arise because of this kind of blurring of perimeters between parents and children. Such parents abandon their children even as they remain dutiful providers and genuinely believe they love their kids. But their love is a self-love that never really extends beyond their own private hall of mirrors.

When the mirror tells the proud queen that Snow White is the fairest of all, objective attention is shifting from the queen to the stepdaughter. The narcissist cannot endure such a recognition of the other person. It is an impossibility, something that simply cannot be acknowledged or tolerated. The only reaction to such a focus on the other person is envy, anxiety, angry resentment, and fear of self-oblivion, for the narcissist has no self of her own.

3

As time passed, jealousy and conceit sprouted taller and taller in the queen's heart like an ugly weed, so that she was restless day and night. Finally, the queen called her huntsman and exclaimed, "Take that girl away into the deepest part of the wood. I can't bear to see her any longer! Kill her and bring back her lungs and liver as proof!" The huntsman obeyed the queen and took Snow White away; but when he had pulled out his knife, and was ready to stab Snow White's innocent heart, the little girl cried, "Oh, my dear huntsman, let me keep my life! I'll run further away into the dark wood, and never come back again."

And because she was so beautiful, the huntsman took pity on Snow White and said, "Run away, then, you poor thing." "The wild animals will soon eat you," he thought, and yet it seemed to him like a stone had been lifted from his heart because he no longer had to kill the girl. Just then, a young boar came rushing past. He stabbed it with his knife, cut out its lungs and liver, and carried them back to the queen. The cook was told to salt them, and then the wicked queen sat down in her great hall and ate them for dinner, believing that she had eaten the lungs and liver of little Snow White.

The selfish stepmother decides to rid herself of little Snow White once and for all! In some ways, it is amusing to read this part of the tale because we so often think that denial or banishing something from our minds gets rid of it. Not so! To extradite or kill off something is only to repress it into the unconscious. There, an idea or a feeling continues to fester beneath the shallow field of our biased awareness. Our whole self encompasses far more than the range of those things we think we know. All of the fullness of life lies within us, and ultimately we are compelled to deal with the whole spectrum of it, both in the conscious and the unconscious. In the language of folklore, to put something or someone into the dark forest is to reject them into the twilight regions of the psyche, to the dark, uncultivated, raw nature within us. But those matters that need recognition or development inside of us cannot be stopped so easily. They have far deeper roots that are fed by powerful energies from our hidden depths. Their existence is part of the overall flow of life arranged by the higher powers, so if we attempt to block them, their rich growth will persist in secret, unbeknownst to the prideful, self-aggrandizing ME. From there, they will cause plenty of trouble as they seek validation and fulfillment, even if they must ruin our habitual lives in order to do so! In this manner, their overall effect is to cause bewildering complications and frustrations; and this is precisely as it should be, because the tyrannical lordship of *me, myself, and I* finally must be unseated if our lives are to become whole and healthy. Our psychological troubles are often the very healing solutions that we insist upon rejecting. If we reject heaven, we get the consolation prize, which is hell! There is nothing much in between.

There are certain unusual places in the world where a stream of water flows placidly through the countryside and then suddenly disappears into an underground cavern, where its course continues, hidden from view. Only many miles later and far downstream does the river surface again into the clear light of day. Snow White is that current of life that her stepmother so detests. As the tale unfolds, we will see that nothing and no one can stop her from reaching her ultimate destination.

The vain queen uses beauty and sexual allure to manipulate. But as we all know, true love and beauty are incompatible with egotistical power motives. Where there is absolute power, love is absent. Where love exists, raw power cannot be. For power is invariably to use and abuse another person or a God-given talent for selfish ends. In this sense, the queen is the dominant attitude in consciousness that makes self-centered magnificence the highest value, so that love, innocence, and vulnerability are consumed by strident exploitation. We employ the modern lingo for this disposition when we remark that somebody is "on a power trip." However, there appears to be a moral tendency built into the human psyche. This is not a sense of ethics or fairness that is socially constructed by human will alone. Somewhere, there is an inner law that says that if power and self-importance go far enough to the extreme, then a correction is likely to occur—namely, the tables will turn on the culprit sooner or later. It is some kind of primal justice deep in the human personality that is beyond all manipulations. In medieval times it was commonly called "the wheel of fortune," where eventually, the highest became the lowest, and the lowest, the highest.

There is a most intriguing tale, also in the Grimm's collection, entitled "The Devil with the Three Golden Hairs" (No. 29), that perfectly illustrates this principle. Here we see an analogous theme of irrepressible achievement on the part of an innocent young hero who is contending with a tyrant. A simple peasant boy is born heralded by an omen proclaiming that he is a Child of Good Fortune who will grow up to marry the king's daughter. The king, traveling nearby, gets wind of this and, deeply troubled by such a prospect, tries to do away with this boy. He pretends to be friendly and gives the youth a sealed letter which is ostensibly a document approving of the marriage. But actually, it is an order of execution, commanding the queen to have the boy killed as soon as he arrives. On his long trek to the palace, the Child of Good Fortune gets lost in the forest and ends up in a den of robbers. While the boy is sleeping, the robbers open the letter, read the contents, and then, taking a kindly interest in the boy's welfare, exchange the original letter for another. The new letter commands the queen to have the boy married to the king's daughter immediately upon his arrival!

The robbers have completely turned the tables on the selfish old king, and it will soon become obvious that a similar phenomenon is occurring in our tale of Snow White. When we are on the wrong side of fortune, opposing the flow of life within ourselves, then predictably we will suffer frustration and opposition, ensuring the failure of our wrong-headed plans.

Filled with compassion for the little seven-year-old girl, the huntsman spares her life and kills a wild boar instead, substituting its lungs and liver for Snow White's.

The wild boar traditionally has symbolized ferocity and immorality in many old myths. In the old days, swine seemed particularly adept at gratifying themselves through gluttonous eating and copulating. In Near Eastern and Roman antiquity, the sow was a fertility symbol, associated with the mother-earth goddesses. Pigs were typically sacrificed to Demeter in the rituals of antiquity. For this reason, and not because of the disease called trichinosis, pork was considered unclean and therefore forbidden by the food laws of Jews and Muslims, who were militantly patriarchal, and who, like the Christians, viewed the old earth-mother cults as evil abominations. Because the pig, like the hippopotamus, is fatter than many other animals, its corpulence suggested continuous pregnancy, which accentuated the pig's tie to fecundity.

The wicked stepmother wanted the lungs and liver of Snow White. In the science and psychology of the ancient world, the mind was not identified with the head, as it is today. Rather, the lungs, with the diaphragm, together called the *phrenes*, were considered the seat of thought. The Greek poet Homer, for instance, likened the finely articulated branches and intricate tracery of the lungs to the delicate quality and complexity of the mind. In classical times, mental thought was supposed to occur somewhere in the chest, within the cardio-respiratory region, not in the head!

27

J. N. H. Perkins

The liver, on the other hand, was believed to be the seat of the soul and the emotional center of the body, from which spring the deepest feelings and passions.

An Irish tale, collected from Gaelic-Celtic oral tradition as recently as 1935 by Séamus Ó Duilearga, depicts an ancient hero named Ceatach, son of King Cor, who, in a succession of battles with mythic challengers, had his lungs and liver torn out by the Great Cat of the Cave. The Great Cat hung Caetach's organs as trophies on the wall of the cave. Somehow Caetach survived long enough to kill the monstrous beast before he himself died. Finding both Caetach and the Cat dead, his wife and warrior companions brought him back to life with a magic salve, but by mistake they gave Caetach the lungs and liver of the cat instead of his own. He awakened strong and fit, yet with a peculiarly fierce look in his eyes. On the way home when a rat crossed their path, Caetach chased the rat, and Caetach's supporters then realized their mistake. Returning to the Great Cat of the Cave's lair, they replaced the feline organs with Caetach's own, administered the healing balm again, and the strong hero regained his normal personality.

Many Native American practices involved the eating of the internal organs of a captured enemy hero, in order to assimilate his mana or spiritual force. This is the significance of most cannibalistic practices in traditional cultures around the world. According to this logic, you become precisely what you eat. In the higher religions, such a rite develops into a form of holy communion with a divine person, whose body and blood are symbolically consumed in a ritual meal.

In the ancient Egyptian embalming rituals, the internal organs of the deceased king and other royal and noble persons were removed and interred separately in four clay vases called "canopic jars." It was believed that when resurrection occurred, these organs would be reunited with the body of the revived individual. The vital determinates of psychological temperament, later considered the four *humors,* blood (sanguine—lively), yellow bile (choleric—hot tempered), phlegm (phlegmatic—apathetic) and black bile (melancholic—depressed), were identified with these internal organs.

In the Snow White tale, it is plain that the evil stepmother's intention to cannibalize the little girl's organs represents an attempt at psychological digestion and incorporation. What we have here is a possessive mother attempting to devour the mental and affective substance of her daughter. The evil queen wants to seize, internalize, and then identify with the very essence of Snow White. She will tolerate absolutely no competition from outside. But, due to the huntsman's deception, she eats the organs of a wild boar, not those of beautiful Snow White. The vain stepmother may be attractive on the outside in terms of her physical beauty, but inside, she has the disposition of a fierce and greedy brute. In her soul and mind, she is a gluttonous and ferocious boar, not a human being. It is a flagrant attempt by the disposition of *me, myself, and I* to stop what fate, destiny, or providence has in store for us as our lives gradually develop. Such a flagrant possessiveness represents our tendency to inflation, which happens when narcissistic ego devours everything into itself and uses everything and everyone for the purposes of power, self-esteem and personal security. Probably one of the most important forms of fasting is the refusal to eat up people!

Of course, everyone knows that animals are not gluttonous, selfish, or oversexed. They are simply themselves, following their own natural, self-regulating programs for living. Such animal metaphors as we are discussing here result from the human psyche's anthropomorphic projections onto animals. In this way, animals come to represent, in figurative language and vivid image, the instinctive tendencies of human nature. In stories and dreams, animals symbolize the visceral impulses of human beings.

When the huntsman kills the ferocious wild boar, he is doing an important service for Snow White. There is more to this act than merely providing a substitute for Snow White's own organs in order to trick the bad queen into believing that her stepdaughter is really dead. The sacrifice of the boar stands for subduing the wild, instinctive energies of the human psyche, so widely celebrated by the old mother religions, and also in the ecstatic cult of Dionysus, the volatile wine-god of Greek antiquity. In story language, for a person to be attacked and devoured by a wild animal means that, psychologically, an individual is overpowered and consumed by his own capricious instincts and impulses. But these impulses are not healthy instincts, because their character and intensity reflect the distorting influence of repression by an idealistic or moralistic consciousness. This imposed regimen has already trampled upon them and changed them artificially. In this circumstance, when he loses control he becomes a taunted and disturbed animal and not a conscious human being. When we are seized by an irrational mood or urge and get "carried away," we are the unwitting victims of our distressed animal impulses. These perverted instincts, which are not characteristic of healthy animal inclinations, appear as overwhelming waves of emotion or impulsivity that drown our lucid awareness and our sane judgment. At this point, these surging desires are our enemies rather than our friends. A good example of a modern-day possession by Dionysus is the impulsive fraternity brother played by John Belushi in the film *Animal House.* Another example is the well-known phenomenon called "road rage."

All cultures and traditions have their own images of *The Peaceable Kingdom,* where the animals live serenely, coexisting with each other and with humans, and "the lion lies down with the lamb." This is an unrealistic fantasy when applied to the actual bloodbath of the natural food chain, but it is wisdom when addressed to the possibility of an integrated human personality, where the higher reflective capacities of the conscious mind and the energies of the instinctive body live together in a balanced, cooperative, and ecological manner.

When the huntsman kills the wild boar, symbolically he is strengthening and guarding the integrity of a new consciousness from onslaught by autonomous instincts. The genius of the old sacred animal sacrifices, which has been absorbed today by the secular meat-packing industry, is that when mankind hunts down the animal, ritually slaughters it, makes an offering to the higher powers, roasts the flesh, and then eats it ceremonially, he is integrating animal instinct within human sensibility. Accordingly, his consciousness is formed, nourished, and sustained by the transformation of volatile animal energy. Conversely, when the animal in a story devours a person, human ego-consciousness momentarily disappears within animal impulsivity, and the individual *goes berserk,* i.e., he is covered by a "bear-shirt," meaning that he loses control and is consumed by his volatile urges and appetites.

J. N. H. Perkins

The ritualized slaughter of the animal represents the creation of a clear field of consciousness and self-control. This gradual emergence of the human spirit from the sheer animal instinct of primal mankind is an evolving course that slowly shapes a higher and more lucid human culture. Even when a religious image appears on the stage of history that presents ritual images of earthy lust and power, like the *baubo* figure of naked Isis, who opens her legs to proudly display her genitals to us while seated on a pig, we know that something new is evolving, where the blind forces of nature are beginning to be appreciated within the reflective mirror of the human mind. When such images appear, where instinct is given artistic expression through imagery, we know that a weak and tenuous human consciousness is attempting to free itself from slavery to the instincts. Through various icons and rituals, some of the instinctive energy is converted into a conscious experience that is capable of self-control, motivation, and most important of all, creative imagination. One might say that, in this manner, our consciousness arises as the lucid picture of instinct, yet now capable of deliberation and choice.

The poor child was now all alone in the dark wood, and so frightened that she looked at the leaves on every tree and didn't know where to turn. Then she started running, and she ran over sharp stones and through thickets of thorns, and the wild animals ran by her, but she came to no harm.

We aren't at all surprised that the beasts did no harm to Snow White, because of the huntsman's deed of slaying the wild boar. In this way, the problem of Snow White's relation to primal instinct has been settled. Even though the wicked stepmother cannibalized what she thought were Snow White's organs, the wild animals of the forest have no

32

interest in harming the little girl. There is a folklore theme in many stories in which the heroic child on his or her quest makes friends with the animals and kind-heartedly helps them out of a difficulty of some sort, so that later, when the hero or heroine is caught in a jam of his own, the animals, who have remembered these good deeds, come to the rescue. After the slaying of the wild boar, the animal instincts have become Snow White's friends rather than her enemies. This demonstrates that the new field of lucid awareness is reciprocally attuned to the instincts rather than opposed to them. Such is our inner or psychological ecology.

This brings to mind a most charming Russian icon, depicting the popular nineteenth-century saint, Seraphim of Sarov. A little elf-like fellow is shown seated on a log in the dark forest, where he feeds a large bear that eats peacefully from his hands. An ax is leaning against the log next to the little man, which he has been using to cut wood and clear a space among the trees for a bit of sunlight to shine through. One glimpses the corner of a rustic log hut through the green boughs nearby. This structure is the house of our human consciousness where we reside in a safe, orderly place in the midst of uncultivated, unadulterated nature. To be on good terms with the animals means that we are both spontaneously instinctive and fully conscious at the same time. The animals within us are alive and healthy and our minds are clear and vigilant. Neither one harms or abuses the other. Such is The Peaceable Kingdom of enlightened humanity.

4

Snow White ran as long as her feet would last until nightfall. Then she saw a little cottage, went up to it, opened the door, and stepped inside to rest. Everything inside the cottage was tiny, but very neat and very clean, with everything in its place. There was a table, and on it was a white cloth, and seven tiny plates, and resting upon each plate was a tiny spoon. There were also seven tiny knives and forks, and seven tiny mugs. Along the wall stood seven tiny beds in a row, and each one was covered by a snow-white quilt.

Like the sun crossing the sky, little Snow White runs the course of the day (remember that earlier she was described as "more beautiful than the day") until evening, when she finds a safe haven in the forest. At this point in the story, we are deluged with the number seven. Later we are told that the dwarves' cottage lies over "seven mountains." Snow White herself is seven years old, and everything in the cottage is in multiples of seven. The figure seven is *the* mystical number in all of mythology. It seems to permeate everything. In pre-Copernican astronomy, there were seven "planets" then visible to the naked eye that were believed to circle the earth: Sun, Moon, Mars, Mercury, Jupiter, Venus, and Saturn; from these come the names (in the Latin-based languages) for the seven days of the week and the seven tones (A-G) of the musical scale. These seven planets were also associated with the seven basic metals mined from the earth: Sun: gold; Moon: silver; Mars: iron; Mercury: mercury; Jupiter: tin; Venus: copper; and Saturn: lead. In East Indian yoga there are seven *chakras*, or nodes of consciousness, on the ascending scale of enlightenment. In Christian theology there are seven virtues: Faith, Hope, Charity, Fortitude, Justice, Prudence and Temperance; and seven deadly sins: Pride, Envy, Gluttony, Lust, Anger, Greed and Sloth. In our story, little Snow White represents the virtues and the evil stepmother the sins.

In the interest of our psychological appreciation, it is helpful to see the seven virtues not so much as moralistic traits but as symptoms of a liberated human spirit that is no longer simply the tool or pawn of the capricious appetites. We are talking about free will, responsibility, and the human capacity to make choices and impose a certain amount of order and clarity on the circumstances of our lives, as well as to live peacefully with those around us.

Our tale says that everything in the cottage was neat and clean, as well as small. Here you have an order that is not merely the tidy arrangement of an actual domestic scene, but the straight pattern of our thoughts in the house of the lucid mind. And everything is small. In myth, story, and various speculative systems like alchemy, there is a long tradition that celebrates the irony of little things that turn out to be very great things indeed. Part of this is the realization that what the conscious mind minimizes, or so easily overlooks, often proves to have dramatic and far-reaching consequences. A mere child, relatively impotent and innocent and without great influence in the world, often turns out to be the heroic harbinger of vast cultural change. We see this principle exemplified in the little peasant boy in the tale "The Devil's Three Golden Hairs," to which we referred earlier, who overcomes all odds to marry the king's daughter and attain the throne. And we are all familiar with the innocent babe of Bethlehem who is later welcomed as the Messiah, the Sun of Righteousness and the King of Kings. The tiny mustard seed grows into a great tree. The stone that was rejected becomes the chief cornerstone. In Hindu philosophy, it is the *Atman*, the tiny kernel in the bottom of the soul, that is also the *Self*, the fullness of the entire cosmos. Here the rule is: micro is also macro (and vice versa), and as we say, "small is beautiful," for as we are told, "those who humble themselves shall be exalted." Little Snow White, in the little cottage, with the little furnishings, and soon to be visited by her seven little hosts, is the inexorable new development that will change everything. One day she will be queen, which means that she will transform the mentality of the era and take leadership in a new cultural consciousness that is foreordained by the higher powers.

5

Little Snow White was so hungry that she ate some of the vegetables and bread from each tiny plate and drank a drop of wine from each tiny mug, since she did not want to eat everything from one place alone. Then, because she was tired, she lay down on one of the little beds, but neither that one nor the next suited her. Each was either too long or too short, but at last she came to the seventh bed and she found that it was just right. So she stayed in it, said her prayers, and then fell fast asleep.

Snow White, now aged seven, finally rests in the seventh bed, as Goldilocks did in the third. But this is no ordinary bed, for it corresponds to the seventh planet, which is Saturn, the patron of Saturday, the seventh day of the week. Saturn is the god associated with the harvest and with the demise and death that precedes renewal and rejuvenation, since the day following Saturn's day is Sunday, the radiant, so-called "eighth day" of the week. Sunday stands for the highest and final culmination of all transformations in the series of seven. This first day of the week is associated with the royal metal gold, whereas Saturn's metal is lead, the heaviest and the most corrosive of all the metals. Its silvery sheen soon turns black like a corpse when exposed to the air, whereas unalloyed gold retains its original brilliance for thousands of years, as evidenced by ancient Sumerian and

Egyptian artifacts. So Saturn stands for the periodic death in cycles of time that is succeeded by a Sunday of lucid mental and spiritual awareness that is eternal, and thus beyond the vicissitudes of life. In Christian symbolism, Sunday is at once both the first day of creation and the day of the resurrection to eternal life, once and for all.

Psychologically, Saturn stands for a changeable consciousness that, ruled by our unpredictable mood swings and emotions, is unstable and chaotic, and thus *saturnine*—depressed, morose, mysterious—a perfect reflection of seven-year-old Snow White's temperament while she is lost in the wild forest. In contrast, the untarnishable gold of Sunday stands for an enlightened awareness that remains constant, true, and stable throughout the many fluctuating states of our minds and fortunes in the successive seasons of our lives.

Snow White samples a little food and wine from each place setting, not wishing to take all from one only. This may demonstrate her consideration for the needs of others, but the deeper significance is that, by tasting from each plate and cup and trying each of the little beds, she makes the rounds of all the seven planets, together with the metals associated with each. Passing through all seven days of the week, which also correspond to the seven tones of the diatonic musical scale, she comprehends the entire harmony of life. Now she is in a position to enter the next phase of her journey toward maturity, culminating, finally, in the golden tiara of monarchy.

Because Snow White finally rests in the seventh bed, we know that she will soon die! This will not be her literal biological death, but rather the final day of her childhood before the beginning of her life as an adult. As a little girl she must die in order to be reborn as a woman. The ancient mytho-poetic mind of humanity does not think in terms of nuanced developments gradually over time. Rather, life is envisioned as a series of discrete episodes, each beginning and ending in succession. When a change of major proportions is addressed, this is expressed and appreciated in the symbolic image of death and rebirth, not steady evolving growth. One of the chief examples of this for the female psyche is the myth of Persephone who must die into the underworld in order to become a mature woman rather than remaining simply her mother's sweet little girl. In entering the Kingdom of Hades beneath the ground, she is not ceasing to live in the literal sense of the word, but rather is passing through a stage of adolescence through being united with the universal principle of fertility—the Goddess Earth, the mother of all.

As we mentioned earlier, this tale in one respect addresses the psychological issues of all adolescent girls, who are making the sometimes confusing passage to adult womanhood. Years ago, when I was teaching a class of fifteen-year-old girls, I was also reading a book titled approximately *The Student-Centered Classroom*. This book was the rage among liberal-leaning teachers of the late sixties, as it advocated tailoring the learning process to the students' own experiences, perspectives, and interests. In my attempt to implement this philosophy, I asked the girls to brainstorm, using all the words and phrases they could imagine to express the topics and themes of most vital importance to them. As they chattered away enthusiastically, I listed all these on the blackboard. Later, I recorded this list on a sheet of paper that I reproduced and distributed to each student, asking them to rank the ten major topics in order of their importance. After collation, the first three turned out to be: love, sex, and death. At that very moment, the contemporary significance of age-old Persephone, Psyche, Snow White, and all the other dead maidens and sleeping beauties of myth and legend was made glaringly evident to me!

6

When it was quite dark, the owners of the cottage came back. They were seven dwarves who quarried in the mountains, searching for ore. The dwarves lit their seven candles, and because the cottage was now full of light, they saw that someone had been there, for nothing was in quite the same order as it had been when they had left the cottage that morning.

The first said: "Who has been sitting in my chair?"
The second: "Who has been eating off my plate?"
The third: "Who has been taking some of my bread?"
The fourth: "Who has been eating my vegetables?"
The fifth: "Who has been using my fork?"
The sixth: "Who has been cutting with my knife?"
The seventh: "Who has been drinking out of my mug?"

When the first dwarf looked around and saw that there was a little hollow on his bed, he said, "Who has been getting into my bed?" The other dwarves came up and each cried out, "Somebody has been sleeping in my bed too." But when the seventh dwarf looked at his bed, he spied little Snow White, who was lying in it asleep. He called the other dwarves, who came running over, and they chattered in astonishment and brought their seven little candles and let the light shine on Snow White. "Oh, heavens above! Oh, heavens above!" they cried. "What a lovely child!" Because they were so glad, they did not wake her, but allowed her to sleep soundly in the bed. The seventh dwarf slept with his companions, one hour with each one of them, and so he spent the night.

In the morning, little Snow White woke up and was frightened when she saw the seven dwarves. But they were very friendly and asked her what her name was. "My name is Snow White," she answered. "How did you find our house?" asked the dwarves. Then she explained that her stepmother had tried to kill her, but that a huntsman had spared her, and that she had then run all day long until she discovered their cottage. The dwarves said, "If you will take care of our cottage, cook, make the beds, do the washing, sew and knit, and if you promise to keep everything neat and clean, you can stay with us, and you will have everything you need." "Yes," said Snow White, "I will with all my heart," and she remained with them. She kept order in the house, and in the mornings the dwarves went out into the mountains and searched for copper and gold. At night, they came back, and by that time their supper had to be ready. The girl was all alone during the long days, so the good dwarves gave her a warning and said, "Beware of your proud stepmother. Before long she will discover that you are here, so make sure you don't let anyone inside."

Notice the great emphasis on order in this part of the tale. When Snow White first entered the little cottage, she noticed how clean and neat everything was. After the dwarves came home and discovered her, the next morning they offered hospitality and invited her to stay, on the condition that she would keep the house clean and tidy and cook their meals. We should recall again that the German word *fegen*, recorded by the two Grimm brothers and translated into English as the word "fair," means to clean and sweep, to tidy up and put things aright. So the sense of regular order is very important in this story. Snow White's "fairness" is not seductive beauty. That sort of erotic magnetism is represented by the vain and evil stepmother.

As we have said, the number seven is particularly important in this segment of the story because the seven original planets that were believed to encircle the earth exemplified the symmetrical order of the universe.

Just imagine the profound impression made upon the human mind in earliest antiquity (c. 3000 BCE), when the first astronomers and mathematicians began to observe the precise movement of these seven celestial bodies as they passed regularly through twelve recognized patterns of light in the background of the fixed stars. In ancient Mesopotamian Sumer (present-day southern Iraq), the exact mathematical regularity of heavenly motions was measured and recorded. It is no doubt likely that the whole field of mathematics, and of music, arose in conjunction with the observations of the sky and the need of these first stargazers to compute their findings with precision. We owe our "sexagesimal" (based on the number 60) system for measuring time and space and the sevenfold tones of our diatonic musical scale to the arithmetic of these very calculations. Whenever we glance at our watches or compasses, or play the piano, we may thank these ancient Babylonian astronomers.

So what impact did the measurement of these sidereal events have upon the early Mesopotamians? Why were such matters so hugely important? The answer lies in the fact that terrestrial life is capricious. The weather, crucially important to agricultural folk, is not predictable, even with today's advanced meteorology. Much is uncertain. There is good fortune and bad fortune. Illness afflicts some people and some animals, but not others. Certain people live to be old; others die young. Crops flourish, but then may be ruined by famine or locusts. Moods change as well. There are people who seem in a different frame of mind today than they were yesterday. For instance, only this morning, I "got out of the wrong side of the bed," and was moody and irritable, but yesterday I was cheerful and relaxed. One tries to be as careful as possible, but there are still accidents and mishaps. Life is full of vicissitudes and quirks, and one can never be sure of what will happen next.

But look! Up there in the sky, beyond and behind all this terrestrial flux and erratic human fortune, nothing is like that at all! Certain regular patterns are observed, and to the naked eye, they occur in cycles that are exactly predictable, never veering one iota. Here we see the same patterns yesterday, today, and tomorrow, and seemingly for all of eternity. How impressive and satisfying—a neat and orderly system up there! What did this mean to early astronomical man? It meant that life down here on earth was an inferior and imperfect rendition of that heavenly prototype up there that is perfect and therefore divine, evidenced by its impressive order and predictability—the perfectly timed and tuned clockwork of God. So every effort must be made to make *this* world be like *that* world.

To the ancients, the most successful plan of living on earth was one that imitated, as fully as possible, the patterns observed in the heavens. The idea of "Thy kingdom come, Thy will be done, on earth as it is in heaven" existed long before Jesus of Nazareth, even long before his earliest Hebrew forebears. The people of the first city-states of the Near East set up an elaborate system, developing myths, symbols, and ceremonies that ritually enacted the events of the sky in the social patterns of the human community. The first hierarchical designs of a royal government and elaborate courtly etiquette were set up in imitation of the heavenly planets.[6]

As Sir Charles Leonard Wooley (1880-1960) discovered with amazement when he excavated the sixteen royal tombs of Ur (3200-2000 BCE) around 1925, the skeleton of Queen *Shub-ad,* lay surrounded by her ladies-in-waiting, accompanied by her girl court minstrels. On her deathbed—in a grave that was discovered eighteen feet below ground level—this queen wore an ornate headdress made of a long gold hair ribbon covered by beaded wreaths with gold pendants, heavy earrings of unalloyed gold, and a golden Spanish-type comb with five points ending in lapis-centered flowers of gold. These patrician ladies, festooned in similar but slightly less elaborate headgear, appeared to have died willingly with their sovereign, allowing themselves to be buried alive, perhaps after having taken a potent drug from a goblet of pure gold discovered among the artifacts. Considered an early rite of *suttee* (Sanskrit for "perfect being"), this sacrificial burial occurred either after the king himself was ritually slain or had died of natural causes. The few surviving digits of the court minstrel's fingers still rested on her instrument exactly where the thin gut strings formerly stretched. The purpose of this ghastly burial rite, which was certainly a voluntary human sacrifice, was to enable the queen and her royal court faithfully to accompany their divine moon-king on his celestial journey back home again into eternity. From there, all would reappear in the great cycle of eternal return, just as does the moon after three days of darkness in its periodic monthly passage. All this was considered, of course, to be the ultimate and the most perfect reality possible. To do otherwise would have been considered *a-sat*, not true, or false being.[7]

At some later date, when this earliest astrological-astronomical system emerged into the first psychology in the classical to medieval European period, a third cosmic level came into realization: the *microcosm* (little cosmos) of human interiority—the soul—that gradually came to be known as the depth of individual personality. All the levels follow, or should follow, the same divine plan. And what a perfect system! What occurs in heaven, in society, and inside me are all beautifully coordinated, made essentially of the same stuff behaving in the same way. Any discrepancies are due simply to an implicit terrestrial inferiority, not to the divine prototype itself, which was considered to be *the* ultimate Truth. As I am writing this, I am reminded that our word "consider," which I used just this second, means literally "to be with or follow the stars" (from *sidus*, star or constellation). Accordingly, the ancient thinking survives implicitly in the etymology of our ordinary language to this very day.

One should not underestimate the tremendous aura of security and profound meaning provided by such an orderly cosmos. Humanity belonged in a perfectly regulated universe and resided within an equivalently designed state. If mankind had cared to look deeply enough, he would have found within himself a micro-cosmic wholeness and an integrity that was equally perfect, reliable, and satisfying. No existential angst here. This was definitely not a Woody Allen world!

In this episode of Snow White, notice also that the seven dwarves came home when it was quite dark. Don't think that this is simply a reflection of the typical workday in northern Europe. These seven dwarves appear only after dark because the planets and stars of the sky do not become visible until after dark. What appears at night is precisely what is invisible during the day—in other words, to ordinary human consciousness. Consequently, it is at night, when the sky is blazing with stellar light and when our heads are stuffed full of dreams, that the cosmic or archetypal region of the generic human personality reveals itself in all its complex splendor.

The dwarves each carry their own candles as they look about the cottage to see who has disturbed the order of their domestic scene. These candles are their individual lights—the planets—that appear in the sky at night. As Snow White is first observed by the light of these "candles," rather than by ordinary daylight, she can be likened to a dream figure, not an actual person. She is a character appearing within the *microcosmic* interiority of the human psyche, that little world that lies within us. This also explains why everything in the cottage, including the dwarves, is so *little*. It has to be, in order to fit inside us.

Our story mentions that, during the day, these dwarves dig and delve for ore in the mountains. A little later it is revealed that they dig specifically for the metals gold and copper, which stand for the Sun and the planet Venus. Just as the celestial sun was believed to be born from the abyss of the watery netherworld each morning, so the little dwarves functioned as midwives. As little obstetricians, they brought forth the gold from the womb of their terrestrial mother, the earth.

J. N. H. Perkins

Earlier, we alluded to the tale called "The Devil's Three Golden Hairs," in which a peasant Child of Good Fortune, against all odds, finally marries the king's daughter. After realizing that his trick has failed, the jealous king seems to relent, but secretly he tries to rid himself of this unwanted son-in-law by employing a clever ruse. He sends the youth on a fatal mission to retrieve three golden hairs from the head of the devil. If the young man is successful, the king promises to officially ratify the marriage.

After several adventures, the youth finally arrives at the sooty mouth of hell. He enters and discovers only an old woman who explains that she is the devil's grandmother, and that the devil won't be home till after work. The youth describes his mission, and the kindly grandmother says she will get the three golden hairs for him. At nightfall, just as the devil comes storming in, ranting and raving and shouting "Where's my dinner?" the old woman transforms the youth into an ant and hides him in the folds of her voluminous skirt (the night sky). Then she proceeds to feed her grandson, and afterward, with his head in her lap, she begins to pluck the lice from his hair. As the devil snores thunderously, the old woman successively pulls each of the required three golden hairs from his head. In the morning after the devil has gone out (sunrise), the boy receives the required hairs, politely thanks the grandmother, and successfully goes on his way.

It is easy to see that this temperamental fellow is not really the devil at all, but the celestial sun, Helios, coming home to sleep in the underworld after a long day's work journeying across the sky. His golden hairs are the luminous rays of sunlight that shine on the earth. So when the youthful hero of "The Devil's Three Golden Hairs" gets the blond strands, he is like the seven dwarves of Snow White, mining the metallic gold from out of the cavern of the underworld. And like them, he must become little, very small relative to Big Mama, in order to succeed. Notice that the devil sleeps in the lap of his grandmother. During the day, he is high and mighty and powerful, but at night, he weakens, regresses, becomes a child again, starts bossing everyone around, and requires maternal attention. This alone should convince us that there is sublime wisdom in fairy tales. The fact that the young hero gets just three golden hairs from the sun god rather than the whole scalp teaches us that only a wee bit of intellect or mental brilliance is sufficient to illuminate our entire human nature, enabling us to become fully conscious human beings. We don't all need a doctoral degree.

We will return to the theme of the transformation of gold again and again. Gold is the sun-consciousness hidden deep inside the earth. Equipped with this kind of wisdom, one has no need to substitute brainy, airy abstractions for down-to-earth common sense. The wisdom is already in the gut! One may remain a natural human being with feet planted firmly on the ground and at the same time grow in sublime intelligence within one's self! It is not necessary to travel far up into the sky, or ascend an ivory tower, or become spiritually ethereal, in order to achieve enlightenment. Heaven is already here, near to hand, on earth and in the earth, if we will but see it and value it. The pearl of great price lies buried within us. The Jewish-Christian notion that human beings are created originally in the image of God and contain this divine image within themselves is an expression of the same idea. "The Kingdom of Heaven is within you."[8]

According to the old myth, when the sun sets in the west, enormously weakened after his long flight across the sky, he falls into the arms of the great mother of the underworld. In this embrace, he impregnates her and simultaneously she devours him, just as the black widow spider consumes her mate. Paradoxically, he survives because the tomb of the great mother's stomach is synonymous with her maternal womb in which he, now the fetal sun (son of himself!), gestates during the night. From her womb, he finally bursts forth onto the eastern horizon as the brilliant new day. In this so-called "matriarchal" mythic scheme, the son is "of one essence with the Father." But here, unlike in the Christian formula, the son is his own father, who is his own son, who is his own father, in a succession of alternations, in the endless cycle of eternal return. The sun god continually renews himself through his own death and rebirth. The one unchangeable and eternal figure overarching all, ever the same day after day, night after night, is not the Great Father, "maker of heaven and earth," but the Great Mother, into whom and through whom and out of whom all of life passes from beginning to end, through limitless generations of living, dying, and living once again, forever. In short, she *is* eternity!

7

When Snow White reaches the cottage of the seven dwarves, she encounters the principle of gold and solar light that is being mined from deep within the mother-mountain. Here she is getting connected with the masculine principles within herself that can retrieve and achieve mental brilliance, but still allow her to remain rooted in organic, earthy nature as a woman.

Like the devil in "The Devil's Three Golden Hairs," or the sun that falls into the great arms of the mother goddess each night when he sets, the seven little men are really eternal children who are in need of a maternal provider. They function exclusively in the great "eternal return" cycles of Mother Nature, within which they live, move, and have their being.

The dwarves represent the age-old system of what some have termed a "feminine awareness," arising from the ecological depths of nature and Mother Earth. The profound genius of raising the gold from within the earth is an approach to living that is intrinsically organic, integrated, holistic, and wise—one that is highly intelligent, yet never unduly abstract. The psychological function of this mythic theme is to prevent a dissociation of the mind, especially of the will and the intellect, from our overall human nature. For both men and women, it is a dangerous and unhealthy tendency to detach the higher mental faculties completely from the body and from the visceral instincts. For in this case, integration of mind and body, of spirit and nature, is impossible, and human beings of both sexes are left in a condition of dualistic fragmentation so that psychological and physical health are both jeopardized. So that is why, when we encounter a person who lives *both* from their wise intellect *and* from their earthy guts, we are so impressed.

Our tale says that the dwarves mine copper as well as gold. The word copper, *cuprum*, comes from the name of the Mediterranean island of Cyprus, thought to be the birthplace of Venus, known in Greece as Aphrodite. That explains why copper is associated with Venus, whose day is the sixth of the week, Friday (in French, *vendredi*). So the little dwarves are digging up the divine emblems of both eternal consciousness—which we associate with clarity of intellect—and the organic fertility of nature, which we encounter as the magic of love. Not a bad combination, both smart and sexy!

It helps to make a shift and think mythologically and symbolically to appreciate matters such as these. We have already mentioned the three-decker notion of cosmic levels or regions: big sky, middle society, and little personality. With the development of the early science of metallurgy, an additional layer was inserted into the first three. The seven planets of the sky were believed also to appear in subterranean analogous form as the seven basic metals that may be dug from the earth. Silver, iron, mercury, tin, copper, lead, and gold are then the chthonic or underworld reflections of the seven heavenly planets that rule all of existence.

Two more examples from the rule of "mother right" will round out our discussion. One comes from the classical world of the Greek mysteries, the other from the Catholic rite of Holy Saturday.

In the heavily attended religious celebrations (c. 1500 BCE–400? CE) of Demeter and Persephone at Eleusis, a town located about thirty miles west-northwest of Athens, the most sacred moment occurred when, in the utter darkness of an underground room, a torch was lit, representing the periodic return of Persephone from the underworld. This marked the rise of the new spring vegetation each year. In the Middle Ages, as is still enacted today on the eve of the first Mass of Easter, the church lies in total darkness. Suddenly a light appears, struck from flint. It is the light of the great Paschal Candle, six feet tall and about four inches in diameter. This immense candle is carried in procession by the deacon, who chants, "Lumen Christi" (The Light of Christ) three times successively, after which he plunges this giant illuminating phallus another three times into the waters of the maternal baptismal font in order to fructify its uterine waters by the power of the Holy Spirit.

In both instances, the light appears first in the darkness and emerges as if arising from the depths of the underworld prison, termed by the Greeks, Hades, and by the Jews, Sheol. It is " ... a light that shines in the dark, a light that darkness could not overpower," and as the Evangelist John said, " ... the true light that enlightens all men."[9] Both of these are examples from the mother religions, the first in honor of Demeter, the corn goddess, and the second, a celebration by Holy Mother the Church, begun in early medieval Europe.

On the horizon of the present episode of Snow White lurks the ever-present stepmother. She will try to put Snow White into an Aphrodite death-trance, insuring that as this little girl passes into adolescence, she will become and remain the passive and unconscious icon of sexual allure and visceral fertility, deathly beautiful and unchanging like Persephone, and not a conscious human being in her own right.

8

But the queen, who thought that she had eaten Snow White's lungs and liver, was sure that she was once again the most beautiful of all; and so she went to her magic looking glass and said, "Mirror, Mirror on the wall, who in this land is the fairest of all?" and the looking glass answered, "Oh, Queen, thou art fairest of all I see, but over the mountains, where the seven dwarves dwell, Snow

J. N. H. Perkins

White is still alive and well, and none is so fair as she." Then the queen was stunned and amazed because the looking glass never, ever lied, and so she knew that the huntsman had disobeyed her, and that little Snow White was still alive.

Before we get to the wicked queen's next piece of mischief, we ought to pause briefly and say something about the amazing looking glass, which the queen consults with regularity. Now it is not the mirror's fault that the stepmother is so vain. In fact, the looking glass is highly accurate and tells the truth. It never lies. It is the queen's attitude toward herself and the use she makes of the mirror that is the problem.

On one level, the looking glass refers to the mind's capacity to reflect, to form within one's waking consciousness a subjective image of what is out there in the world. It is interesting to note that our word "mirror" derives from the Latin adjective *mirus* signifying "wonderful," "astonishing," "extraordinary." The verb *mirari* means "to wonder at." Our words "admire" and "miracle" give the same sense.

Our earliest ancestors were indeed astonished at what the mind could do when it could *re-flect*, flex or bend back upon itself, and thus build an interior awareness of self and world as experienced from inside the personality. One imagines that there was indeed an historic moment when the miracle of subjective consciousness first came into existence. This is exemplified in the myth of Prometheus, who stole fire from the gods for humanity's use. What previously had been considered the prerogative solely of the divine now became a human possibility, and a step was made in which man, and not the gods alone, would became the measure of all things. As we shall see, humanity, like Prometheus of old, will eventually be required to pay the freight for this usurpation.

In prior generations, mental deliberations were lodged in a system characterized by us moderns as *animism.* Truth was determined through mystical interpretations, prophesies, oracles, and auguries. On a more sophisticated intellectual level, Plato and the neo-Platonist philosophers determined truth by a finely tuned and perceptive intuition of the *nous* or higher mind. Here, archetypal Truth was considered an independent, objective, spiritual reality, in no sense a man-made construction. Existing in a sort of paradise far beyond the human brain and material reality, this ultimate sphere could be perceived, if we believe Plato, by those gifted folk called philosophers, who functioned somewhat like seers and soothsayers, though on a far more rational and sophisticated level than the simple folk diviners, who were considered superstitious by comparison.

We mentioned earlier that the word "consider" means to follow the patterns of the stars (*sidus,* the starry firmament). Employed in an altered sense, *sidum* means "pride" or "glory." What had been the pride and glory of the gods or of the majesty of the stellar universe and of the Divine Mind came to be the magnificence of our brainy heads, the presumptuous "I am" of enlightened, ego-oriented humanity.

The gradual development of reflective consciousness in humans entailed a progressive internalization or incorporation of the enchanted cosmos into a field of subjective psychological awareness. During many centuries of cultural and scientific advancement, this process gradually produced an immense inflation or aggrandizing of the human person. Having attained personal self-consciousness, man came to identify with God and then to displace God. Sir Isaac Newton, rejoicing in his successful determination of the laws of mechanics, remarked, "Now we know how God works!" Within a generation, his own successors were saying, "Now we know that it is not God, but instead physical laws, which make everything happen." The die had been cast.

With monstrous audacity, heaven, once considered the realm of transcendent spiritual reality, was debased to a subjective "psychological" experience, and what was once divine omniscience became simply prodigious human intelligence. What was formerly the omnipotence of God reappeared as willful human purpose. And what was formerly divine Providence became the human aspiration to both private achievement and predestined (utopian) social progress. In short, human consciousness had displaced the divine mind.

In this manner, the human ego-mind became the pride and glory of itself. The "Thou" became the "I." In our tale, the new queen's own reflection in the looking glass, that object signifying "wonderful-astonishing-extraordinary," served, for her and for us, as a divine image, an icon of personalistic self-glorification. The proud and narcissistic stepmother of life is, in fact, we ourselves!

The mirror theme is crucial in Snow White. An old Greek story recorded in Ovid's *Metamorphosis* relates that a naiad (water nymph), Liriope, was ravaged by a river god, Cephisus. In time she bore an extraordinarily beautiful boy-child, whom she called Narcissus. Liriope, wondering about her little son's future, consulted the blind sage,

Tiresius, asking him if the boy would live to a ripe old age. Tiresius answered, "Yes, if he never knows himself." With this oracular pronouncement, Tiresius was forecasting the danger inherent in the rise of human self-consciousness, for we are all, every one of us, Narcissus, gazing at the mirage of our own reflection in the mirror of life, believing all the while that we are witnessing objective reality! But we are sadly deluded.

Modern psychology has often cited the Narcissus tale as a characterization of prideful self-involvement. Until realization comes, Narcissus has no idea that he has fallen in love with himself. He believes that the face he sees behind the mirror of the water's surface is another person altogether. When he finally realizes that the boy he sees is his own reflection and not another person, he can no longer tolerate life, and sinking to the greensward, his face now pale and wan, he closes his eyes. This myth explains why narcissists rarely do well in therapy. To come to terms with themselves, to take responsibility and deal with their own problems, is simply intolerable. Narcissists prefer their delusions to reality. To them, self-awareness is as frightening a prospect as death! For they, no doubt, sense that if they were to take a careful look inside themselves, they would discover *nothing.*

Narcissists use other people for personal security. Because they have little selfhood of their own, others must function as satellites to provide an ersatz sense of security and vicarious personal identity. Narcissists are dependent upon other people to play their assigned roles in the projected drama of their own empty lives. Narcissists have no way to check on their own reality. They must use other people manipulatively to do this. Narcissists can't tolerate other people existing *in their own right,* for others can only be mirror reflections of themselves. If enough people refuse to play their dutiful roles, the narcissist simply goes to pieces, for he has no intrinsic reality. You, and his relations with you, are who he is. If the narcissist ever comes to "know himself," as the myth states, he finds the experience unbearable. If a narcissist likes you, it is all about him, not about you. If he hates you, it's because you won't play his game on his terms, according to his needs, and so he is convinced that there is something wrong with *you,* not with *him!* Narcissists live exclusively *through* other people, not inside their own skins. Narcissists are the preeminent "Hollow Men."[10]

When we exaggeratedly admire or idolize another person in such a manner that we ourselves feel inferior or lacking in substance, and then are seized by envy and competitiveness, this is simply our unconscious narcissism, our unacknowledged grandiosity that hides in the dark basement of our minds. We project this narcissism onto another person, admire him or her, and then feel insignificant and inferior by comparison. It is this gnawing sense of inferiority and creeping malaise that signals the narcissism that lies behind our exaggerated reverence toward the other person. If you truly rejoice in another's gifts and still feel okay about yourself, then chances are you are not a victim of unconscious pride, but are making an accurate appraisal.

The distinguishing characteristic of the stepmother is her unbridled vanity. She must be the most beautiful woman in the world, or else! She views her foster daughter (who is a real person in her own right) solely as a rival to her incomparable resplendence, for she can only exist through her mirrored image.

In the German writer Franz Werfel's historical novel, *The Song of Bernadette*, a Lourdes *douagiere*, Madame Millet, is curious about the news of Bernadette's first visions of a beautiful and vivacious young lady who appears to her at a cavern near the town. Madame Millet suspects that the radiant girl who appears to Bernadette is the spirit or ghost of her own deceased niece, Elise. Thinking to enhance Bernadette's appearance during future visitations, Madame Millet takes Bernadette, a fourteen-year-old who lives with her family in abject poverty, into her rich household and, on one occasion, persuades Bernadette to try on the long white confirmation gown that had once belonged to Elise. Bernadette, attired in this festive frock, is shoved by Madame Millet before a sumptuous full-length mirror. For the first time in her life, Bernadette gazes in utter astonishment at the silver reflection. "Pretty as a picture!" gushes Madame Millet excitedly. But as Franz Werfel describes this poignant scene, "[At home] … there was a broken bit of looking glass but no real mirror. Hence Bernadette knew the figure, face, and garment of the Lady [in the Grotto] far more exactly and in detail than she had known herself. It could have been said that the lovely one in the niche [of the grotto] was far less a 'vision' to her than her own image in the mirror."[11] This acute observation should help us appreciate the fundamental difference between Snow White and her vain stepmother.

With the assimilation of the supreme mythic order of the universe into the subjective mentality of secular man, all discrimination of levels between the personal and the transpersonal, between the human and the divine, between earth and heaven, have been obliterated. Today, we naively assume that all hierarchical distinctions are elitist, just as we believe that all visions are psychotic hallucinations and all myths are superstitions. By reducing the divine to the level of the human ego, enlightened postmodern humanity has profaned and privatized the mythological and divine strata of experience to one plane. The modern mind has become a monstrous man-god, a contemporary Minotaur, imprisoned in the labyrinth of its own obsessive self-reflection. Our fixation with celebrities, projecting godlike attributes onto them; our mania for an ageless youth culture; our language when we fall in love: "He's divine. I'm in heaven"—all reveal our unacknowledged grandiosity. In this manner, our idolatry displays our psychological inflation.

In this respect, it is important to recall the theme of littleness that we have seen over and over again. Little Snow White, the little dwarves in their little cottage with their little furnishings, and the child of good fortune who must be changed into a little ant before he may receive the three golden hairs. Such littleness refers to the absolute necessity of shrinking the grandiose and inflated human ego down to a very small size. This smallness represents the immense need for humility. Humility is not so difficult when one is worshiping the great God up there in the sky, or just filling one's assigned role in a traditional society. But with the assimilation of the mythic universe and the omniscience of heaven into the human soul, to the proud mind of modern "lifestyle" man, whose cold eye is continually searching for opportunities to advance himself, the danger is certain that man will risk becoming a sphinx-like fiend, "slouching toward Bethlehem to be born."[12] This Second Coming will be not the reappearance of the good Redeemer and Man of Peace, but of the dangerous and bloodthirsty monstrosity of contemporary humanity.

Finding God or the supreme wisdom within us is an unimaginably dangerous endeavor, which, in the typical instance, is doomed to failure precisely because of the human penchant for egotism and grandiosity. It is for this reason that the great mystics and seers of history all over the world have invariably practiced some severe form of ascetical self-denial in order to discipline the ego's insatiable desire for power and self-importance. The rule seems to be: the smaller you can make yourself, the greater and truer will be your mind.

There is a dangerous degree of inflation in the contemporary "New Age," human potential, spirituality movements, especially in those currents that stress Eastern philosophy and religion as imports into the grandiose Western culture of *me, myself, and I.* Western society can only appreciate the divinity of the personality as an inflated ego phenomenon. It has no idea that there could be something beyond one's self inside one's far greater Self. That is too much for our childish, self-achieving mentality. A patient's dream illustrates this very phenomenon:

I was in a classroom and looking up to the wall above the blackboard, I saw the most beautiful golden letters. They weren't just gold paint, but real gold. I reached out and took one of these letters, but suddenly, this letter and all the others turned black. All the gold was now gone and I had the feeling that I had ruined everything.

The gold disappeared when the dreamer tried to *possess* the letters by taking them as his personal property. The most sublime things in life are precisely those that we "can't get a hold on," for they belong to *life,* not to *us.*

But then, who in the world is this Snow White, in relation to our proud consciousness? She is neither "I" nor "me," not what *I want* or what *I will get*, but, in fact, the objective image of beautiful life itself. Not your life or my life, but the fullness of the Life that lives itself through all of our meager selves, what people of former times called the soul. In a subsequent story we shall examine in this book, we learn that Snow White's colors: red, white and black, stand for the bright sun, the clear light of day, and the darkness of night. In this sense, they are not the personal characteristics of any private individual, but are celestial qualities that extend far beyond "me, myself, and I."

Little Snow White is not a strident and aggressive hero, with weapons and armor, marching intrepidly toward her goal with power and might. Rather, she is life itself as it submits itself to the higher powers, who know far more regarding her real significance, needs, and destiny than she alone could possibly fathom. This young lady is not the single cause of victory, but rather the lovely and sublime result of it. We moderns, both women and men, have misplaced our Snow White souls. We desperately need to recover them. Snow White's smallness (she is only seven years old) and the dwarves' diminutive size reflect the importance of humility—the shrinking of the grandiose ego down to modest size.

9

The queen thought more and more about how she might kill her fair stepdaughter, for as long as the queen was not the most beautiful woman in the whole kingdom, jealousy kept her from even a moment's rest. At last, the queen thought of a way to carry out her plan. She made up her face and dressed herself to look like an old peddler woman, so that nobody would know who she really was. In this disguise she traveled over the seven mountains to the seven dwarves' cottage and knocked on their door and shouted, "Pretty things to sell, very cheap, very cheap." Little Snow White looked out the window and cried, "Good day, my good woman, what have you got to sell?" "Good things, pretty things," replied the old woman. "Stay-laces of many colors," and she pulled out one of them which was made of bright-colored silk. "I may let the harmless old woman in," Snow White thought, and she bought the pretty laces. "Child," said the old woman, "how awful you look; come, I will lace you the right way for once." Snow White didn't suspect anything, but stood in front of the old woman and let herself be laced with the new laces. But the old woman laced so quickly and so tightly that Snow White couldn't breathe, and she fell down and looked dead. "Now I am the most beautiful," murmured the proud queen to herself, and she ran away.

When the dwarves came home and found Snow White lifeless, they examined her carefully, and when they loosened the stay-laces, Snow White began to breathe once more and woke up. The dwarves warned her a second time never to let anyone into the cottage while they were at work in the mountains. But the proud stepmother, after consulting her looking glass, knew that her attempt to kill Snow White had failed yet again, so this time, employing a secret magic craft, she contrived a comb filled with poison and made herself up in a different way and returned as before. After at first hesitating, Snow White let the peddler woman in and allowed her to comb her hair. But as soon as the comb touched her hair, Snow White fell down dead. When the dwarves came home, they found her lying senselessly on the floor. Examining her again and searching thoroughly, they at last saw the comb, and when they removed it, Snow White woke up. This time the dwarves warned her even more strongly not to allow anyone into the cottage while they were away during the day.

J. N. H. Perkins

The envious queen tries to kill Snow White, first with the corset laces, then with a poisoned comb, and later, as we know, she succeeds with a cleverly poisoned apple. We'll talk about the apple in a while, but first we need to deal with death—not actual death, but death as a metaphor.

If a boat "lies dead in the water," it has lost its power and is no longer moving forward. If you "kill the motor" of your car, you turn off the engine. So when Snow White "dies," she stops being the person she was previously. The course of her life comes to a halt. We have already suggested that this tale is connected with the passage or transition from childhood to adulthood. Adolescence is not something unique to an individual; it is universal. When Snow White "dies," an actual person does not cease living, but rather, the girl reaches the end of her childhood. It is her childhood that dies. This is necessary in order for her to become a woman. Although most parents rejoice in this progressive change in their children, there lingers a certain bittersweet feeling about it. They produced a child and loved that child for eleven or twelve years, and then one day they look up and realize that this child is gone, or almost gone, and will never return. Somewhere in the depths of their hearts they begin to mourn the loss. The old Greek tale of Persephone is in a similar vein. Her mother, Demeter, in deep mourning, roams the world looking everywhere for her little girl, even to this day.

As in most folk tales, the negative or evil force is invariably problematic. It is double-sided, both positive and negative. It acts in a destructive way, yet in the end, we realize that without this input, the adventure could never be completed. Hansel and Gretel would never have gained the fortune in jewels from the old witch un-

62

less their mother had not first cruelly abandoned them in the forest. Without the proud queen, Snow White would stay an innocent child and remain at the immature level of development that we have already described regarding the stunted little dwarves. They are misshapen adults who never fully matured. They belong to the mother and live and work strictly within her boundaries. They will never go on to find wives of their own. Without the jealous queen, Snow White would remain always Mama's sweet little girl, fulfilling her dream of the white, the red, and the black, but in a juvenile manner. I have encountered not a few women of this type, with a sugary disposition and that characteristic soft, high, tiny voice. Such women forever mourn the passing of their mothers.

So the encounter with the wicked stepmother is merely a step along the way of a dangerous journey through "death" that is necessary for reaching the ultimate destination of full womanhood. We see the same thing in the tale popularly known as "Sleeping Beauty," the original name of which was "Little Briar Rose." In that story, at the instigation of a witch-like godmother, the daughter pricks her finger and falls asleep for a hundred years. The death-prick heralds the onslaught of puberty. This is the awakening of the image of virile masculinity and its effect within the girl's imagination. First the girl must have an inner image of the man of her dreams. Then she will be able to recognize the semblance of him in the outer world. But as we all know from cruel experience, there is a universe of difference between the "dream man" and actual men. Some women linger in the unconscious fantasy of the "dream man," and overlook numerous opportunities to form good partnerships in the real world. A few women remain in the so-called death trance all of their lives. No man ever quite measures up. So, still in the death-trance, they wait, and wait, and wait, certain that some day ...

In a healthy transition, this "death trance" should be a temporary condition of deep unconsciousness of self and of world. We could say that it is the rule, the automatic psychological law, that when a girl verges on womanhood and begins to appreciate herself erotically as a woman, her awareness of herself as an individual will become diffused. Instead, remaining "asleep," nature will take over and she will be under the influence of hormonally driven energies within her body and mind whose purpose is to attract a man with whom she may propagate the human race. Her heart and head will swim with wondrous images of nature and romance, and she will often seem to be "somewhere else."

As we have indicated, the stepmother is a version of Aphrodite, the goddess of love. It is intolerable that any mortal woman could be beautiful and charming in her own right as a fully conscious human being, for that would be a usurpation of Aphrodite's divine power. When a human woman is competing with a goddess, human consciousness is attempting to assert its lucid awareness over and against a life of blind, unconscious impulse, where choice is non-existent and the personality is entirely under the influence of enthralling romance and the nesting instinct. The rare genius is to be earthy and conscious simultaneously, rather than exchanging one for the other.

The tale of Snow White focuses on the transition from unconscious, automatic femininity (the principle of elemental fecundity ruled exclusively by Aphrodite) to one of awakened wisdom and individual self-determination. Our tale is very clear about this. Snow White is rendered unconscious by female cosmetic items, whose purpose is to artificially enhance a woman's external erotic appeal, especially in the eyes of men. When feminine adornment is successful, men themselves personify the looking glass that never lies. Their various reactions to what they see become the "true" image of the woman's worth. This is the "Carmencita"[13] sex magic that irresistibly attracts the male, and it is through this Aphrodisian means, and this means alone, that an unconscious woman may gain self-appreciation and self-respect. A woman so bewitched and so bewitching can find validation only in becoming the target of men's desires. She simply is as men see her, yet is herself mentally vacuous, "dead" to her own life. Such a woman cannot live out of her intelligence, but is an actor on a stage, programmed by her instinctive nature to fish for attention from men. No man by himself can force a woman to become a sex object. He may certainly try, but for him to succeed, he must persuade the woman to cooperate fully and eagerly, or she must offer herself to him as a beguiling sex object in the first place. In either instance, she must want to be a seductress. If she offers this pose at the time, but later blames the sexist chauvinism of men for her subsequent unhappiness, she has not moved one inch out of her death-trance. The woman must take full responsibility for all of this where her own femininity is concerned.

I once knew a man named Steve, a writer, who was divorced and then married Gail, a much younger woman. In her twenties, she was beautiful and sexy and liked to assume the pose of a 1930-40s vamp. Gail adored her father who was fifty when she was born. Gail was a fashion designer and looked marvelous in her clothes, some of which were her own retrospective '30s creations. In these outfits, she would play Tommy Dorsey dance music on the stereo and mix up a pitcher of martinis, just like Myrna Loy in the old *Thin Man* films. She was so alluring that people would stop and gaze at her in the street. Even after they were married, Steve and Gail were often observed in the company of their friends smooching and kissing, a public display of affection that proved increasingly distracting to the rest of the group. Steve was very possessive of her and demanded her attention all the time. But after about two years, Gail began to feel suffocated and imprisoned by Steve's riveting attentions. Trapped like a bird in a cage, she increasingly realized that Steve never really knew who she was as a person, but was sexually fascinated with the outer role she played. Unable to get him to understand the problem, she finally left him. It was obvious that Gail was romancing her father, recreating the 1930s when he himself was young, not forming a realistic relationship to a contemporary man, and that Steve was in love with his own possessive fantasy about women, not the actual Gail. In this predicament, Gail and Steve were equally responsible for the difficulties of their obsessive liaison.

Too often in the past, the notion of "femininity" has been a male fantasy which women have devoured and imitated. This was certainly true for Gail and Steve. In this sense, women have been pandering themselves even if they haven't actually walked the streets. But there is a huge and glaring difference between male fantasy and womanly femininity itself. This is what Gail painfully came to realize. There is, in fact, an essential or inherent femininity and sexuality appropriate to a woman who has sovereignty over her own life and her own body, and whose sense of womanhood emerges from her biology and authentically from within her own psychic and spiritual life. It is a woman's own sexuality, consciously realized, that must be acknowledged, and not displaced by the male's imagined version of woman's eros. A woman can only safely belong with a man if she first belongs to herself and realizes this clearly in her mind!

So there is this instinctive tendency in women to flirt with men by appealing to their erotic interest. However, much folk literature leads us to believe that it eventually becomes necessary for a woman to own her soul and take a stand in her intrinsic womanhood with a certain clear separation from male influence. This involves a relative detachment from instinct in order to achieve a field of conscious reflection that will produce a more objective view of self and world. All the story images of housekeeping and seed sorting point to this need for mental discrimination. In a later chapter, we will examine a tale called "The Iron Stove," a less-known tale from Grimm, but one which brings out clearly the long and arduous journey that a woman must travel on her own to prepare herself for marriage.

When Aphrodite holds complete sway, it is impossible for two people to achieve a relationship where both consciously acknowledge each other, yet retain their separate boundaries and their personal limits. When they retain their boundaries, the two individuals are each persons in their own right, and their connection does not require the loss of their respective identities. Unlike Catherine in Emily Bronte's steamy Victorian novel, *Wuthering Heights*, no conscious woman could make the outrageous declaration, "If I were dead and Heathcliff were alive, I would be alive. If I were alive and Heathcliff were dead, I would be dead. I am Heathcliff!" Such talk suggests an identity or a fusion of persons, and this phenomenon is the direct opposite of relationship. It is also not love but a form of narcissistic and possessive self-idolatry. One sees an extreme example of such a fusion in cases where a lover murders his or her partner when their intense passion is no longer reciprocated. In *Carmen,* the final curtain falls just as the young corporal Don Jose stabs Carmen to death because she has repeatedly shunned his offer of absolute love and devotion. And the film *Fatal Attraction* gives a similar, though inverse, result.

The wicked queen succeeds in her ploy by impersonating a peddler woman. This makes us reflect upon what is being "peddled" to us in contemporary life. Our culture sells us a bill of goods, and, therefore, we become convinced that, if we spend enough money on various accoutrements to enhance our external appearance, we will be better, more successful people, with enhanced self-esteem, so we can achieve recognition from others. But instead, we get a death-trance, the reverse of the awakening we seek.

10

After attempting to kill Snow White, first with the stay-laces and then with the poisoned comb, the queen again consulted her looking glass. When she was told that Snow White was yet still alive, the queen trembled and shook with rage. Then she went into a very lonely room in a closed-off section of the castle, a place where no one ever went. There, using conjuring and witchcraft, the proud stepmother contrived a poisoned apple, white with a red cheek, that looked so pretty that anyone seeing it would be seized with a great desire to taste it. Afterward, she made herself up to look like a farmer's wife and traveled over the seven mountains to the cottage of the seven dwarves. When she knocked, Snow White put her head out the window and said she was forbidden to let anyone in. Then the queen offered to give her an apple, but Snow White refused. So the queen said, "What? Are you afraid of poison? Look, I shall eat one half myself, and you may have the other." She cut the apple in two and said to Snow White, "Here, you may have the red cheek and I shall eat the white." Now the apple was so cleverly constructed that only the red cheek was poisoned. When Snow White saw the old woman eat her half she could resist no more. She reached out and took the red half. But the second she got a bite of the apple in her mouth, she fell down dead. Then the queen, with a terrible look on her face, crowed with delight, "White as snow, red as blood, black as ebony wood! This time the dwarves will not wake you again." As soon as the queen had reached home, she once more consulted her looking glass and it answered, "Oh Queen, in this land thou art the fairest of all."

The poisoned apple death trance of Snow White re-minds us of the Biblical story of Adam and Eve. Eve was tempted by the serpent to take and eat an apple from the tree of the knowledge of good and evil, a fruit that had been forbidden by God. In Eden the beguiler was a serpent rath-er than a jealous old queen disguised as a farmer's wife, but the two characters amount to the same thing. The mythic tradition says that, with the eating of this fruit, death came into the world for the first time. Later in the tale we learn that a piece of the poisoned apple became lodged in Snow White's throat, the so-called "Adam's apple," which is the larynx or voice box. Snow White is consequently a kind of second Eve.

In old Mesopotamia (3,500 BCE), which is the prima-ry source of this garden scene, the snake was considered the spirit of vegetation. There was nothing in the least evil about him. He simply personified the energies of nature, the spirit that makes things grow. In this sense, he was a sort of tree numen, standing for the life force of the vegetation. Those who included this mythic tale in the cannon of Hebrew Scriptures established three thousand years later (about 500–600 BCE) inverted its original significance. Rather than signifying enlightenment by the spirit of nature, for instance in the manner of a Buddhist awakening, it now became the first occasion of moral disobedience. These two mythic dispositions, the nature-oriented Eastern and the ethical-social Western, arose almost contemporaneously in the sixth century BCE. They both had deep roots before, but in the middle of this first millennium BCE— also the period of the Greek poet Aeschylus, the Greek philosopher and mathematician Pythagoras, the Indian Buddha, and the Chinese sages, Confucius and Lao-tse—their forms began to crystallize.

The mythological eye sees Snow White's death as a transitioning passage rather than an actual and physical death, for as long as organisms have lived upon the earth, they have always died. Scientifically speaking, there was never a time in the history of our planet when people or animals lived eternally. The death of Adam and Eve and their descendants, and the death trance of Snow White signify an acute psychological deprivation, the loss of a simple child-like wholeness and integrity in which humanity lives naively, completely at home and trusting, in sympathy with nature.

In this disposition there is nothing to think about or worry about. Life just *is*. Neither the dichotomy nor the precariousness of life and death is yet a concern. Actual hunger and thirst, suffering and death, good and bad, certainly exist, but they have no vital significance to an unreflecting mind. At this stage, human existence is closer to a pattern of self-regulating instinctive behavior. The artist Charles M. Schultz caught this perfectly in one of his *Peanuts* cartoon strips. The little dog Snoopy is stretched out napping on the roof of his doghouse. Charlie Brown comes bounding out of the kitchen door one morning and inquires, "Hi Snoopy, what are your plans for today?" Snoopy replies, "Plans? … Well … I … er … I guess I never really … " Snoopy isn't in the habit of making plans, for plans require a sense of past, present, and future with the ability to imagine them. Plans require that we have desires and crave a way to satisfy them. Plans involve worry and frustration as well as anticipated satisfaction in the field of time. To live in the contented eternity of the present with no thought of progress is a different matter altogether.

When seven-year-old Snow White is poisoned by the red side of the apple, it is the child in the emerging woman that dies. Externally, she remains beautiful and life-like, not at all like a bloodless corpse, but her animated spirit seems to have departed, and she remains passive and inert, her body still as ice. Joseph Campbell has speculated that the first notions of an imagined afterlife may well have arisen when primal man began to reflect on what could have happened to an intimate friend or relative after they died. A person who was once warm, spontaneous, and lively now lies silent and cold. The same external form with its familiar features is there, but the memorable animating person who once inhabited that body is gone. What remains is merely the abandoned shell of a life once lived. Where did that life go? Even today, with all our scientific sensibilities, we have the same feeling when we view the mortal remains of a friend or relative lying so terrifyingly still in a coffin at the funeral parlor.

J. N. H. Perkins

We all know the story of Snow White and how, in the very end, she awakens from her death trance and becomes once more her lively self. The question is, why is it necessary for her soul to depart from her body for a certain space of time? What mysterious thing is occurring in the interim between life, and then life again, while she is so utterly still and mute? As we have previously suggested, this is an instance of Persephone in Hades, the descent of the young maiden daughter of Demeter (Ceres), the grain goddess, into the realm of the departed spirits.

The Snow White tale, with its mother-daughter complications and the centrality of its fruit image (Persephone could have fully returned from Hades but for the fact that she took a bite of pomegranate) reflects an ancient mythology that vastly predates Christian Europe, just as the paradisiacal fruit of the Biblical Genesis story harks back to a much earlier Neolithic age of earliest Mesopotamia, two thousand years before there was any Hebrew history at all.

In the mythology of those desert and semi-desert peoples who worshipped the transcendent sky god exclusively, the lower regions were given no positive value. Although the earth itself was believed to be the creation of the great god of the heavens, in and of itself alone it had no positive spiritual importance. In fact, to the migrating herdsmen and those numerous others who adopted their cosmology, the underworld was a region of diabolic creatures and events. Humanity had to be constantly on guard to protect itself from the dangerous genii and sprites of the earth—in other words, the realm of the powerful feminine goddess. For this reason, richly embroidered rugs, which we in the West call "oriental," were laid down on the bare ground inside the Bedouin tents as protection from the earth demons. In later Christian mythology, the underworld, now a fiery Hell, became the abode of the devil himself. Eternal imprisonment, unending punishment, and estrangement from all that is good lay beneath the surface of the earth. In contrast, truth and salvation were believed to come from the heavens above. This is a strictly masculine view of the cosmos, one that severely demeans the earthy feminine dimension of existence, and it has contributed to the evolving psychology of the human personality that is implicit in much of our cultural heritage.

The perpetual misogyny inherent in our culture strongly prejudices our evaluation of the aptitudes of women and men respectively, just as it distorts the significance and the value of masculine and feminine themes of living intrinsic to both sexes. Doing, knowing, and controlling—conventional masculine traits (left-brain)—are valued more highly than the traditional feminine traits of being, living, and relating (right-brain). Detached will and clear purpose are considered superior to vulnerability, involvement, and empathy. Resisting nature, even to the point of repressing it or brutally exploiting it for the sake of power, convenience, or profit is considered preferable to aligning one's self with the inherent patterns and rhythms of the environment. These later characteristics fall into the secondary categories of life enrichment, personal enjoyment, and recreation, just as courses in the fine arts tend to be peripheral to critical-analytical subjects in topics like science, history, and math. Enjoying life deeply is a luxury that one only deserves after years of hard work and careful discipline, in one's "free time." Of course, this principle is flouted regularly, but all the while, something in secret gnaws at the conscience. Within the American political spectrum, the right tends to side with a masculine or patriarchal disposition (John Houseman says, in an old Smith Barney Wall Street commercial, "We make money the old fashioned way—we EARN it!"), whereas the left tends to identify itself with the feminine or maternal character (for example, the welfare state).

However, the foregoing cosmic setup is not nearly as old as the mythology of the settled planters, whose lives were preoccupied with the raising of cereal grains like wheat and barley, and eventually tuberous plants and fruits. The lives of these agricultural villagers, who traced their origins back to Neolithic times, revolved around the seasons of harvest and planting and the cycles of rainfall that provided irrigation for the crops. These peoples depended upon the earth for their whole livelihood. They envisioned the cycle of the seasons, the coming and going of the vegetation, the springtime planting of the seeds in the earth and the harvest of the autumn as the Great Round of the Earth Goddess. Here, the farmer envisioned himself as the spouse of his livestock and the fertile land. Our present-day agricultural terminology still reflects that sense in the expression "animal husbandry." This was a feminine cosmology, where the seasonal passages into and out of the earth reflected the creative bodily rhythms of the Mother of All. Attuning oneself to these rhythms was the path to truth and the fullness of life. It is precisely these creative bodily rhythms within the depths of Snow White that are surfacing as she passes through her transitional death trance.

In certain primal cultures, when a girl first menstruated, she was shut up in a little hut away from the rest of the tribal community. There she sat alone, meditating on nothing but herself and her own physical body. In an analogous manner, Snow White is being shut up inside herself, oblivious to the larger world outside, where she will be initiated into the mystery of her own body and the momentous transformations occurring therein. The close parallel between the events transpiring within her and the observed rhythms of the surrounding natural environment, including the phases of the moon (the source of our term *menstruation)* will gradually become obvious to her. Alignment with nature is the age-old feminine way. Alignment with a divinely imposed law—especially regulations applied to social structures and imposed morality—is the age-old masculine.

In the old Neolithic to Bronze Age Near East (c. 5000-1200 BCE), when the wandering herdsmen appeared toward the end of the second millennium BCE, they viewed these settled agricultural peoples—these planters and breeders of barnyard livestock—as diabolical and inferior. To migrating herdsmen such as these, who practiced a transcendent Father religion of the thunderous storm cloud and the lightning bolt (Indra, Yahweh, Zeus, Odin, et al), the fertility rites of those who ploughed the earth were considered the worst abominations of all. Worshipping the Great Mother as the mistress of the regenerating seasons of planting and harvest was seen to be nothing other than idolatrous. Eternal death, not new life, could be the only result of such disgusting beliefs and practices, for these rites of fecundity alluded to a mythology centered upon a figurative mother-son incest, a ritual theme which, as we now know, was the ancient source of the Oedipus drama in much later Greece, where it had taken on a negative connotation. Here, the agricultural cycle of the dying and rising vegetation was anthropomorphized (symbolized in human terms) as the continual fructification of Mother Earth by her own offspring, thus making the great Father seemingly irrelevant.

In this context, a cosmology and theology of utter *transcendence* came into a sharp collision with a cosmology of natural *immanence*. For the planters, it was within the human body and within the larger body of plants and animals that one encountered the profoundest mysteries, rather than above in the airy atmospheric heavens. Life comes from the visible and concrete Mother, not from the invisible and intangible Father. Life is natural, not ethereal; the spirit is *in* nature, and within its intrinsic events, not *outside* of it. It would be a serious error to interpret this scheme as a kind of materialistic *pantheism*, for among such folk, there was no sense that the divine had somehow been *reduced* to nature or that the natural world had supplanted the divine. Rather, the whole environment was considered to be bursting with an enchanting numinosity, fueled by a powerful daemon that worked inside the body of nature rather than outside of it, yet was not to be confused with it.

In an imaginative sense this seems to be an entirely rational explanation. Mother Earth gives birth to vegetation. But at harvest time, some of the grain is saved to be planted in the spring. So what Mother Earth produces from her body is also that which inseminates her for the next season. Such a Great Woman has no need of an equivalent male partner, for she is fully capable of producing a little phallic boy lover independently within herself. That lover is the seed that she herself produces. By eating the apple of death, Snow White is being drawn into this profound regenerating system of nature, not as the male fructifier, but as the all-encompassing Woman. The little phallic boys appear in our tale as the seven dwarves, who dig and delve in the mountains for gold. By carrying their light deep into the mines, they impregnate the goddess, so that with their help she may give birth to copper and gold.

The planting of the seed in the earth was likened to its death and burial in the tomb-womb of the Mother. In the feminine mythology of the earth goddess, this seed was personified as a divine son, fruit of the womb of his all-encompassing mother. In order for agricultural life to prosper, this son had to be ritually sacrificed to her in order to make the seasons go round in the production of food grains. That "son" who stands for the vegetation is the source of the mythology of the dying and rising god, the antique beginning of the religious theme of death and resurrection three thousand years before the Christian era. This Divine Child of the Divine Mother was variously worshipped all across the ancient Near East as Osiris, Tammuz, Adonis, or Attis. In Babylonia, Tammuz appears as the youthful spouse and lover of Ishtar, the great mother goddess, the embodiment of the reproductive energies of nature.[14]

Among the rootless Syro-Arabian Semitic herders who migrated across the land, the male tribal ancestors and the blustering warrior sky god are primary themes. Here the key to identity is in the social group led by the dominant males, and sanctified time, expressed in the imagined origins and destiny of the people. This scheme constitutes the first notion of history and the idea of progress and providential development, including territorial expansionism. The appropriately regulated relations between the member folk of this group is the beginning of law and ethics as we know them today.

Among the planters and their successors, the nature gods are primary and the emphasis on the maternity of the earth is paramount. Tribal ancestors and social-historical developments over time are secondary and of peripheral importance. Among the nomadic herders, moral behavior according to the dictates of the Great Father is the key to validation in the common life of the society, and the purpose of the group's lordship over creation is to control and manipulate natural resources for social survival. By and large the male notion of truth is extrinsic to nature and is spiritual and disembodied, much as our abstract intellectuality is today. Conversely, in the mother-religions, truth is intrinsic or inherent within the eternal rhythms of the seasons and the masculine deity is imaged as a virile animal. Here, in the old mother religions of the embodied spirit of the earth's vegetation, we have the foretelling of modern ecology. Nature itself is a divine person with a soul, not merely a created *product*, intended primarily for our convenience and consumption!

In the Canaanite religion of the eastern Mediterranean, existing from about 3000 BCE, this boy lover was worshipped as the divine Baal, son of the goddess Baalath, a form of the Semitic goddess Astarte.[15] In Greece these two were called approximately Adonis (who was killed by a wild boar!) and his mother Aphrodite (the goddess herself as boar sacrifices her own son to herself in the act of self-fertilization or auto-impregnation). At this point we should recognize the connection between the old mythology of the planters and the significance of the stepmother queen, who "kills" Snow White with the luscious apple. In so doing, she is drawing the little girl into the erotic, high-energy field of natural fertility. Here, what is sacrificed is not a feminine person herself but her masculine creative consciousness— a process represented by the mytho-poetic symbolism of death. In her glass-enclosed coffin, she is still lifelike, yet her capacity for conscious awareness is "dead."

Snow White's death trance is the means by which her body and her feminine soul are being aligned with the principle of the Great Woman. She must "die" (lose consciousness) and, like a rotting fruit, become immersed in the body of nature before she can evolve into her adult feminine identity. Recalling what we have observed before, Snow White's fully developed femininity will encompass her subsidiary masculinity as a form of interior creative and self-inseminating energy. This harks back to the "littleness" of everything in the cottage, and particularly the diminutive size of the dwarves, who work and serve the interests of the Mother in the mountains. Here, in a sense, the masculine consciousness lives inside the woman. Within her, he is her creative spirit, the wise serpent in the Garden of Eden of her soul.

Snow White is a girl, not a boy, so she is aligned with the goddess. By coming under the aegis of the Great Mother, Snow White will have access to the creative masculine cycle within herself, and thus will avoid falling under the externally oppressive power of the male. If we apply this to our psychology, then within a woman's psyche, the strength and wisdom of femaleness must be superior to maleness, and the purpose of mental consciousness is to recognize, appreciate, and ecologically validate the richness of organic life within the personality and in the surrounding natural environment, rather than trying to dominate and exploit it for extrinsic purposes.

The death of Adam and Eve, together with the death of Snow White, is the preliminary and necessary event, the *felix culpa*, or "happy fault," that must precede a coming to new life. When Adam and Eve tasted the fruit of the knowledge of good and evil, they were punished by being ejected from Paradise, where, subsequently, Adam was consigned to the hard work of tilling the soil by the sweat of his brow. In other words, he was demoted from the superior status of herdsman to the inferior status of farmer. Much later, Jesus's gospel parables are filled with agricultural imagery concerning seeds and treasures buried in the fields as well as allusions to the arcane mysteries of the vineyard. In the sacramental rite he established, he proclaimed his symbolic identity with bread (Demeter) and wine (Dionysus)—food images straight out of the old High-Neolithic tradition. Here, the despised farmer mentality seems to have been, to a degree, redeemed. Christianity could be characterized as a union of sky god and earth mother, producing a new, holistic spirituality, transcendent and immanent all at once, both human (*humus*—earth) and divine, both man and God. In anthropological and theological language this is termed *panentheism*—the paradoxical union of immanence and transcendence.

It is the mythology of the farmer that forms the mythic underpinnings of Snow White's life. That is why the poison-transforming apple is delivered by a "farmer's wife." The stepmother in disguise is simply code language for the ruthless and jealous purposes of Mother Nature.

Snow White is now in the underworld, to which her soul has departed, while in the upper region, her body lies as still as a stone. She is "dead," which means that she is in the womb of her second, prototypical mother, the earth goddess Demeter. This is all in order for her to endure and accomplish the gestation of her adult womanhood. Being so immersed and buried in the mother, the daughter will finally be capable of being a mother herself. This second gestation is the beginning of a cultural and psychological appreciation of her existence, in this case the implication of her adolescence from girlhood to womanhood. Being taken against her will "through the portal of death" (Persephone's abduction by Hades) is the mythological means to understand what is occurring when certain hormones begin to change, not only the body of a girl, but also her emotions and her mental outlook on life. In this no-exit predicament, something irreversible is happening to her. It is not a selection on her part nor does it arise because of any personal intentions, purposes, goals, or deliberate choices.

The apple with the red cheek is the fertility fruit that represents Snow White's present metamorphosis from girl to woman. With her own glowing red cheeks, she is herself that fruit. It is poisonous because in order to become fertile, Snow White must die into the underworld, just as the fruit must fall from the maternal tree and rot on the ground if the seed-germ is to grow in the soil. Such is the "poison" of sexuality that kills the innocent dependence of childhood as it prepares the girl for the possibility of pregnancy. Like Euridice, Snow White has descended to the Land of the Shades. In the enchanting lines of Ranier Maria Rilke (as he depicts Euridice):

> Wrapt in [enraptured by] herself she wandered. And her deadness was filling her like fullness. Full as a fruit with sweetness and darkness was she with her great death, which was so new that for some time she could take nothing in.[16]

The major achievement of this tale is not the death trance, but the fact that Snow White is able to pass through this stage of initiation and finally awaken from it. In a sense, this is a major cultural transition for womanhood because, rather than becoming an imitation man, she finally arrives at the conscious realization of herself as an erotic, earthy woman, capable of holding her own with a man. As frustrating as this must sound, however, Snow White isn't a model for womanhood in any secular ego sense, but simply an image of the creative soul within both women and men, as each comes to realize the vitality of the fresh life within them, rather than becoming the pawns of societal patriarchy.

11

When the dwarves came home in the evening, they found Snow White lying on the ground. She was breathing no more and was dead. They lifted her up, unlaced her, looked to see if they could find anything poisonous, combed her hair, and washed her with water and wine, but it was no use. The poor child was dead and remained dead. They laid her upon a bier, and all seven of them sat around it and wept for her, and they wept for three days.

They were going to bury her, but she looked as if she were living and still had her pretty red cheeks. They said, "We could not bury her in the dark ground," and they had a transparent coffin of glass made, so that she could be seen from all sides, and they laid her in it and wrote her name on it in gold letters, and they added that she was a king's daughter. Then they put the coffin out upon the mountain, and one of them always stayed with it, standing watch. And birds came, too, and wept for Snow White, first an owl, then a raven, and last a dove.

In the medieval period in which this tale no doubt circulated, before it later reached the collectors Jacob and Wilhelm Grimm in the nineteenth century, a dead person in a glass-covered coffin or a casket with a little quartz or thin translucent window of shell, would have been a renowned saint or a holy relic, both of which were commonly venerated by pious Christian pilgrims as they visited the great shrines of Europe: Canterbury and Walsingham in England, Chartres in France, Santiago de Compostela in Spain, and the like. The material body of the saint was believed to be the dwelling place here on earth of the Spirit of the transcendent God, and like a living icon, this body—even in death—was considered a source of ghostly light, so that even after the spirit had departed, the body, the honored place where the spirit had once resided and to which it was expected to return again at the General Resurrection, continued to remain as a holy vessel. Consequently, the body of the saint served as a local and edifying focal point of inspiration and enlightenment. To the pious believer, in some mysterious way, the eerie presence of the divine seemed still to hover about the corpse, patiently awaiting its reunion with the physical body on the day of resurrection. It is obvious that in this sort of piety, the old Neolithic nature mythology has survived in the medieval Catholic practices of Holy Mother the Church.

Today, we might also interpret Snow White's glassed-in coffin as an image of nature and of the organic, material world itself, acknowledged as a vessel radiating something from within that is far greater than its ostensible, matter of fact, form.

Snow White is *behind* the glass, not *in front of* it, as was the stepmother queen before her looking glass. When she awakens, she gazes *through* the glass, not at a reflection of herself, but at a *perception* of the world. And when others observe her, they see her *through* the glass, at *her,* not as a *reflection* of themselves. This is all about seeing beyond the surface of appearances to that which lies beyond and within—to a deeper connotation of life, of both self and others, and most importantly, to a profounder appreciation of woman. Here, self-enclosed narcissism has been transmuted to an objective perception of the real. It may be likened to the transformation of Maya (illusion) into an enlightened encounter with truth. As the esoteric Buddhist scripture, the Surangama Sutra, states, "Things are not what they appear to be: nor are they otherwise." What we see is still there. It has not changed. But we have changed, and our view of it has changed, and so its significance for us is markedly different.

We have referred to all these historic mythic and religious associations to amplify the symbolism of the coffin stage in the Snow White tale. Something of majestic importance, a substance of most precious value, without which our existence is a living death of depression and ennui, resides within the glass coffin that the little dwarves have placed upon the mountain, and by which, in turn, they stand in silent vigil, day and night. On one level at least, we might say that here lies the soul of all our humanity, awaiting its emergence from unconscious nature to lucid personhood.

We should take note of one interesting detail. The dwarves wrote in gold letters that Snow White was "a king's daughter." Yet in the opening lines of this tale, the king is not mentioned, and later on he plays no protective role whatsoever in the painful vicissitudes of Snow White's struggles with her ferocious stepmother. Initially, Snow White is presented more as a "queen's daughter" (a woman's woman) than as "a king's daughter," and her paternity seems to be from above, from the abode from which the snowflakes descend, rather than from a human father, who would symbolize the culturally enforced conventions of the patriarchate.

In addition to the coffin, the birds—the owl, the raven, and the dove—carry mythological significance. In Egyptian symbolism, the owl stands for death, night, cold, and passivity, namely the condition of the sun after it has set in the west and descended into the underworld below the horizon. This is when the masculine power of Helios is dead inside the maw of the dark goddess who has consumed him into the great abyss of her tomb-womb. The owl is associated with Osiris, the dead pharaoh, identical with the solar deity in the underworld, *night-sea* portion of his daily cycle, just as his son, the reigning king, appears as the falcon, emblem of the bright sun god Horus, soaring brilliantly across the heavens above. The owl, as the goddess Athena's bird, is also the emblem of wisdom, because of his large eyes and his ability to see in the virtual darkness of night. So the owl stands for the enigmatic nighttime vision associated with womanhood, when the sun is dark in the outer terrestrial world of daylight consciousness, but is more softly illuminating the interior of the personality, as happens at night when our heads are flooded by dreams. As any therapist will tell you, women, on average, have a greater interest and willingness for psychological insight than men, who feel they know plenty enough already without any further aid. For so many men, insight, self-examination, and help from another are tinged with the notion of weakness, ineptitude, and confusion. Osiris, the sun god in the underworld, is associated with the Greek god Hades, who abducted Persephone to the Land of the Shades. We have seen a version of him in "The Devil's Three Golden Hairs" tale. Consequently, these amplifications on the theme of the owl give us a picture of consciousness hidden away in the darkness of night and the underworld, i.e., a condition of profound unconsciousness that is likened to death.

The black raven, on the other hand, is the bird of the Scandinavian god Odin, known among the old Germans as Wotan. Some have considered Odin to be the Norse version of the Greek Zeus, father of the other gods. Odin was accompanied by two ravens, one seated on either shoulder: Huginn and Muninn, *thought* and *memory*.

Ravens also represent deep, dark thoughts and intuitions, not necessarily evil, but more connected to the shadowy, depressed side of human mentality, illuminating thoughts that come to us in our darker, lonelier moods. In this sense, the raven is associated with profound yet melancholic insight into the divine and into the obscure depths of the human condition.

We see this dark mood in Edgar Allen Poe's gloomy poem, "The Raven." The author, seated alone one night in his study, longs for a departed lady, Lenore ("the queenliest dead that ever died so young"), and wonders if he shall ever see her again, but the raven, who has flown into his study and perches on the head of a bust of Pallas Athena (goddess of wisdom), when asked its name, replies, "Nevermore." Such dark, forlorn thoughts are part of the normal spectrum of human mentality. In our enlightened modern day, however, in which happiness and optimism are stressed, we tend to run from our raven moods. Positive thinking, a disposition that restricts itself to the above-ground daylight world of optimistic and rational explanation, requires that we must suppress depression or escape it through medications. This is a one-sidedly masculine point of view that is unable to appreciate dark moods as a form of emotional intelligence. Depression in some circumstances can have the ultimate effect of lowering consciousness to a more fundamental and realistic level close to nature. This is especially the case if it is a realistic reaction to actual circumstances rather than a pervasive collapse of interest. If something depressing happens to us and we jump to the conclusion that it's all our own fault or that we really shouldn't feel this way, then we have made a colossal mistake. We become the victims of our moods rather than using them as a means of insight.

Dark thoughts can put us in touch with ourselves, especially if we keep them in perspective and try to appreciate their significance, so that they do not completely submerge us. The grandiose and confident person with big expectations, who lives far too high up, always experiences the vicissitudes of life as frustrating ordeals, unworthy of his exalted destiny. His motto is "independence, power, bliss and success!" If a raven mood appears, this is a sure sign of weakness or ineptitude. So right away, it must be fumigated from consciousness.

Some people, who are accustomed to coping with misfortune, are able to take a wiser, more detached attitude. Some years ago, when I encountered an old Irish farmer on the road, I mentioned how disappointing it must have been when heavy rains that year interfered with the harvesting of the crops. With a droll smile in his eyes, he replied, "Well, that would be true if I were an optimist." Such an individual has learned to take the bad with the good as part of the normal mix of life.

Among the Celts, the raven was the bird associated with the death of the great Irish hero, Cu Chulainn (pronounced "Coo-Hullen"). The raven had been the bird form of the goddess *Morrigan*, wild-woman patroness of battle, strife, and fertility. The ecstasy and intoxication of war and sex fell into her province. This may sound strange to our modern ears, but among these ancient Celts, the furious impulses of the bloodthirsty warrior and the seething desire of sexual arousal were intertwined. This may account for the tendency toward rape and pillaging among warriors in all periods of history.

The Cu Chulain legend, mentioned above, goes as follows: Morrigan, one of the powerful tribe of goddesses called the *Tuatha De Danaan* offered her love to Cu Chulainn. Not recognizing who she was, he rejected her. In reprisal, she vowed to hinder him at some future time when he went into battle. Later, when Cu Culainn was killed in a fight, Morrigan, in the form of a crow or raven, came to perch victoriously on his shoulder, signifying his predestined death at her hands.

The divine battle ravens, like the female fates of old, were thought to choose which warriors would die in battle, and afterward, like the carrion they are, were seen to pick over the bloody corpses in the field. There is an impressive bronze statue of the dead Cu Chulainn, with the Raven of Morrigan perched on his shoulder, displayed in a window of the General Post Office of Dublin on lower O'Connell Street, just north of the Liffey. It is a memorial to the fallen members of the Irish Citizens Army, who, led by the poet, Patrick Pearse, gave their lives in the name of Irish independence during the disastrous Easter Rising of 1916. The figurative lesson of Cu Chulainn's death is that if either women or men fail to recognize and appreciate the fateful power of the feminine threads of life, they will indeed be hindered and destined to fail. Then the best quality of earthly existence will slip from their grasp.

The white dove stands for purity, gentleness, guileless honesty, serenity, and truthfulness. In Christian lore, the dove is an emblem of the Holy Spirit, which serves to connect the divine realm with the human. However, in more ancient, pre-Christian times, the dove was the lovebird of Aphrodite. The goddess's sacred priestesses were known as "doves." These women, however, were not prostitutes in the modern meaning of the word, for it was their duty to symbolically enact a divine, transpersonal fecundity, a sacrament of sexuality, whose purpose was to further the fruitfulness of the harvest and animal husbandry. There is considerable controversy regarding whether such rites of prostitution were ever enacted literally and physically—Herodotus' *Histories* notwithstanding. It is possible that what Herodotus reported was really more symbolic than actual. At any rate, these "love birds" were religious ministrants and not for secular hire, as they were set apart and dedicated to the earth goddess. Such *heirodules*, or holy slaves, belonged to the Great Mother, never to men. They were considered virgins, in the old sense of the term, not because they had refrained from sex, but because they remained unmarried, with no matrimonial fetters.

The birds that hover around Snow White's coffin are reminiscent of the *ba* souls, observed in the Egyptian tomb paintings and statuary. These *bas* are the avian forms of the soul of the deceased, comparable to the externalized totem souls, familiar in our own Native American traditions. While Snow White is in the death trance, her psychological capacities for mental awareness that compose the characteristics of her personality exist apart, *in ecstasis,* in bird form.

Such a combination of birds is certainly a rich one. Snow White is surrounded by Athena (owl), the virgin goddess of wisdom, Morrigan (raven), the goddess of battle who wields the sword of life and death, and Aphrodite (dove), the goddess of sensuous love. Brains, courageous strength, and sexual allure all rolled into one! These are the innate characteristics of Snow White's personality, the aspects of her inner soul that, taken together, make her such a beautiful, three-dimensional human being. One has the impression of an enormous comprehension here, of the paradoxical union of heaven and earth, of spirit and nature, of lucidity and inscrutability, of the ideal and of the organic, of the worlds of light and of darkness. Here is woman (and humanity) still within nature, neither abstracted from it nor distorted by any extrinsic male motives, awaiting her great awakening.

The coffin rests on the mountain and within it reposes a lovely, new flower of womanhood. In ancient times, there was a process known as *exposure*, which was sometimes practiced under unusual circumstances, such as in times of severe famine or unusual oracular forecasting. For instance, as we have previously mentioned, when Oedipus was born, it was prophesied that he would grow up to kill his father and marry his mother (the old mythology of the planters: the new season follows the death of the old season). His parents, therefore, abandoned their infant child in the lonely countryside. In Hansel and Gretel, the mother, fearing her family would perish from starvation, deserted her two children in the deep forest, where they wandered alone. In the Biblical story of Moses, the tiny babe was placed in a little reed-and-pitch basket and floated alone among the bulrushes of the Nile. Snow White, by being put on the mountain, is exposed to a superior force as an offering to God. If such a child is abandoned alone, then a destiny arranged by the Higher Powers will be free to act.

Today we could say that exposure is the necessary process of letting go of jealous ownership and rigid plans in order for something bigger and better to occur, something beyond what *me, myself, and I* could imagine. This occurs usually when a big transition to another stage or important period of life is required. The old habit or program must die to make room for the next creative phase. We must become receptive to the great change that is about to take place. Sitting still and waiting to see what will happen next is sometimes the perfect strategy, for otherwise we might fail to catch the significance of a sudden event.

12

Snow White lay a long, long time in the coffin, and she did not change, but looked as if she were asleep; for she was as white as snow, as red as blood, and her hair was as black as ebony.

It happened, however, that a king's son came into the forest and went to the dwarves' house to spend the night. He saw the coffin on the mountain and the beautiful Snow White within it, and he read what was written upon it in golden letters, that she was a king's daughter. Then he said to the dwarves, "Let me have the coffin; I will give you whatever you want for it." But the dwarves answered, "We will not part with it for all the gold in the world." Then the prince said, "Let me have it as a gift, for I cannot live without seeing Snow White. I will honor and prize her as my dearest possession." Since he spoke in this way, the good dwarves took pity on him and gave him the coffin.

J. N. H. Perkins

The king's son had his servants carry it away on their shoulders. And it happened that they stumbled over a tree stump, and the shock jolted the coffin so much that the poisonous piece of apple came bursting out of Snow White's throat. And before long, she opened her eyes, lifted up the lid of the coffin, sat up, and was once more alive. "Oh, heavens, where am I?" she cried. The king's son, full of joy, said, "You are with me," and he told her what had happened, and then he said, "I love you more than everything in the world; come with me to my father's palace, and you shall be my wife." And Snow White was willing, and went with him, and their wedding was held with great show and splendor.

In this penultimate stage of the story's development, we begin to see an ironic twist, namely that the dead unconsciousness of Snow White is a necessary preparation for the visit of the prince who falls in love with her passive, lifelike corpse.

Hard as this is to understand and accept, there are certain moments in our lives when it is necessary to "fall asleep" and be overtaken by the higher powers of the psyche, those transpersonal forces that energize our human nature from deep within our instinctive and spiritual foundations. Some transitions must happen at an unconscious level first, and then it is the task of our meager consciousness to catch up with what is already in progress. In *The Divine Comedy*, Dante travels down through Hell and back upward again, where he climbs the peak of Mount Purgatory. There he falls asleep and, in a dream, is transported to Paradise. When he awakens, he gazes at the glorious White Rose of God surrounded by angelic choirs. The great love of his life, Beatrice, is nearby and greets him joyfully. Then she fades from view as Dante steps forward in contemplation of this breathtaking scene, which is the culminating episode of the work.

When we fall asleep in this way, it is our striving ego level that is held in abeyance. We say we are "carried away" or that we "forget ourselves" for a time. In the end, our willful sovereignty and our so-called self-determination turn out to be only partial and limited influences on our overall destinies as humans. The genetics of our biology and the age-old structuring of the brain and nervous system hold the lion's share of influence. Yet mankind has always suspected that there is something more than just our biology pure and simple, something ineffable that is difficult to capture or fully understand. That is the numinous power that lies beyond the limits of our human consciousness, but which has, from time immemorial, given us strong hints from around the shadowy edges of our experience.

When the king's son sees Snow White in her coffin, he finally tells the dwarves that he "cannot live without seeing Snow White," and then they have compassion for him. Now, if a man acted this way in real life, we would think of him as quite disturbed and possibly dangerous, a person suffering from fatal attraction, or worse, a necrophiliac.

But if we think of it in a mythic, transpersonal manner, then it makes a great deal of emotional sense. Snow White, even in death, is the image of Life Itself that gives the king's son such delight. In that sense, she is not a human being at all, but rather, represents inward fulfillment—the inspiring soul that brings to us all the rapture of being alive. This paradise on earth appears to consciousness in the mask of a lovely princess. The prince is that noble function of the psyche that comes to recognize and value magnificent Lady

Life, awakening her from her deep sleep in the soul. Their marriage represents the union of being and knowing, the two essential dimensions of every human person, whether male or female. To *be* requires that we are deeply immersed in the instinctive and emotional foundations of life. To *know* requires that we develop a certain spiritual detachment from this elemental stuff of nature so that we may appreciate it and take conscious responsibility for it without, however, severing our umbilical lifeline to the Mother Nature within. There are literally thousands of folk tales the world over in all languages and ethnic dispositions that deal with this theme of the conscious realization of elemental life.

In Emily Bronte's *Wuthering Heights*, Catherine Linton dies, and her stepbrother-lover Heathcliff cries out vehemently, "Be with me always—take any form—drive me mad! Only do not leave me in this abyss, where I cannot find you! Oh, God! It is unutterable! I cannot live without my life! I cannot live without my soul!"[17]

Some years ago, a young man told me the story of his recently failed relationship with a woman. At first he was extremely drawn to her and felt he had met the love of this life. But eventually she rejected him, admitted she didn't feel the same way at all, and they parted. Perhaps his having fallen so intensely in love unnerved her—an occasion to which she didn't feel capable of rising. Nevertheless, this very sensitive man was grief-stricken for months, often feeling the tears well up in his eyes as he pondered why the love affair hadn't worked, because he had felt so certain about it. One night he missed her so much that he descended into a crying jag, and his deepest feelings and emotions poured out of him as he shrieked and wailed in agony all alone in his apartment. Before long, his cries flipped over into intense laughter. At that moment, he worried that he might be losing his mind. The intense laughter continued until he could breathe no more and finally he quieted down, exhausted. He stared out the window of his apartment for a long, long time in utter silence, and then he heard himself say aloud, "I have never been as happy in all my life as I am right now. I have everything I so desperately need inside me now and I know I am really in love with life, not with her!" This man's emotional turmoil shifted the displacement of his soul from his girlfriend back to himself where it belonged, so that he could recapture the rapture of being alive. I might add that, at the time, his realization occurred without the help of a therapist. By fully acknowledging his pain down to the very dregs, he passed from hell to heaven.

The inner core of sublime romance is true. The inner lovers as prototypical players in the drama of life are essential to our existence. It is the projections or transferences of these sublime figures to actual mortal persons that is sometimes illusory and often dangerous.

In Hindu India, marrying couples dress up in ritual costumes, beflowered as the god Shiva and his lovely divine partner Parvati. Although the man and woman are ordinary people on the societal level, their costumes stand for the transpersonal partnership that lies in the deep background of their commitment to life-long friendship. In the most inner sanctuary of the Shiviate temple, however, stands the high-voltage symbol of erotic romance par excellence, the *lingam* and the *yoni*, the divine genitalia of the god and goddess, depicted in coitus. If I am Hindu, I live all my life in a committed sexual relation with my friend, who is my husband or my wife. But for high romance and ultimate erotic excitement (what we in the repressed West would call pornographic titillation), I go to church! It fairly scrambles our Western brains to appreciate that in India, intense sexualized romance is considered a spiritual experience, worthy only of the gods. In the home shrine of many Hindu families, one may see a bronze statue of the lovely Parvati, depicted as a lithe dancer, gracefully displaying her voluptuous naked breasts, narrow waist, and flaring hips. We could learn something from this ancient and venerable culture of introverted, contemplative people, who long ago discovered the profound truth that, ultimately, sex is divine. I have such a statue of Parvati, brought back as a present from India years ago by a dear friend. When men come to our house, I have to remind them please not to touch her ample breasts!

Snow White as royal sleeping beauty finally wakes up to life. When the prince's servants stumbled on a tree stump, the apple of good and evil that had lodged in her throat came popping out.

This awakening, as we have suggested earlier, is an awakening from the sheer elemental fecundity of primal woman, so well exemplified in the old agricultural societies even long before male dominance. Aphrodite stepmother tried to immerse Snow White in the *unconscious* grip of sexual fecundity. This expression of femininity would have served only the narrower interests of reproduction. As Snow White awakens from this sexual beauty-as-utter-passivity-and-receptivity to the male, womanhood itself gains a conscious appreciation of its significance and meaning in relation to men.

It was the Aphrodite stepmother herself, not any dominating males, who by the way are completely absent from the scene until the last episode, who wanted to keep women as *objects* of sexual desire, *objects* subjected to her own image, not free *subjects* in their own right with personalities all their own. Snow White's awakening symbolizes woman becoming active and realistic, carrying the old wisdom of fertility forward to a new level of creative realization. Now woman can achieve legitimate identity and significance in the world and become linked to a man as an equal partner. The fact that this occurs to a person of royal station and not to a commoner suggests that such an awakening is not for everyone, which means not for every aspect of any one person. It is the royal part of humanity, what we have termed the deeper prototypical dimension of the soul. The narcissistic ego, the *me, myself, and I,* in such a circumstance is only inclined to the sort of presumption and arrogance exemplified by the vain stepmother. The ego is distinctly a "commoner" in the larger drama of life. When Snow White finally opens her eyes, as do also Adam and Eve in the Eden episode of the Bible, her awareness does not bring division, guilt, condemnation, and death, which are symptoms of dissociation, but salvation and enlightenment, represented by her union with the young prince. This connotes the final rejection of the male type of dualistic consciousness in favor of one that is more sympathetic to nature, an intrinsic awareness rather than an intellectual or moralistic ideology that is brusquely imposed upon life. Here, the mind returns to the heart, to the home of love, its source. Our cerebral faculties have a way of flying at a fairly high altitude. But it is to our advantage to come down to earth, to ground level, in order to get back in touch with tangible, elemental existence.

Snow White is awakened by a mistake, when the prince's servants accidentally stumble on a tree stump. The

J. N. H. Perkins

coffin is severely jarred, causing the poisoned bit of apple to be ejected from Snow White's throat. Soon she wakes up and is conscious again after her long death-trance.

At the risk of overdoing etymologies, it might be interesting to review the meaning of our English word "stump" (Old High German *stumpf*).

When a person is "stumped," or mentally defeated in all attempts to solve a problem, he or she appears confused. So often it is precisely when we are baffled or disoriented that something new has room to enter our heads. In the end this will be a new perspective that differs markedly from our previous assumptions. It has been said often that we must first get lost in order to find ourselves. When we come to question ourselves and realize that we don't have all the answers, that is just when growth and true wisdom appears to move us to a newer and more enlightened point of view. When we make a serious mistake—a slip—or incur some failure in our lives that embarrasses or otherwise disturbs us, that is precisely when the inner world wakes up and speaks to us. This is especially true of men. It is particularly hard for men to cope with failure, such as losing a job or going through a divorce, for their proud, ego-oriented masculinity is easily threatened at such a time.

Snow White's wicked stepmother was also invited to the marriage feast. After she dressed herself in beautiful clothes, she stood before the looking glass, and said, "Mirror, Mirror, on the wall, who is the fairest of all?" The looking glass answered, "Oh, Queen, of all who are here, the fairest art thou, but the young queen is fairer by far as I trow."

Then the wicked woman uttered a curse and was so wretched, so utterly wretched and frightened, that she knew not what to do. At first she would not go to the wedding at all, but she had no peace, and could not resist the urge to see the new young queen. And when she entered the great hall of the palace and recognized Snow White, she stood frozen with rage and fear, and could not move. But iron slippers had already been put over the fire, and they were carried in with tongs, and were set before the proud stepmother. Then the royal footmen forced her to put on the red-hot shoes, and made her dance in them until she fell down dead.

If you will recall, the third day of the week (Mardi or Tuesday) was sacred to Mars (Greek, Ares) whose metal was iron. Although the Greek Ares was nothing more than a swashbuckling swordsman, the Roman god Mars had broader cultural attributes associated with agriculture, per-haps due to the iron blade of the plough. Mars was also linked to the function of righteous vengeance, the sharp retribution by the gods for an injustice among men. So here we see evidence of the intervention of one of the higher powers who have been looking after little Snow White as she has grown from childhood to adulthood and finally entered into the bonds of marriage. Now Mars/Ares was widely acknowledged to be the lover and the cult-spouse of Aphrodite. So the irony here, the tragic-comic irony and the chilling correctness of the retribution which the wicked stepmother has brought upon herself, is that, at the very wedding feast she had hoped would never occur, a feast that really signifies her own absolute and final displacement from preeminence, she is forced to dance in the iron shoes of Mars, her own lover and cult partner. Here, witnessed by all, she herself suffers a gruesome wedding feast of her own, a horrible and excruciating dance with death, a death from which she, unlike Snow White, will never awaken.

2

The Iron Stove

In this chapter we are going to consider a less well-known Grimm's tale (No. 127) called "The Iron Stove." After studying the tale in its details, I am tempted to call it "The Butterfly Princess." When we get to the end of the interpretation you will understand why I have mentioned this.

This tale provides us with a glimpse into a strange and mysterious set of events that may be viewed as occurring inside of the human personality—episodes that compensate the prevailing culture. As this is not an individualistic tale composed by one person, but rather the creation of an age-old societal tradition, all of the characters in this story can be considered as elements contained within the psyche of our common humanity. As in a gestalt dream analysis, we are everybody in the story of ourselves, and even the negative figures are necessary players in the overall action, which charts a course from an out-of-balance, dysfunctional situation, to a place where healing and wholeness may occur.

As before, let's look at the whole tale first, and then take it section by section for comment.

A king's son was bewitched by an old witch, and for many years he was shut up in an iron stove in a forest, where there was no one to rescue him. Finally, one day a king's daughter got lost in the forest and discovered the iron stove.

J. N. H. Perkins

A voice spoke from within the stove, telling the girl that it would give her directions to get home if she would promise to come back again with a knife and free it by scraping a hole in the stove.

The princess returned home and immediately told the whole adventure to her father, the king. He, however, upon hearing this, was not at all pleased and insisted on substituting two peasant girls to do the job instead of his own daughter. But each time the peasant girls journeyed into the forest and scraped, the voice in the stove knew immediately that neither of them was the real king's daughter. Finally, the princess grabbed a knife, put it into her own pocket, and stole away into the forest, found the iron stove, and after much hard work scraping, made a hole in the stove big enough to peep inside. There she saw a handsome prince, brilliant with gold and precious jewels. Delighted, she continued scraping until the hole was big enough for him to climb out. When they saw each other, they fell completely in love.

The prince wanted to run off with the princess right away, but she begged to be allowed first to return home and bid her father farewell. The prince agreed to this, but he made her promise that when she got home she must not say more than three words to her father. The princess returned home, but talked far too much, and told the king every last detail of her adventure, and then some. As a consequence, the stove, with the prince in it, was mysteriously transported far away across the sea to a strange and distant land.

Returning to the forest, the princess searched and searched nine days for the stove but it was nowhere to be found. She grew exhausted and weak with hunger and one night, sitting in a tree for safety, she detected light shining through the windows of a little hut in the distance. After descending, she soon reached the cottage, peeped in, and saw a toad family eating from a table well supplied with meat and wine. Invited to stay the night, the princess told her story, ate her fill, and slept. The next morning, the kindly toad lady presented the maiden with three needles, which she said would help the princess climb over a high glass mountain. Then the mother toad gave the princess a plough wheel to carry her safely over three swords. Finally, she explained to the princess that she must cross a vast lake. If the princess could do these things, she would get her lover back again. In addition to the needles and the plough wheel, the princess was given three nuts and was told to keep them safely in her pocket until needed.

The needles, attached to her shoes like crampons, got her over the glass mountain. On the plough wheel, she rolled safely over the three swords.

Crossing the lake, she came to a large castle. Hired in the castle as a humble scullery maid, the princess knew that her true lover was somewhere within. But now he had another maiden by his side that he intended to marry. In the evening, the princess-maid cracked one of her little nuts to eat, but discovered tucked inside, all compressed into a tiny bundle, a stately royal garment. When the prince's new lover saw this dress, she found the gown so beguiling that she pleaded to wear it. The princess kitchenmaid agreed on condition that she, herself, be allowed to sleep in the same room with the prince for just one night. This was permitted, but the false bride put a sleeping potion in the prince's drink, and all night he slept in a stupor, so that even his true love could not awaken him. The identical thing happened the following night with a different nut that contained an even more beautiful gown. Drugged by the false lover, the prince slept on, unaware of his true love's fervent attempts to awaken him. All the while, the princess wept bitter tears, crying, "I freed you from the iron stove, and I searched and searched for you, and walked over a glass mountain, three sharp swords, and crossed a lake besides, before I found you; and still you will not hear me!"

During these nights, however, the servants, listening just outside the door, overheard the pleading and lamenting coming from the prince's bedroom, and knew how the maiden had tried in vain to awaken him. The next morning they told all this to their master. On the third night, the prince threw away the drugged beverage and remained on his guard. This time, when the princess opened her third nut, she found a gown of indescribable beauty sparkling like the very stars of heaven. The false lover couldn't wait to wear this dress as well and the same bargain was made as previously. When the princess entered the darkened chamber, the prince pretended to be asleep as before. Soon the princess began to weep and protest about her long-suffering search for the prince over a tall glass mountain, three sharp swords and a lake, and how he had still refused to hear her. At these words, the prince suddenly leapt to his feet wide awake and, exploding with joy, declared, "You, dear Princess, are the true and rightful bride. You are mine and I am yours!"

Stealing the false bride's clothing to keep her from following them, the true lovers crossed the lake, the three swords, the glass mountain, and then they came to the toads' little hut. But miraculously, it had been transformed into a magnificent castle. The toads, who years before had been bewitched by a witch, had now resumed their original human form as happy king's children. The wedding was celebrated, and the old king, the true bride's father, was summoned. He remained with them, and the couple lived in happy wedlock for the rest of their lives.

"The Iron Stove" has the ring of a woman's story, a tale of feminine psychology, although it no doubt applies equally to the interior side of men. Earlier we mentioned that a royal marriage represents the holistic union of consciousness with the unconscious, of spirit with nature, of the masculine and the feminine aspects of existence, functioning together in a balanced and creative way. We also observed that these masculine and feminine themes must not be directly sex linked. Each exists, respectively, in the personalities of women and men alike. The health and the empowerment of each sex rest upon the creative interpenetration of these masculine and feminine principles. For individuals and for society at large to be healthy, there must be a reciprocal, cooperative marriage of these hidden companions inside every woman and every man, so that doing and knowing may be related to living and loving.

Now let's return again to the first section:

A king's son was bewitched by an old witch, and for many years he was shut up in an iron stove in a forest, where there was no one to rescue him. Finally, one day a king's daughter got lost in the forest and discovered the iron stove. A voice spoke from within the stove, telling the girl that it would give her directions to get home if she would promise to come back again with a knife and free it by scraping a hole in the stove.

J. N. H. Perkins

The princess returned home and immediately told the whole adventure to her father, the king. He, however, upon hearing this was not at all pleased and insisted on substituting two peasant girls to do the job instead of his own daughter. But, each time the peasant girls journeyed into the forest and scraped, the voice in the stove knew immediately that neither of them was the real king's daughter. Finally the princess grabbed a knife, put it into her own pocket, and stole away into the forest, found the iron stove, and after much hard work scraping, made a hole in the stove big enough to peep inside. There she saw a handsome prince, brilliant with gold and precious jewels. Delighted, she continued scraping until the hole was big enough for him to climb out. When they saw each other, they fell completely in love.

The prince wanted to run off with the princess right away, but she begged to be allowed first to return home and bid her father farewell. The prince agreed to this, but he made her promise that when she got home she must not say more than three words to her father, the king. The princess returned home, but talked far too much, and told the king every last detail of her adventure, and then some. As a consequence, the stove, with the prince in it, was mysteriously transported far away across the sea to a strange and distant land.

As we study this tale, notice that the story makes no mention of the princess's mother. The only parent referred to is the princess's father, the king. When one parent is conspicuously absent, this hints at the underlying trouble. The queen is strangely missing, yet at the same time, there is a negative female figure in the background, namely the witch, who incarcerated the prince in an iron stove, and as we subsequently learn, turned the rest of his family into toads. She appears later in the tale disguised as a false bride who drugs the prince into a stupor.

106

So, the transpersonal feminine figure that should be a partner to the king has disappeared from consciousness and turned up as a negative character somewhere else. Such a circumstance is typical of a cultural predicament in which everything is excessively masculine, ruled by the programmatic masculine values of doing, possessing and controlling, an inflexible system of absolute formulas for living. The more organic, holistic, and flexible feminine side that forms the genius of love and relationship, which contributes to the rapture of being alive, reacts and begins to cause trouble. The queen, sensing that she has been harshly ruled by male values turns into a witch and imprisons the prince in her stove. This deep feminine negativity lurks in the background of many women's lives today. Our tale makes this dilemma more understandable and also hints at the proper solution, which requires much feminine effort and courage, fueled and inspired by a passionate and tenacious love and by the need to live up to the ultimate, mountain-sized truth of one's feminine self as an equal partner to the masculine.

There are two levels involved in the liberation of women. One is social, political, and historical, where actual women struggle for equal opportunity and sovereignty of their lives in the external world. This sociological level has received plenty of attention in recent years. But there is another level, the inner companion to the first. This is the internal or intra-psychic realm of liberation, the freeing and the strengthening of the whole woman, of both the masculine and the feminine aspects within a woman's inner depths. Such a dimension lies concealed within the unconscious shadow side of our "equal rights" preoccupations. In order for such a rebalancing to be convincing and effective, it must succeed inside each human personality as well as outside in the human community.

Our tale is about something feminine saving something masculine and integrating it in a balanced way. In the initial situation, a king's daughter gets lost in the forest and discovers an iron stove.

The theme of getting lost in the forest is a common predicament in many folk tales. This suggests that the chief character in the tale, in this case the king's daughter, has somehow departed from the standard program for living, where her father, the King—the one who governs the collective mentality of the culture—is fully in charge. Here, the whole cultural mindset is identified completely with masculine values and ways of living.

In psychological language we could say that the king's daughter, representing the challenges of feminine development that need to be met at a given stage of culture, has gone "beyond the pale" or proper bounds, dropped out, and entered the territory of the supra-cultural values of the unconscious, represented by the dark forest. She has wandered away from the discipline and the beliefs that have been inculcated in the official masculinized society and has disappeared into the hinterlands of the human psyche, into the realm of pure nature below normal awareness. This makes her a heroine, a classic female protagonist whose task is to reintegrate the unbalanced, one-sided, dysfunctional personality.

The following dream comes from a young woman artist who was overly dependent upon her parents and anxious about navigating her own life.

I was riding in the car with my parents in the country. I was sitting in the back seat listening to their conversation. I think at first I was interested in going with them on their excursion, but then I changed my mind. My mom was nagging me about something and I decided that I could stand it no longer. I asked them to pull over. I got out and said that I would find my way home. I walked back and followed the path for a little while. Then I realized I had a long way to go, so I decided to cut into the woods and see where it would take me. Deep in the woods, I found a house that was hidden away between the trees and looked in to see if anyone was there. I saw a girl my age who asked me where I was going. She wanted to come with me, and I was thrilled.

As you can see, the dreamer abruptly leaves the path of her parents' life and strikes out on her own into the forest, just like the princess in "The Iron Stove." There she discovers a house in which she meets, not a prince, but an important dimension of herself, a part that couldn't be included or lived as long as she conformed to the standard program of her parents. In a sense we could say that the dreamer "found herself" when she courageously took a risk by leaving her parents. The new friend asks her where she is going. That is precisely the question the dreamer herself should ask, namely, "Where am I headed in my life–in *my* life?" None of us will ever know the answer until we ask the right question!

The heroine's job is to retrieve what has been lost to consciousness, or to bring up something new that is needed for the further development of a culture or an individual. Since ancient times, we humans have recognized that there is something about the feminine personality that is both mediumistic and remarkably intuitive. In the tale of "The Iron Stove," the king's daughter, like the *shamaness* or medicine-woman of many traditional cultures, rambles into the land of the spirits, which is the uncharted prime-val forest. She must get away from her father if the dilem-ma of the negative, extremely possessive witch queen is to be solved. She must also get away from this domination *within herself.*

Without the king's daughter, the prince is lost. The development of a new and transformed masculine dimen-sion of wholeness has been repressed or suppressed into the unconscious. The subterranean inner world has held it as a prisoner, locked inside the iron stove. The tale says the prince has been bewitched by a witch.

The new masculine attitude, one that is capable of making a creative relationship to the world of the feminine, is "in the oven." We know that the "oven" is a figurative term for the uterus. If a woman has "one in the oven," that means she is pregnant. The unconscious, the maternal source of the new attitude, is holding it fast in her womb. This is, of course, the negative mother, the stepmother, who, like the witch in "Hansel and Gretel" wants to cook Hansel and eat him. It is only Gretel, the sister and feminine half of whole-ness, that can save him from the fate of the oven. So in our tale, the king's daughter is an aristocratic version of Gretel, and the prince is a patrician representation of Hansel.

The incarcerated prince tells the king's daughter to go home and get a knife and return to scrape a hole in the iron stove so he can escape. The knife is a symbol for the rational mind, the power that can cut one thing from another, making mental separations, decisions, or discrimi-nations. We sometimes speak of an *incisive* mind, or a *razor sharp* mind, or of a *keen* mind. Apparently, only the sharp mind of a woman can do the job in this particular predicament. This is because the male mind is completely helpless, caught in the mother-complex.

In the late nineteenth century, the German ethnologist, Leo Frobenius, in his book entitled *The Era of the Sun Gods (Das Zeitalter des Sonnengottes)*, described the old mythology of antiquity regarding the death and resurrection of the sun. We have alluded to this theme before, but let us revisit it again. As I relate this mythologem, a very precious jewel in the history of the human imagination, keep your mind on the situation of the prince imprisoned in the iron stove in the deep, dark forest.

It was believed that the celestial sun god, Helios, was born out of the eastern ocean, where he had escaped imprisonment in the underworld. Reaching the apogee at mid-day, he began a gradual, ever weakening afternoon descent toward the western horizon. At evening sunset, exhausted of his energy, he entered the sinister zone of the underworld, where he was devoured by an ogress mother-bride—a personification of the primeval waters of chaos. Paradoxically, this entrance into the netherworld was envisioned as the simultaneous death-burial and coitus with the dark goddess of night. In this instance, both the finality of the grave and the nascent possibilities of the womb are a single ironic mystery, two sides of the one coin of truth. Here, to die, is to inseminate the underworld and thus start the process of conception, gestation, and birth all over again. Like the mate of the black widow spider, the conjugal embrace cost the male sun god his life. As the personification of yesterday, Helios dies, never to live again. Yet as the seed of tomorrow, he is paradoxically alive as his own offspring, now a fetus in the womb of the dark goddess of the abyss. Like all young gods, being a fellow of prodigious resources and strength, the new fetal Helios struggles and finally breaks the bonds of his gestational imprisonment, escapes, and soon appears on the horizon as the new and brilliant hero of the dawn.

Frobenius called this mythic adventure through the underworld, dividing one day from the next, "The Night-Sea Journey." Versions of this myth are found all over the ancient world, and in many primal cultures. This is no doubt the deep mythic background for the Christian doctrine of the death and resurrection of Christ, the God-Man, forecasted in the Hebrew Scriptures (Malachi 4) as "the Sun of Righteousness," who was destined to appear with "healing in his wings."

One could then say that the prince, the son of a king, is similar to the imprisoned sun god. The prevalence of the shining gold and sparkling gems that the princess observes through the hole in the stove points to the prince's solar and stellar significance, just as did the golden hairs of the devil in "The Three Golden Hairs" tale. Symbolically, the prince's rescue from his iron jail in the forest correlates to the power of renewed consciousness breaking free from the regressive, bewitching power of the mother that holds back the child emotionally from his proper development toward adulthood. The castrating maternal embrace must be broken if human consciousness is to gain a new and freer existence beyond primal instinct alone.[18]

The journey from birth to midlife and on into old age and death involves a constant series of deaths and rebirths, of a series of changing conscious attitudes, one succeeding the other, as our human mentality keeps pace with the differing demands of each stage of existence. But cultures also develop and move from stage to stage. They follow an analogous pattern of change on the plane of history. Just as there is a personal or individual development, so there is also a series of collective cultural deaths and rebirths on the historic plane. The German philosopher of history, Oswald Spengler, outlined this process in his great work, *The Decline of the West.*

Some years ago I heard a woman's dream that spoke of this same transformation.

I find myself in an unfamiliar house. I pass along a hallway, and through an open door I see my husband and our daughter who is twelve years old, reclining on a sofa. They are entertaining themselves by reading stories and playing games. It is a warm and pleasant scene. But I do not linger; rather, I continue down the hall to the end and pass through a door leading to a different area of the house. As I try to close this door behind me, I have difficulty, and notice that the lock itself and the part affixed to the door frame do not coincide, so the door will not latch shut properly.

Although the dreamer is in her fifties with children in their twenties, it is clear that inside her personality, she is making a transition from a "father's daughter" sense of herself to a more mature, authoritative development of her womanhood. The dream depicts a father-daughter intimacy, but since it is not a photograph of actual outer reality (literally the husband and the daughter), but rather a subjective psychological occurrence, it depicts the dreamer's interior predicament. She, herself, is aligned too closely with the father principle. Latching the door is required so that the woman in question will not linger in a situation where her relation to her husband is like a daughter to a

113

father. If a woman does not make a sufficient separation inside herself between her feminine side and the masculine father-image of traditional authority, in real life she will remain overly dutiful and childlike or unreasonably opinionated, and this will also determine the character of her marriage relationship. The husband will be considered always to know best, and the wife will passively follow her husband's leadership, with, of course, irritable outbursts and gnawing resentment. A twelve-year-old relationship to father is a good thing if you are, in fact, twelve, but insufficient for an adult woman. The dreamer is having trouble "closing the door" on this immature period of her life.

In our tale, the prince tells the princess that she must not speak more than three words to her father before returning to join him. Remaining on too familiar terms with the old father authority will jeopardize the princess's chances for the new lease on life signified by her future marriage. She can't proceed with her life if she remains simply her father's daughter. If the princess talks too much with her father, if she becomes too familiar and comfortable with him and his sphere of influence, then she will be stuck in the old value system and thus unable to participate in the new venture with the prince.

Much of what her father represents is, of course, incorporated into the child's own psyche early on. It is this interior complex of paternal authority that must be transcended if a woman is to find her own way. No matter how outwardly rejecting she is of male authority, a woman will not develop a healthy feminine standpoint until she discovers it for herself *inwardly*. Much of the touchy, judgmental bias and inflexible opinions voiced by some women are caused by the failure to free themselves from a ruthless male dominance within, just as so much male emotionality and moodiness stems from possession by the mother-complex. Women who can't separate from the inner father are typically possessed by unquestioned and unevaluated thoughts, as if these ideas amount to some kind of god-like absolute truth. Women so possessed either beat up on others with ready-made pronouncements because they think they always know best, or else they become the victims of such distressing ideas inside themselves and suffer a ruthless self-doubt with consequent anxiety and incapacitating depression and self-loathing.

Lucy was a Boston investment banker in her early forties, with an unresolved father-complex. Lucy believed that she should model her life on her father. She was in grave danger of succumbing to a completely masculine way of living, a social identity where her own rich femininity would have no place but utter subservience. Then she had the following dream:

I dreamt I was in a terrorist's castle. I was with a lady. She was veiled in white, so I did not see her features. We were sitting in a small room—it was a cross between a police interrogation room and a priest's cell used for confessions. A charismatic Middle Eastern man was sitting opposite us. He was talking a lot about how excited he was that we were joining his family.

He said that this family had strict rules, but that everyone in it lived a spiritual and virtuous life, and as spiritual and virtuous people ourselves, we would fit right in. I wasn't buying it. I kept getting a bad feeling and thinking that this place was more of a cult than a family. When he finished his long-winded lecture on the pros of joining his family, he whipped out two contracts, and asked us to sign our names.

Both the veiled lady and I looked at the documents and felt a sense of dread. While we were reading, the terrorist priest leaned forward and asked us to confess our secrets. This raised some alarm bells inside me. I looked at him and asked him why I should share my secrets, since, if I did, they would no longer be secrets. He got impatient and angry and said that in one family there should be no secrets. As head of the family, he would carry our secrets, as well as our conscience, for us.

I was appalled. I felt like I saw through him clearly—who he really was—for the first time. I also felt that I was in danger. I looked at the white veiled lady and felt that she agreed with me. I had to buy time and get us out of this situation without arousing too much suspicion. So I told the terrorist priest that I wanted more time to think about it and put my affairs in order before I joined. Then we got up and started walking toward the exit.

The castle was huge—it had the feel of a police station or army barracks: impersonal, cool, and authoritarian. I was dressed in business attire (skirt, stockings and high heels), so I could not walk as fast as I usually do in my casual clothes. As we got out of the building and started walking across the drawbridge, which was made of sheer rock, I looked over each side and saw that there was a deep abyss beneath the bridge. I was frightened but decided to stay cool by looking ahead; the end of the bridge was near and would bring us back to civilization among "normal" people.

In order to walk faster, I told the lady in white to get rid of everything that she did not value. In my case, I threw my shoes, stockings, and my expensive designer purse into the abyss. I only kept my wallet, which had my identity cards and some money. I could now walk more freely and faster.

Lucy's dream is a dreadful version of *Father Knows Best!* This dream warns her that in her personal life she must shed her business role, which is the superficial personality she has adopted in order to follow in the footsteps of her father. Unless she pitches those dressy heels and fashionable handbag, i.e., her business uniform, she will not escape from the terrorist paternalism that infects her soul. Instead, Lucy will retain an army barracks mentality and approach to living, i.e., top-down rigid lines of authority. The veiled woman in white is no doubt the guarded mystery of Lucy's warm feminine temperament, the sensitive part of her that can relate to people and enjoy a rich, emotional existence, which means to enjoy life as a complete woman, a wise woman, with *both* a sharp mind and a gentle heart, rather than as an imitation man. In the cool male atmosphere of the priest-police barracks, Lucy cannot see these feminine features clearly behind the white veil. These are, of course, Lucy's own feminine characteristics, which she must keep carefully hidden while in the business world.

Lucy's problem is not that she earns a living as a professional business woman. Rather, it is that her father-business complex is about to possess her entire personality, imprisoning her psychologically in a cult-like terrorist setting. Here she will be completely brainwashed by an inflexible masculine stereotype that will do the thinking for both of them. The irony of the situation is that, if this were to occur, the outer world would continue to admire Lucy as a liberated woman making big bucks in the financial world. The inner truth, however, would be that she was just a docile Near Eastern woman subservient to the masculine forces who wield power and authority over her. We have mentioned Lucy's circumstance because it is so much like the situation

J. N. H. Perkins

of our princess in "The Iron Stove" tale, who can't seem to make a separation from her father, the king.

Because the princess lingers too long in intimacy with her father, she loses her chance to be with her lover, the prince. What might have been easy has now become difficult. Fortunately, in the myths and dreams of the human imagination there is always another chance, though with each missed opportunity the trouble becomes greater.

The princess's father, the king, wants to substitute peasant girls for his noble daughter. This signifies his wish to keep the situation at a low level of importance so it does not alter the ruling attitudes of the realm. We, ourselves, do this all the time when we believe one thing officially yet behave differently. It's okay for an uneducated peasant woman, the earthy person in us all who lives close to visceral impulse, to indulge herself and have a little adventure, but this should not be allowed to change anything of vital importance in our lives. In this way, a hard dualism is preserved. This type of psychological dissociation is the source of most of our hypocrisy. Like the princess, we must often "steal" ourselves away from the narrowness of conventional ideals, even the most respected and honored ones, if we are to achieve a major transformation in our lives. As we do this, however, we should realize that this is not a matter of succumbing to personal whim or idle craving, but is in reality our faithful obedience to those higher powers that govern the true course of our lives.

Joan, a sixty-five-year-old patient who held me in extremely high esteem as her analyst, dreamt the following:

118

Death and the Maiden

I arrive at my therapist, and when it is time to leave, I pick up the beautiful flowers from a vase on the table and plan to take them home with me. I wrap them in blue paper, the same shade as my favorite tablecloth at home. I think the flowers will look wonderful there.

Joan's dream showed that she needed to "steal" herself from my influence and become her own person, rather than living dependently in the aura of the compassion and the understanding which she felt she was receiving from me in our work together. As her father had died when she was just nine years old, I had obviously become a substitute for him. In a certain psychological sense, Joan had never passed completely through adolescence in order to become her own person. But in appropriating the flowers, she was taking an important step toward moving beyond her father—whom she adulated—to an adult life of her own. As flowers are age-old symbols of femininity, she was inclined, as the dream so well put it, to take her blossoming femaleness away from the province of the father-figure analyst, and live it herself. Dependency upon people perceived as wise, wonderful, and loving is the hardest kind to break! Joan needed to sever her tie to me as an authoritative parent—just as the princess needed to leave her father in the past and proceed with her own life—so that her therapy could proceed on a new, more mature level.

These superior forces of wisdom that hover behind traditional stories and our contemporary dreams help us immeasurably in navigating our journey toward wholeness. If you descend to the bedrock foundation of any of the world's great symbolic traditions, such wisdom will be plainly apparent.

J. N. H. Perkins

Returning to the forest, the princess searched and searched nine days for the stove but it was nowhere to be found. She grew exhausted and weak with hunger and one night, sitting in a tree for safety, she detected light shining through the windows of a little hut in the distance. After descending, soon she reached the cottage, peeped in, and saw a toad family eating from a table well supplied with meat and wine. Invited to stay the night, the princess told her story, ate her fill, and slept. The next morning, the kindly toad lady presented the maiden with three needles, which she said would help the princess climb over a high glass mountain. Then the toad lady gave the princess a plough wheel to carry her safely over three swords. Finally, she explained to the princess that she must cross a vast lake. If the princess could do these things, she would get her lover back again. In addition to the needles and the plough wheel, the princess was given three nuts and was told to keep them safely in her pocket until needed.

The needles, attached to her shoes like crampons, got her over the glass mountain. On the plough wheel, she rolled safely over the three swords. Then she crossed the lake.

The princess returned to the forest and searched far and wide for the prince, but he was nowhere to be found. She searched exactly nine days. It is interesting to note that the number nine is the foundation mystical number of the Hebrews, for just as three times three equals nine, so nine times nine equals eighty-one, and, according to numerological addition, the eight and the one of eighty-one equals nine. Nine is also the multiplication of the three cosmic levels, underworld, terrestrial world and heavenly world, combined with the three traditional dimensions of the human personality: body, mind and spirit. Of course, the number nine is also the number of months of human gestation in the womb. This suggests that the time during which the princess searches in the forest is a period of a major psychological development that prepares for a new lease on life, in this case, her emancipation from her father, the king.

Finally, after the princess's long vigil in the tree, a toad lady (a positive, helpful mother figure) offers solace and wisdom and explains what must be done to find the prince. A toad would represent primal feminine instinct. Among traditional peoples, the toad carried the meaning of fertility. The peculiar shape of the toad's body and legs resembles the female reproductive system. The mouth and head are like the labia and the vagina, the torso like the uterus, and the long legs and the slender toes suggest the fallopian tubes that extend up to enfold the ovaries. In medieval times, a peasant woman who was having trouble getting pregnant would make a little clay image of a toad and place it near a statue of the Virgin in the church. In this way, she offered her fertility to the Mother of God in the hope of being blessed with a child. Though the princess lingered too long with her father, she at last ventured into the forest and made a connection with feminine instinct, which would guide her on the journey to the wholeness of marriage.

The toad lady described the difficult hurdles the princess must overcome and gave her three needles, a plough wheel, and three nuts. The needles help her climb over the glass mountain. The wheel conveys her safely over the sharp swords before she must navigate a lake without such technical assistance.

The mountain has traditionally symbolized a higher state of consciousness or illumination; that place in the clouds where earth and heaven meet. Wise folk and prophets often received their divine revelations while on top of mountains. On the summit, one is completely earthy and completely spiritual at the same time, because the mountain stands for the intersection of the highest and the lowest, the ethereal and the material dimensions of life. And as we mentioned before, mountains also symbolize the great breasts of Mother Earth. Glass, indicating clarity and spiritual transfiguration, is connected to the spirit and to the highest ideals.

The princess's challenging adventure corresponds to a woman's unique inner journey in contrast to the absorption by and influence of the conventional ideas and prescriptions emanating from the father ideals of the standard culture.

The needle has long been a metaphor for the intellect. The needle and thread together refer to the sewing of thoughts. A thread (in Sanskrit, "sutra") of thought means a developing sequence or procession of ideas. The surgeon sews up a wound or incision with a "suture," which is a stitched thread. The needle relates to the knife we saw earlier, when the princess scraped a hole in the stove, but the needle functions somewhat differently. The knife cuts, scrapes or divides, but the needle probes and can be used for making connections. The probing of the needle is creative, for it may be used to stitch together pieces of material. The needle symbolizes the means to *make a point* in the process of discrete thinking and exposition. The needle is connected to feminine intuition.

So the journey over the glass mountain with the help of the needles refers to mental development using the sharp, probing capacity of the mind. Also, the needles, used in sewing together fabrics, protect us from a tendency to dissociation caused by the kind of thinking that depreciates feeling, emotion, and the intimacy of human relationship, or inordinately isolates one region of living from another. It is impressive that a toad offers this sharp exploring competence! Since the end of the story reveals that the toad was really an enchanted human being, who had been reduced to an animal incarnation, it must be that a truly feminine consciousness, formerly active, has become stifled to unconsciousness. What once represented a feminine capacity for creative awareness and mental achievement has regressed to mere animal fecundity. Our tale speaks of the reversal of this dilemma; of the liberation of a woman's mind from the prison of instinct, without at the same time severing her links to her visceral nature.

Apparently there is danger from the three swords, which will be averted by the plough wheel rolling over them. We may become the victims of our intellectual faculties, dominated by a peculiarly cold rationalistic bent that squelches all emotion and feeling. This relates to the problem of a negative mentality, where quarrelsome or pedantic intellectuality thwarts all opportunity for humane cooperation. Some people, men included, insist upon prevailing in the debate at any price. Here discussion must become a squabble, a ferocious fight to the finish. It never remains a fair exchange of views where people listen to one another patiently with mutual respect. In this sense the sword stands for naked power, which is always incompatible with relationship, and particularly with love.

The princess is to roll over the destructive swords, avoiding injury. The wheel stands for wholeness, the symmetrical circle that has no one-sidedness. But this is not just any wheel. It is specifically the wheel of a plough, which

J. N. H. Perkins

has a sharp blade designed to cut a furrow into the earth. As we have seen, this farmer's implement was sacred to the war and agricultural god, Mars. So the wheel is linked to the blade as an aggressive tool of fertility. This suggests the keen mind used not for destructive, war-like purposes or in strictly intellectualized debate, but to foster life by supplying nourishment for humans and animals in the organic agricultural cycle—"food for thought." Such is the meaning of "they shall beat their swords into ploughshares, and their spears into pruning hooks. Nation will not lift sword against nation, there will be no more training for war." (Isaiah 2:4)

Here, our penetrating mental faculties are used in partnership with the earthy ground of our instinctive life, to interact creatively with nature and instinct. Ploughing the furrow has long been a sexual metaphor. Among traditional peoples, cultivating the soil with a blade was likened to a conjugal union between the farmer and his land, in which the ground was fertilized; in archetypal terms, this amounts to a marriage of spirit with nature, a creative, responsible and ecological partnership between the mind and the body, between human industry and the natural environment.

Our tale fails to mention that any special tools are given to the princess to help her cross the great lake, for instance, an oar, raft, or boat. The lake is a challenge, but not quite as destructive or dangerous as are the swords and the slippery glass mountain. Apparently, with the first two hurdles solved, the third is less difficult. Crossing a great body of water generally signifies a change of attitude or a movement to a new standpoint in consciousness. After such a transition, when one has finally arrived on the other side,

124

one's mental outlook is completely different. Crossing the surface of the water means that a person is able to maintain the stability of consciousness, "keep one's head above water," during a chaotic psychological change. Big psychological shifts can be stressful, if not dangerous. One may lose one's bearings and be swept under by turbulent emotion or confusing thoughts, as one explores unfamiliar territory. So crossing the lake is a test of mental steadiness and buoyancy necessary for navigating life.

Crossing the lake, she came to a large castle. Hired in the castle as a humble scullery maid, the princess knew that her true lover was somewhere within. But now he had another maiden by his side that he intended to marry. In the evening, the princess-maid cracked one of her little nuts to eat, but discovered that tucked inside, all compressed into a tiny bundle, was a stately royal garment. When the prince's new lover saw this dress, she found the gown so beguiling that she pleaded to wear it. The princess kitchenmaid agreed on condition that she, herself, be allowed to sleep in the same room with the prince for just one night. This was permitted, but the false bride put a sleeping potion in the prince's drink, and all night he slept in a stupor, so that even his true love could not awaken him. The identical thing happened the following night with a different nut that contained an even more beautiful gown. Drugged by the false lover, the prince slept on, unaware of his true love's fervent attempts to awaken him. All the while, she wept bitter tears, crying, "I freed you from the iron stove, and I searched and searched for you and walked over a glass mountain, three sharp swords, and crossed a lake besides, before I found you; and still you will not hear me!"

The princess has surmounted all the obstacles and arrived at a strange castle in a far distant land, where her lover has been transported because the princess spoke more than three words to her father. Here, she discovered her

true love, but he had apparently forgotten her and was engaged to another woman. When the princess attempted to
make contact with the prince, the new lover put a sleeping
potion in his bedtime drink, causing him to fall into a stupor from which he could not be awakened.

We sense that the prince has fallen victim to some
kind of negative enchantment related to the new lover.
We should recall that, originally, the prince had been bewitched by a witch and imprisoned in a stove. Apparently
the bewitchment continues, and the new lover's sleeping
potion and the prince's forgetfulness are another instance
of diabolical possession. Being trapped in the oven-womb
of the goddess and then drugged by the false lover are
successive predicaments that point to a progression of the
male from the protective incarceration of Mother to subservience to a dominant female partner. It is very difficult for a
young woman to break through such a barrier, because this
type of man is too emotionally dependent and insecure in
his own right to form a mature relationship with a partner.

A royal marriage indicates equality between the masculine and the feminine complexes residing within every
person, male or female. An out-of-balance situation where
one pole dominates, possesses, or seduces the other is incompatible with this marriage of wholeness. We see the opposite problem in the *Swan Lake* myth, where the wicked
magician, Rothbart, in the form of an owl, changes prin-
cesses into beautiful dumb swans, and thereby holds them
captive. This expresses the negative domination of femininity by masculine energies in the psyche, one that keeps a
woman's femininity unconscious, in animal or bird form,
rather than human, so that her personality remains errat-

ic and "flighty," with no power to reflect or think clearly, steadily, or systematically.

However, in this tale of "The Iron Stove" we have the inverse of the *Swan Lake* myth. Here, it is the possessive domination of the masculine principle by the feminine side—the witch of the forest—that carries the prince away from all possible contact with his true love. One gets the sense at this point that the witch, working stealthily in the background, finds that the Princess's continued allegiance to her father excludes her from the candidacy to function in the big transformation that is necessary—for if a strong and courageous woman were to become active in the drama, then the witch's own existence would become unnecessary, and her job would be done. As the heroine begins to succeed in her arduous efforts to find her rightful partner, it is revealed to her that the prince has been seduced and drugged by a new yet false lover. Consequently, he has forgotten all about the one who is destined to be his true bride and liberator. The princess is the only one who can free him from his delusion, for, as a woman, only she may exercise loving devotion in tenacious strength. If we can't grasp this, we don't appreciate the voracious power of which a woman's love is capable.

In real life, there are men who are, psychologically speaking, seduced and drugged. For example we're familiar with the man who worships his wife, doting on her and attending to her every requirement, with little regard for his own interests or needs, as if under a spell. He has fallen into a state of overly sensitive emotionality, and is in danger of being controlled and manipulated by his female partner. All common sense goes out the window and the man soon has a ring through his nose. In slang language he is "pussy whipped by pussy power." In this way he misapprehends servile obsequiousness as love and devotion. Drugs and poisons are always the tools of the negative mother in myths and folk tales, for they stand for power, not exercised openly and forthrightly, but stealthily and circumspectly, subtly maneuvering the man to just where the woman wants him.

Such is the problem of a man who is unable to get away from his mother. The inner problem of mother is that the primitive power of the unconscious devours the masculine potential to be consciously aware and proactive. Here, mood, whether it be fear or pining desire or low self-esteem, dominates all good sense. There is no mental detachment or perspective. Such a man's masculinity is "in the oven." In this state the male will react emotionally, with unrealistic caution or inordinate yearning, but in neither case sensibly or effectively. He typically throws up his hands, "goes ballistic," or sinks into a depression and withdraws. In such a psychological state he can take no real responsibility for his own life, nor can he summon the energy to exert himself with any forceful purpose. All he can do is mope and complain and blame others, fall into a slough of despondency or in some cases simply wither on the vine.

During these nights, however, the servants, listening just outside the door, overheard the pleading and lamenting coming from the Prince's bedroom, and knew how the maiden had tried in vain to awaken the prince. The next morning they told all this to their master. On the third night, the prince threw away the drugged beverage and remained on his guard. This time, when the princess opened her third nut, she found a gown of indescribable beauty sparkling like the very stars of heaven. The false lover couldn't wait to wear this dress as well and the same bargain was made as previously. When the princess entered the darkened chamber, the Prince pretended to be asleep as before. Soon the princess began to weep and protest about her long-suffering search for the prince over a tall glass mountain, three sharp swords and a lake, and how he had still refused to hear her. At these words, the prince suddenly leapt to his feet wide-awake and, exploding with joy, declared, "You, dear princess, are the true and rightful bride. You are mine and I am yours!"

Stealing the false bride's clothing to keep her from following them, the true lovers crossed the lake, the three swords, the glass mountain, and then they came to the toads' little hut. But miraculously, it had been transformed into a magnificent castle. The toads, who had been bewitched years before by a witch, had now resumed their original human form as happy king's children. The wedding was celebrated, and the old king, the true bride's father, was summoned. He remained with them, and the couple lived in happy wedlock for the rest of their lives.

While the prince is drugged into a stupor and the princess tries without success to awaken him, the servants in the hallway outside the door hear what is happening in the sleeping chamber, and they finally reveal the true situation to their master. The servants save the day. Then the prince wises up, gets a little sense, and throws away the sleeping draught so as to remain vigilant during the night.

Many myths and tales feature a curious and suspicious servant. Usually their prying brings on a disaster, but invariably the final resolution of the tale is dependent upon such a snoopy attitude, which serves the purpose of waking up an individual who has remained naïve for too long. These servants have the intuitive "street smarts" that sharpen the wits of the hero or heroine. Such an awakening brings a major resolution or helps to navigate a critical transition that is necessary before the big dilemma can be recognized and resolved. In the present instance, the prince begins to doubt his relation to his newly intended bride. The servants help him to "smell a rat" somewhere. The rat is, of course, the false lover, a kind of sex witch, who has entrapped him, hypnotized him with her voluptuous charms. Circe "of the braided locks," who, in Homer's *Odyssey*, could turn men into pigs, is the classic example of this archetypal, alluring femme-fatale.

The true bride appears in the castle in the role of a servant. She functions just like Snow White, who serves as a housekeeper in the cottage of the dwarves, or Cinderella, who becomes a menial servant in the household of her deceased mother. The heroine of our present tale trades the magnificent gowns that come from the nuts for the opportunity to spend time with the prince during the night. Although the true princess is of royal blood, she does not identify with the trappings of nobility. Her approach to her destined husband is as a menial kitchen maid. This is a version of the folklore theme called "the king (or queen) in disguise." We will encounter this theme again in four other stories in this book.

The theme of the three, ever more beautiful gowns is a typical motif. Usually it is successively a silver dress glowing like the moon, then a gown of gold shimmering with the light of the sun, and finally—the most magnificent of all—a diamond-studded robe that glitters like starlight. Such robes represent an archetypal or transpersonal role, signifying that the royal person is the earthly incarnation of a stellar, heavenly being. All royal vestments represent this high, celestial status, "on earth as it is in heaven." These archetypal vestments belong appropriately to the princess

Death and the Maiden

who is seeking her true love. We must remember that the princess is not an actual person, but a prototypical figure in the world of the human spirit.

The wonder of this imagery is that in our tale, these incredible celestial robes come from three nuts! The nut is the feminine womb of nature, where the seed of new life awaits development. The notion that an ultimate and limitless reality (here we have the emblems of the moon, the sun, and the stars) is contained in a minuscule seed is also well known in the myths of the world. In the Hindu scriptures, it is said that *Brahman*, the supreme spirit, the One Absolute Being, the entire, macrocosmic, limitless universe of ultimate reality, is also contained within the microcosmic human soul as a tiny germ, namely *Atman*, sometimes called the *Self*. In one of his parables, Jesus refers to the Kingdom of Heaven as like a tiny mustard seed that is destined to grow into a great tree. In medieval Christian iconography, Christ and his mother, the Virgin Mary, are often depicted as the king and queen of heaven. The Mother of God is typically shown wearing a crown of stars (as "Maria Stella") like the Statue of Liberty in New York Harbor. These refer, of course, neither to the human ego, nor to the self-centered "me," nor to the narcissistic "I," but to a transcendent and timeless Person that resides at the center of one's innermost being. The king and queen of the universe, though transcendent, also reside immanently within each human soul, yet they remain invisible to the sophisticated, worldly eye. The celestial person appears disguised, masked as an ordinary, unremarkable fellow. Traditional wisdom advises that one should be careful how one treats such folk. It could happen that the next down-and-out beggar, or commonplace unremarkable person you meet, is an almighty king or queen in disguise. That is a time-honored belief. The

131

J. N. H. Perkins

Christian teaching is that every human being on earth is an icon—an image of God—and thus each single person deserves our special care and respect, not because he or she has political "rights," or subscribes to the right religion or politics, but because, down underneath it all, the source of all our lives is from the divine.

This is, of course, to say that one's ordinary, apparent, surface self is not the ultimate measure of one's value or importance. We are all are kings and queens in disguise. Behind the exterior façade is the evidence of eternity.

The princess, who is of royal station, has every right to wear the noble robes of monarchy. Such garb reflects accurately who she really is, so far as her prototypical character is concerned.

The false lover, however, finds the beautiful gowns irresistible. She is filled with vain desire to wear them in order to aggrandize herself. But ironically this is to the princess's advantage, as she may thus bargain with these robes to enter the prince's chamber. Because the princess is a noble woman, she is the true bride whether or not she wears the outward costume of royalty. The false bride can only assume the role superficially, play-acting the part. She is the opposite of the queen in disguise. Psychologically the false bride alludes to an ordinary person, an egocentric person, all puffed up, arrogantly masquerading as a transcendent symbol—"putting on airs." This is the man or woman who merely plays a role in an otherwise empty suit. Yet inside, beneath the exterior scenery, as the tale "The Emperor's New Clothes" demonstrates, there is nothing there at all, but just an ordinary bloke like everybody else! Here, the divine image has been displaced by a grandiose pose, what Robert Coles was fond of calling a "phony" personality.

This phenomenon of the phony bride or bridegroom is at the root of so much of the conceited, self-centered grandiosity in our modern lives. We all have a tendency to masquerade as some kind of god or goddess and cease to live our simple, down-to-earth humanity. Our personal lives get puffed up or inflated and assume a degree of importance and prerogative that is not justified. Much of the advertising industry operates on the premise that if you can sell people a grandiose, luxurious self-image that is symbolized by a commercial product, then they will buy the product, believing that in getting it, they are acquiring a heightened status. If they can possess this or that, they can become kings or queens. The Buckingham Estates, Kensington Farms, or Versailles Parke suburban housing development is a pretense of nobility. But no royal person resides in these mass-produced neighborhoods. It is only Joe Blow, having made a few bucks, who can indulge such a silly fantasy in a bourgeois version of the standard tract house.

The princess, disguised as a kitchen maid, and her cousin Snow White are royal persons playing the roles of servants. As ordinary people, they protect psychological development from grandiose inflation, which would short-circuit the inheritance of destined royal status. It is a rule of spiritual integrity that humility and ordinariness are the necessary prerequisite for the inheritance of one's intrinsic nobility. In India, the wisdom of Brahman is hidden as a tiny seed in the soul. Here, it is believed that all human beings are intrinsically divine. Various ascetical practices and the renunciation of everything that is externally rich and glorious is a required stage on the way to enlightenment.

In the West, humility, self-denial, and works of mercy must precede sanctification and a deifying union with the Christ within, according to whose image, it is deemed, humanity was originally created. In this sense, one must risk being a *nobody* if one hopes to become a *somebody* in a deeper, more authentic way.

The celestial robes came from three nuts. It is as if these garments were produced organically from nature, in the manner of a colorful butterfly that emerges from its long internment in the cocoon. Something that is produced by an organic natural process is not a thing constructed artificially by culture or ideology. Rather, such a thing is innate to life, a revelation of what was previously hidden within, being a part of the original design. Such a realization is not achieved by being or doing what one should, not by striving, except for the truth of one's deepest self. This is why the princess is the true bride. Here there is no conformity. She does not have to follow a socially or even morally prescribed path, but simply honors her archetypal, inherent nature. Such is the way of all true mysticism.

In this story the princess does all the work. The servants' curiosity gets her out of a predicament, but the effort is all hers. When the tale ends, the princess's father comes to live with the new royal couple in their own castle, not his. The heroine has finally moved out of her father's house and now has a different relationship to him. He is now her dependent guest. The new queen is no longer a woman existing in the context of a one-sided masculine psychology. She now resides in an androgynous kingdom of mutuality, where masculinity and femininity cooperatively reinforce and validate each other. The princess evolved from being her father's daughter to becoming her own woman, struggling valiantly because of her great love and devotion, and finally, after much tenacious searching and frustration, arriving at a stage of shared intimacy with an equal partner. An inward freedom and balance have been achieved, not only between people on the plane of social relations only, but within the landscape of the human soul.

The ultimate purpose of this tale is to bring us to that redeemed condition of mind and heart, as Joseph Campbell defined the purpose of myth, where we may find, not the reasonable *meaning* of our existence, but in truth, experience "the rapture of being alive."

3

The Serpent Mother

The following Cinderella tale is from India. It is called "The Serpent Mother."[19] This time, we will take the whole tale all the way through and then comment.

An orphan girl married the seventh and youngest son of an extended family that included the parents, their six older sons, and their respective wives. The girl brought no dowry, and so her in-laws ignored and despised her. Treated worse than a servant, the girl had to eat leftover crusts from the table after the rest of the family had finished. When the time came to make ceremonial offerings to the ancestors, a sweet milk and rice pudding known as khir was prepared, but when the ritual meal took place, the other family members gobbled it up, leaving only a few burnt crusts at the bottom of the pot.

Uncomplaining, the youngest daughter-in-law, now pregnant, folded her meager khir crusts into a cloth and took them away. She planned to consume them alone after gathering water from the village well. When her turn came at the crowded spring, she placed her crusts near a snake hole and went to fill her jug. Expecting to eat them in peace alone, she returned to find that the crusts were gone. A female serpent had smelled the rich khir and had emerged from her hole to devour it. The snake had decided that she would bite the owner of the crusts if that person cursed her as a thief.

"I never got to eat my crusts," exclaimed the girl. "Maybe there was another unhappy woman, a miserable one like me nearby, who ate them. Since I couldn't have them, maybe at least she enjoyed the meal."

Hearing this, the female serpent was mightily impressed. She emerged from her hole and said, "Young lady, I was the one who ate your khir, but you didn't curse me; instead, you thought of the happiness of others. Who are you, my dear, and why are you so unhappy?"

"O Mother, I am an orphan and hence I am treated like an outcast," the girl replied with tears in her eyes; "and since I don't have any family of my own, there is no one to perform the ceremony for my first pregnancy."

"Don't you worry," replied the kindly serpent mother. "You can belong to our family, and at the appointed time we will come to perform the ceremony. Just leave a note by our hole when you need us, and we will appear at once. I will be your mother and my husband will be your father."

The girl went home and when the time arrived to celebrate her first pregnancy, she asked her mother-in-law for a letter of invitation to give to her own family. The mother-in-law made fun of her and exclaimed, "But you're just an orphan! Who could you possibly invite?" Yet as the girl insisted that she really did have a family, the invitation was grudgingly given. The girl took the letter, put it by the snake hole, and returned home.

When the day for the celebration arrived, the girl's in-laws teased her again, snickering, "Well, this should be quite a show! We can't wait to meet your illustrious kin!" But just then, rich and noble-looking guests began to arrive, bearing lavish gifts. The girl realized that these were the members of her adopted snake family, appearing in human form.

The serpent mother drew the girl aside and told her to serve them only spiced milk, for this was the proper food for their kind. When this was prepared, the snake family retired to the guest room where they resumed their snake form and quickly drank up all the spiced milk. After they became human again, the serpent family returned to the main living quarters and presented the whole family with gifts of gold and silver. At the conclusion of the celebration, the serpent family begged to take their daughter with them for the duration of her pregnancy. When the girl's in-laws had given their consent, the serpents and their adopted daughter departed for their hole.

Back at the opening, the snakes resumed their true form again, and they all descended into the serpent house, within which the girl discovered many magnificent rooms, lavishly furnished and decorated. On a plush silk-covered cushion sat the serpent king, her new father. He wore jewels on his head and had a big moustache. The whole family treated the girl with love and affection, and she enjoyed reclining on a swinging bed made of gold and silver.

The serpent mother was also pregnant, and when she was about to give birth, she warned the girl not to be alarmed at what she would witness, which, she said, was the usual precaution that snake mothers took so that not too many snakes would cover the world. When the serpent mother laid her eggs, she began to eat them up as quickly as they emerged. The girl, disgusted by this dreadful scene, dropped the lamp. In the darkness, two eggs hatched and the baby serpents began to slither away. They moved so quickly that the serpent mother only managed to bite off their tails. So there were two tailless snakes that survived.

Soon the girl gave birth to a beautiful son. When he was old enough to crawl about, the girl begged leave to go home to her husband's family. The good serpent mother overwhelmed her with rich gifts for herself and for her new son. Then she said to the girl, "Before you go, put your arms, one at a time, into the mouth of the serpent king. Don't worry, he won't bite you." Fearfully, the girl did as she was told. When she withdrew her arms, she was amazed to find them covered with many bracelets of pure gold.

Reaching home, the youngest daughter-in-law made a great impression with all of her rich presents and her handsome son. The boy began to grow, and one day as he played, he scattered some of the grain the servants were grinding onto the kitchen floor. Discovering this, the eldest daughter-in-law chastised the boy and his mother for wasting the precious food. Another time, the boy spilled some milk, and again the child's mother and he were rudely scolded. On both occasions the youngest daughter-in-law returned to the snake hole and reported her story. Before long, huge bulls delivered immense bags of grain to the house of the in-laws, followed by an entire herd of milking cows. These were gifts from the serpent king and serpent Queen. The girl's in-laws were astonished.

Meanwhile the tailless serpents asked their mother why they had no tails. She explained that at the very moment she was giving birth to them, their foster sister, who had been holding the lamp, had abruptly dropped it and the light had gone out. In anger, the little snakes said they would go bite the girl for having done this. But the snake mother said, "No, she is a good girl and she would bless you!"

The tailless serpents came to the girl's household, and one hid near the threshold of her room while his brother hid in the watershed. They decided to test their stepsister. If the girl discovered them and cursed them, they would bite her. If she blessed them, they would befriend her.

The girl stumbled near the threshold and accidentally struck one of the serpents. Surprised, she said, "I am a girl without parents. I hope my paternal relatives will forgive me if I have done something wrong. My father is the serpent god, and the serpent mother is my mother, and they have given me silk and jewels for my dowry."

The same thing happened at the watershed, and the girl remarked in an equal manner. In both instances the serpents felt they were being blessed by the girl, so they transformed themselves into human beings, gave her a new sari and blouse and gold anklets for her son, and then slithered away to their hole.

May the serpent mother be as good to us all, as she was good to this girl!

The bride of the seventh and youngest son is an orphan. She has neither family of her own nor a conventional background nor identity, nor does she have the resources that come with these. The "seventh," of course, is a special number, reflecting the full cycle of stages toward enlightenment. Seven is the encounter with nirvana, also called Samadhi, the highest level of divine illumination. The number seven is also used for the individual who does not or cannot conform to the usual, collective mentality and is not dependent upon the familiar psychology of the parents. Such a person is capable of superior wisdom. In the context of the family, it is the least important and respected member that is the connection to greater awareness: "The first shall be last; and the last, first."[20] The Grimm's tale called "The Three Feathers," which we mentioned in a previous chapter, states the same truth. Of course, it is a matter of relative consideration. Wholeness and the riches of the spirit agree neither with the biased attitude of one's ego consciousness alone, nor with popular opinion; wisdom involves something deeper, a unique experience of life that flows up from the deep springs of the unconscious rather than from the collective mentality of the culture.

In India, especially, the snake is associated with water. The undulating movements of this creature are reminiscent of waves and the circuitous course of rivers and streams, which symbolize the vital energy of life.

In our tale, the youngest daughter-in-law encounters the serpent mother near the town well while drawing water for her family. And since snakes live underground, they represent primeval energy surging up from the depths. In a form of hatha yoga called *kundalini*, a mythic female serpent, coiled at the base of the spine, is believed to stir and ascend through seven successive centers of awakening, beginning at a point near the anus, then rising through the sexual organs, the navel, the heart, the larynx, the forehead, and finally arriving at the top of the skull. Accordingly, each of these centers, when awakened by the she-snake, will express impulses and psychological states of mind characteristic of that specific level.

Mankind always has been fascinated by the fact that the snake periodically sloughs its skin. After new hide forms underneath, the outer layer loosens and curls back so that the snake can slither out of its old worn and dried-up hide, revealing the intricate designs of its fresh new coat. To traditional, mythic-minded man, the snake seemed miraculously to be reborn from its own death! It is this particular feature of the snake's significance that has played the biggest role in religious symbolism, namely the capacity to die and be reborn from out of one's old self: "Putting off the old man ... and putting on the new."[21] This snake metamorphosis is a feature particularly in the mythology of royal or divine persons. One may recognize an Egyptian god-king or goddess-queen by the Uraeus serpent that emerges from the royal forehead at Kundalini Chakra level six.

Several years ago, in the year of the locust, I noticed two of these insects on the underside of a small tree leaf near our house. They looked like a pair, side by side, one brown and apparently dead, its partner bright green and slowly moving its antennae. I soon realized that the "dead" one was merely the old outer skin from which the green locust had wriggled during the night. But even then I lingered—clearly amazed at the impression this made upon me.

Reading mythic significance into a scientific situation is not just a matter of primitive superstition. What the inner imagination projects onto nature and the outer world reveals sublime facts of the interior human soul. So my amazement was indeed both appropriate and relevant. I was, in fact, encountering a very deep mythical level within myself, and my strong emotional response signaled it.

The serpent stands for the most profound and powerful energies of life. Its meandering, wave-like motion connects it to the primal waters, the cosmic womb from which everything derives, and into which everything returns for regeneration and renewal. For this reason, the serpent has often been seen as the guardian of the springs of eternal life, where it protects the hidden treasures of the spirit. Its cold and calculating aspect suggests that its divine energy lies far beyond sentimental human feeling. The serpent also was believed to cure as well as to kill, killing, of course, being the initial aspect of renewal through a figurative death and rebirth. In our present tale, the serpent stands for the prototypical strength and the wisdom that is especially available to those persons who lack a safe and comfortable cultural context: the outcasts, the orphans, the so-called idiots and fools of the world, those considered to be inferior, who in one way or another don't measure up or fit in very well with the standard system. Such folk often have—and most certainly symbolize within us—special access to the power and the wisdom of the serpent, who will befriend them and bring the inner resources to help their uncommon odyssey through life, even if their journey proves to be against all odds.

It is the humility and the selflessness of this seventh orphaned wife that makes her available to this sublime level of spiritual richness. To a proud or strident individual, such a door will be closed, or what is worse, the serpent energy will indeed appear, but in a negative or destructive manner, to bite and to kill, rather than to restore and to enrich. In modern psychotherapeutic language, we would say that an inflated person will encounter the very same life-energy of the spirit not as a blessing but as a curse, experiencing neurotic difficulties, depression, and gnawing anxiety and confusion, if not more serious illness. For such people, failure often follows, because they simply can't reverence the larger dimension of life, but wish to own and possess it as their elite personal property.

It is unlikely that this Indian tale, "The Serpent Mother," derives from the well-known Grimm's tale (No. 21) called "Cinderella," and yet the two are remarkably alike. Both suffering maidens lack a personal mother. In addition, the solution to each of their predicaments comes from *underground*. Finally, in both tales, as well as in "Snow White," the personal or human father is relatively absent from the main action.

The Indian tale locates the divine realm inside a serpent's hole, in which there are rich furnishings and luxurious gifts. In "Cinderella," the rich clothing that enables Cinderella to be properly attired when she attends the royal ball is presented to her hanging from a hazel tree whose roots go down into her real mother's grave. In the Middle Ages, hazel wood was considered to have magic powers, especially the capability to find water when used as a dowsing rod. So here again we are back to the underground source of the springs of life, expressed in India by the theme of the serpent's watery undulations. It was during the Indian girl's journey to the village well that she made her first contact with the snake-mother. In the Taoist Chinese symbolism, the *yin* side of the *yin-yang* set of opposites is associated with dampness, darkness, and coolness—the earth principle—and is considered feminine in relation to the dry, hot, and bright celestial character of the masculine *yang* pole. So both these tales are about the *yin* feminine resources of life.

Both the "Cinderella" and "The Serpent Mother" tales are pointing to the idea that when the standard program of life proves to be inadequate and one finds one's self in a blind alley, a door opens into a far deeper realm to make up for the difference and provide a correction and a solution. This theme is not only a matter of individual psychology. It is relevant to the larger culture as well. When the collective mentality is too masculine, abstract and "principled," or too moralistic or regimented, the myths—like the dreams of the individual—make a correction or rectification. In our modern Western culture, doing, knowing, controlling and owning have become so dominant that the art of being, living, loving and belonging are vastly depreciated. So, from the dark and moist depths of the *Yin* comes the transformation or re-balancing of the whole of life. Understanding and analysis are important. So is organization. So is discipline. But it is equally necessary to experience and appreciate the value of our existence in sufficient depth with feeling and emotional conviction. Reason alone can't do that.

Regarding the serpent near the well, we see something similar occurring in the story of Bernadette Soubirous (to whom we referred earlier), the simple maiden of Lourdes in southern France, who in 1858 at the age of fourteen, encountered a lucid vision of a radiant lady in a cave near her village. This beautiful and lively young woman told Bernadette to dig in the hard, dry ground near the entrance to the grotto. Nothing happened immediately, but the following morning a spring began to bubble up and flowed more strongly each day out into the nearby river. To this day, the waters of Lourdes are known for their healing effects. These are the serpentine waters of the earthy depths, which like the Greek medical god, Asclepius, cured many illnesses. Asclepius appeared to the medical patients of old in dreams and in art as a snake wound upon a staff. We still see this symbol affixed to the entrances of hospitals and doctor's offices and emblazoned upon the sides of ambulances, but few people know what this image means or how ancient and profound the symbolism of the curing snake.

The seventh bride in our tale is good-natured, kind, and forgiving, and this brings her into a positive relation with the serpent kingdom. How are we to understand this today? As we have said before and must say again and again, modern people can't take fairy tale figures as simple role models for actual living. To be completely gentle, sympathetic, and utterly merciful is not to say that one should become a doormat for others or just sit passively and submit to everyone. This instruction is for the soul as much as for society. If we give up egotistical control, a new level of awareness will open up. It is helpful to get out of the *me, myself, and I* bubble and trust something bigger and more intelligent than our purely conscious ingenuity that is always trying to force things to happen ahead of time on an imposed schedule, with ourselves as the center of action.

It is indeed good to stop being a control freak and to wonder what might happen next. Such advice must not be taken to suggest that we relinquish all responsibility for ourselves or for our actions. I must indeed show up for work on time, do my job, pay my bills, and take care of the people for whom I am responsible. I must make future plans about some things and try to follow through. But like the winding course of the snake or the river, my existence must be open to a certain amount of chance. One never knows for sure what is around the next bend. Without this sense of openness and wonder, my life will become a rigid ordeal of striving with no adventure, void of the outrageous fortune that gives life its vitality and its mystery.

We try to formulate goals and attain them. But a certain amount of receptivity is also important. I may discover that the bigger and truer goal of my life is somewhat different from what I have formulated. Someone has said that the

Chinese oracle book, the *I Ching*, really gives the answer to only one question. That question is, "What is it that wants to happen now?" This is not what *I* want or what *I* thoroughly expect, because in the final analysis, *it* is in charge, not me. This is not so terribly difficult to put into practice. All I need to do is awake in the morning, take a minute before shaving and ask, "What does God have in store for me today?" I have some sort of schedule to follow, but if I leave enough wiggle room for "it" to enter the picture, my life will be fuller and better, and a lot more interesting. I don't mean that God is just an "it." What "it" suggests is the mysterious unknown or inscrutable tendency that is just in the wings of the theater of life, about to come on stage. Oftentimes, it is precisely what we don't know about that is what God has in mind for us. Theologians are fond of saying that God is always doing a new thing, not just repeating old time-worn patterns. I agree completely with this insight! I have never felt that the "goody-two-shoes," straight-and-narrow, moralistic way of living is very productive, but rather, that it is a kind of prison that severely limits life.

Barbara was smart and a successful professional woman in her late thirties. As she later admitted, she was full of pride, quite self-centered and was hell-bent for big success and big money in a highly competitive marketplace. Gradually, however, she began to suspect that this narrow approach to living simply couldn't last. There was something else in her that she felt was leading her to set different priorities. Part of it was that she suspected that she wasn't really living the deeper, earthy, emotional life of a woman and that, consequently, she needed to make a big life change. She also sensed a profound spiritual yearning that had haunted the edges of her life for several years. Interspersed with many others, Barbara remembered vividly the following three dreams:

DREAM: *I sit in the lotus position surrounded by light. I am centered and very happy. My skin is luminous, like soft, rippling light or mother of pearl. I have just, like a snake, shed my old skin, which lies drying and dead to my right. I feel the presence of a benevolent, powerful black snake inside me. I know that it is He that taught me how to shed my skin. I feel much love and gratitude for him, because I know that he is a gentle, wise, living force.*

Here the *Kundalini* snake is fully awake within Barbara and has already begun her transformation.

A month later:

DREAM: *I was lying on my back inside a huge, round egg. (It was so large that I was comfortably warm and snug). The membrane of the egg was thick and dark. The egg was just below the surface, surrounded by Earth. Just above the egg, touching it and trying to pierce through it, was a huge snake. Its face was like a death mask, with many bones of different colors. It reminded me of Aztec/Mayan sculptures/art style—little pieces suspended together to make a whole. For some reason, the name* Quetzalcoatl *sprang to mind. It was moving its head and talking to me. It kept saying that, in order to live, I have to die. And it was busy burrowing through the membrane. I was looking up at it through the egg in my dream, and at first I was terrified because I thought it would eat me. But then I looked closer, and it did not seem terrifying. I had this odd thought that it was just doing its job, and maybe it wasn't here to eat me at all, and this was a very freeing feeling. I grew calm and heavy and felt that things were going to be okay, even though I wasn't quite sure what would happen. Time seemed to slow to a standstill. I was tense as I waited, and it was hard to stay with the*

149

dream at this point. I felt very small in the face of this creature, like I had to abandon myself to what was going to happen. It was very powerful and very much alive. There was a lot of energy in it, and its scales/bones were vibrating and changing colors from black to red to white and back again. But I did not feel dread or threatened by it, and this was amazing.

Quetzalcoatl (Kets-al-co-at-l) was the Aztec god of wind and air, somewhat reminiscent of the Hebrew *Ruach* or Christian Holy Spirit, as well as the original "light bringer," Lucifer. In this sense, the serpent, as a source of the higher self, is engendering new life in Barbara by fertilizing her soul in the manner of a giant sperm. She is being conceived again from the Great Mother Egg of Life, the Earth, like the Native American hero Hiawatha from his mother, Nakomas, by Mudgekeewee, the West Wind. Quetzalcoatl says Barbara must die in order to live. This gets to the heart of deep transformation. The previous attitudes and outlook on life must come to a permanent end in order for the new development to occur. So Barbara's cold tomb will now become a warm and comfortable womb. Notice Quetzalcoatl's colors. They are the same as Snow White's!

Five months later:

DREAM*: I was flying through a forest. I wasn't really going where I wanted to go. I wanted to reach Merlin, who was an image in the near distance, also floating at the height of the trees. I knew that he was a real man somewhere, but it was like I was projecting the image from my imagination into a reality and chasing that image. A huge black snake, with a single white and a single orange stripe on its back, was resting at the foot of the trees below me. It was watching me and was trying to bite me. I was scared. I think it did bite me, because I vaguely then registered the recognition that*

I really wasn't in any pain. I remember thinking, "Well, this isn't so bad, really!" But I also knew that I needed to get down so that I could proceed. I woke up.

Here Barbara is succumbing to an inflation. The previous dream shows that her ego has become puffed up. She is "flying high" and is in a superior position to the divine snake, that properly rests on the ground near a tree. Because Barbara's *me, myself, and I* is so high, the snake turns negative and bites her! She needs to get down to elemental reality, become grounded, so that she will receive the benefits of the snake's transforming wisdom. Both Barbara and Merlin are too high up, "above it all." It was said of old that Merlin was the offspring of the marriage of an evil spirit with a pure virgin. Because his mother was a simple maiden without guile, all the evil power and crafty intelligence of the power of darkness was miraculously turned toward good! If Barbara could maintain her simple and innocent femininity, with feet on the ground of Mother Earth, she would become the recipient of profound insight and understanding, for, as we know, Lucifer (later associated with the devil) was the original morning star, the "light-bringer," who heralded the dawn of a new day. Insofar as Barbara does not achieve a grounded humility, she will suffer the painful consequences, i.e., the unconscious will poison her. In her outer life Barbara wanted desperately to meet the right man, but so far she had not discovered him. This dream suggests that she is flying too high to be able to connect with an appropriate male partner, substituting her fantasy projection for the real guy as she flies above the trees.

There is one very curious turn in the tale. This is when the serpent mother is devouring her own eggs, and the girl, aghast at this dreadful scene, drops the lamp. In the resulting darkness, two of the eggs hatch and the little baby serpents slither away so quickly that the mother only manages to bite off their tails, rather than eating them whole.

In the days when I used to attend Joseph Campbell's classes at Sarah Lawrence College (at the time, I was teaching in a nearby school), I remember the great impression he made on his students when he told a bizarre old tale from Hindu India.

The tale was about a powerful king, Jalandhara, which means "Water Carrier," who, through severe austerities, had managed to unseat the gods and finally conquer the whole world. Jalandhara got it into his head to carry off Shiva's wife, the lovely and voluptuous goddess Parvati. He sent a monster messenger, Rahu, "The Seizer," to confront Shiva and insist that he surrender Parvati. Faced with this impious demand, Shiva opened his spiritual third eye and caused an intense lightning-bolt to shoot forth. As it stuck the ground, a voracious and emaciated lion-headed demon was instantly manifested. This frightening yet gaunt creature was nearly starved to death for lack of food. It possessed so fierce an appetite that it was capable of devouring whole cities of people and herds of animals in one gulp, yet still remain hungry. Shiva now ordered this ravenous demon to devour Rahu.

But Rahu did the only thing he could. He immediately threw himself down on the ground. Prostrate at Shiva's feet, he begged forgiveness, flinging himself completely on the mercy of this great god and promising obedience forever and forever.

"Now can I eat him," shouted the lion-headed demon.

"Well," replied Shiva, "unfortunately for you, another, unexpected problem has arisen. You see, it is an eternal law of the gods that if anyone throws himself completely upon the mercy of any god and promises absolute fealty, then that god is bound to protect him. Such a law is sacred and cannot be broken."

"You mean I can't eat him after all?" shrieked the demon. "But you promised me this great meal to fill my empty stomach."

"Ah," said the great lord Shiva, "you shall indeed have your meal after all, but in a far better way. You may now eat yourself!"

So in obedience, the demon ate first one of his legs and then the other. Having gulped down these, he ate his arms and then he ravenously devoured his own torso until in the end only his fierce face remained. "Thank you for doing me this exalted favor," said Shiva.

"You are now the greatest before me, and your sublime and radiant face will appear upon the outer posts of all my temples, to remind those who seek entrance to worship me that they must emulate your example of self-sacrifice in order to attain the bliss of the gods. From henceforth and forever your visage shall be called 'The Face of Glory.'"

And so the demon became renowned, honored by millions of Hindus to this day.[22]

If you have assumed that fairy tales and myths are addressed to outer life and are intended as moralistic role

J. N. H. Perkins

models to be imitated literally, you are now cured forever of this bad habit!

The serpent, which is also sacred to Shiva as the Kundalini snake of yoga, is often depicted in mythic images biting his own tail. This means that he is devouring himself, consuming his own psychic substance in the process of the self-transformation of death and renewal. He is the very principle of regeneration in operation. If there is one thing that our little ego-nature cannot stand, it is self-sacrificial change. Ego is based upon the principle of preserving itself as it maintains its power and prerogatives and defends itself against all threats. Like a jealous dragon guarding its hoard of gold, it refuses to relinquish its own hegemony. It can't stand change. So, with this limitation, deep religion and any mystical experience is out of the question for the jealous tendency of our egocentric nature. When ego alone is in charge and thinks that IT is all there is, then nothing profound can occur! That means no psychological development can be permitted beyond the status quo, where everything is frozen at the level of *me, myself, and I,* in a rationalistic mindset of hard fact and flat-footed, literal reality.

The serpent mother devours her own eggs in order to keep down the serpent population in the world—at first glance a sort of monstrous form of birth control. By now you should be getting a hint of what is really happening. The serpent mother's act is self-energizing; it demonstrates that the inner personality—like the serpent biting its own tail—must feed itself upon itself and not produce endlessly for the sake of the ego's various pet projects in the outer, practical world of power, pleasure and duty. Such an idea is behind the whole notion of meditation: the interior personality renews itself and recharges its batteries by commun-

154

ing—by uniting creatively—with itself. This energy is also needed for the health of the human psyche in addition to the resources that are normally expended on living in the outer conscious world, with all of its prospects and challenges. It's really about a sort of inner ecology. Hence, the hermit tradition in all the cultures of the world. We are not talking simply about getting some rest. Yes, a certain amount of rest is necessary. But we must provide for rest *before* we are exhausted and flat out. For it is then that such an introverted quiet brings wisdom and a new lease on life. In this way, the inner landscape of the soul comes into clearer focus.

I once shut myself up in our house and did nothing all day on purpose. It wasn't easy! Guilt nipped at my heels all morning, but I stuck to it and refused to give in and compulsively start doing anything productive, including answering the telephone. It rang several times but no one answered, because in a sense, no one was home, as far as the outer world was concerned. When I reflected on this at the time, it gave me a sort of thrill. Once I took a firm stand, the guilt began to fade and a sort of calm yet ecstatic feeling came over me, a sense of contentment and extreme well-being. I said quietly to myself, "I know I'm really in heaven right now." My turn of phrase appeared spontaneously and was a very accurate description of my state of mind and feelings at the time. Inside me, the serpent mother was eating her eggs! My inner psyche was being re-energized and nourished because no outward demands were being made on it. There was plenty of creative energy swirling around inside me at the time, but it would have been water down the drain if I had gotten busy and tried to accomplish something important in the world. Later that day, I went out onto the front porch, sat down, and listened to the birds' songs and watched the squirrels playing tag in the trees. I was at peace. That night, I had a dramatic dream. The man from the fuel oil company pulled up in his big truck and filled our in-ground tank with 600 gallons of furnace oil, worth about twice what I could earn in a modest day of therapy practice in those days, and enough to heat our house for a big part of the winter. Then he knocked at the door and handed me the receipt, announcing that "today, Mr. Perkins, the delivery is free!" I had accomplished far more than I realized during that quiet meditative day. I had generated a vast amount of energy by doing absolutely nothing! That is meditation. That is the serpent mother eating her own eggs.

The young pregnant mother of our tale dropped her lamp. Her conscious attention failed her at that point. She found the voracious appetite of the serpent mother disgusting. The girl was unused to such a vast depth of experience, and such a profound level of realization was simply too strange and too intense for her at the time. It shocked her and she dropped the lamp, losing consciousness. The Hindus say that yoga is a means of going into the unconscious wide-awake! It is easy to enter the unconscious asleep. But to remain alert and vigilant as we descend to this other level is difficult, because it is so hard to stand one's ground precisely at the point where the two worlds come together into one. It is a veritable crucifixion for the *me, myself, and I*. Few people are capable of this to any great degree, because the ego can't stand paradox and ambivalence. Ego wants it one way or another, but not both ways at the same time. Ego chuckles at Yogi Berra's little quip, "When you come to a fork in the road, take it." But Ego could never manage this absurdity because it is almost like being completely sane and totally psychotic, humbly human and mighty God, all at the same time, and ego is unable to sustain this absurdity. But on a certain sublime level, contradiction is the only way to genius.

Of course, these snakes who live underground near the village well are not just slithering reptiles. They are royal persons—a god and a goddess—upon whose heads, say the ancient Hindus, the entire world rests. They may take any form or incarnation they choose, including human. It is just this capacity to assume any form that is so important in our tale. Being an orphan or in other ways finding oneself bereft in the standard culture is the very door that opens us up access to the divine realm. It is easy for a traditional Indian to realize that all humans are, down deep inside, divine, even if they don't know it or realize it. Among various manifestations, the divine serpent may take up residence even in oneself and begin raising one's awareness. This is why, in the formal Hindu greeting, the hands are joined prayer-like and offered before one's partner. On one level two human beings are meeting. On another level, two gods are encountering each other, or perhaps God is meeting God, so to speak. In the West, where we make a clearer distinction between human and divine on the ordinary plane, we might say, "The image of God meets the image of God," and on this plane mutual veneration (not worship) is entirely appropriate and not the least bit idolatrous.

The poor orphan girl in this Indian tale has no regular parents or wealth from the ordinary channels. But godparents suddenly appear and their contribution is far greater than any ordinary parents could possibly provide. Because she receives the rich blessings of her adopted serpent family, the poor orphan girl is transformed into a young woman of rich heritage and with the best connections imaginable,

J. N. H. Perkins

confirming the worth and the energy that flows up from the deep well of the spirit.

4
Pock Face

T he following Chinese tale, with local variants found from the seventh to the tenth century CE, is of the "Cinderella" type. Over a thousand renditions have been discovered worldwide.[23] The story is entitled "Pock Face." We'll present the whole story first, and then take it section by section for comment.

There were two sisters. One, fine-looking, was called Beauty; the other, ugly and spoiled, was called Pock Face. Beauty's own mother had died and turned into a yellow cow that lived in the garden. Beauty was treated badly by her stepmother, who preferred her own daughter, Pock Face, to her stepdaughter. Beauty adored the yellow cow and visited her often. Pock Face got to go to the theater with her mother. Beauty, who wanted to go too, was ordered to stay home and work, straightening out the hemp.

Beauty, in a fit of tears when she heard she had to straighten out the hemp, took it to her mother, the yellow cow, who devoured it and then spit it out all neatly arranged. But the next day, when Pock Face and her mother again went to the theater, Beauty was ordered to stay behind and separate the sesame seeds from the beans. Having little success, Beauty went out to the cow who said, "You stupid girl! You have to separate them with a fan." So Beauty returned and did the job quickly with a fan. Now Beauty thought the stepmother would surely let her go to the theater. But the stepmother asked Beauty, "How did you do this? Who helped you?" Beauty told her, "The cow helped me." So the stepmother went straight outside and killed the cow and used the meat for food. Unable to eat her own mother's flesh, Beauty later took the cow's bones to her room, where she hid them in an earthenware pot.

Still prevented from attending the theater, Beauty finally became so annoyed that she smashed everything in the house, including the earthenware pot. Suddenly, with a crackling sound, there appeared a white horse, a new dress, and a pair of embroidered shoes. Beauty pulled on the dress and the shoes, jumped on the horse, and rode out through the gate.

While Beauty was riding along, by chance one of her shoes slipped off. First a fishmonger, then a rice salesman, and finally an oil merchant each offered to retrieve her shoe if she would consent to marriage. But Beauty refused them all. However, when at last a handsome young scholar came along, Beauty asked him to get her shoe. He too bargained for marriage. As Beauty liked his looks, she agreed. The handsome scholar promptly returned her shoe, and they went to his house and were married.

Soon the couple went to Beauty's parents' house to pay their respects. Feigning hospitality, the stepmother and Pock Face asked Beauty to stay on a few days and follow her husband later. The next morning Pock Face asked Beauty to join her so they could look into the well to see who was the more beautiful. When Beauty looked over the edge, Pock Face pushed her in and Beauty drowned. When the scholar sent word asking what had detained his wife, the stepmother and Pock Face replied that Beauty had a case of small pox and needed to remain with them until she recovered from her illness. The husband sent delicate morsels of food to help nourish his wife, but Pock Face filled her own stomach with them.

Then the stepmother sent Pock Face to the husband to claim that she herself was, in fact, his wife Beauty, now recovered. It was hard for the husband to agree that this ugly girl was really his wife, but she shrieked and made such a scene that the scholar relented and, half-believing, went along with it.

Meanwhile, after Beauty died, she was transformed into a sparrow, and having flown back to her husband's house, began to call out when Pock Face was combing her hair. "Comb once, peep; comb twice, peep; comb thrice, to the spine of Pock Face," chirped the sparrow. Pock Face answered, "Comb once, comb twice, comb thrice, to the spine of Beauty." The scholar was very curious and asked the sparrow, "Why do you sing like that? Are you by any chance my wife? If you are, call three times and I will put you in a golden cage and keep you as a pet." The sparrow called three times and the scholar bought a golden cage and put the sparrow inside.

In anger, the ugly sister killed the sparrow and threw it into the garden. The dead sparrow transformed into bamboo shoots, which began to sprout in the soil. They hurt Pock Face's mouth when she ate them, but tasted delightful to the husband. Then, in anger, Pock Face had the bamboo cut down and made into a bed. But the bed pricked Pock Face in the night while the husband rested comfortably.

Pock Face became cross and threw the bed onto the trash heap.

An old peddler woman who lived next door, a seller of moneybags, took the bed into her house and used it. Every night she had a comfortable sleep. But mysterious things occurred. Each day when she came home from selling her wares and began to fix dinner, she discovered food already prepared and cooked. One day, the old lady returned to her house earlier than usual and discovered a dark shadow washing rice. The old woman asked the shadow why she was doing this, and the shadow told the whole story of Beauty. "Please give me a rice pot for a head, a stick for a hand, a dish cloth for entrails, and fire hooks for feet, and then I can regain my former shape." As soon as the old woman provided these things, suddenly a startlingly beautiful and charming girl appeared. She gave the old woman an embroidered bag and asked her to please take it next door and sell it to her husband.

The old woman went out and made a big noise in the lane and the husband finally came out and asked the old woman where she had gotten the bag, which he recognized as the very one he had earlier given to his wife. The old woman told the story of the dark shadow in her house that had turned into the beautiful girl. The old woman then repeated the whole story of Beauty's life, just as she had heard it from the lips of the girl herself. The husband put a red cloth on the ground and brought Beauty back to the house.

Pock Face, however, grumbled that this woman was just a spirit pretending to be Beauty. Pock face wanted a trial to see who was the true wife. Beauty, who knew she was the real bride, readily agreed. They had to walk on eggs and climb a ladder of sharp knives. When Beauty trod on the eggs, they remained whole, but when Pock Face stepped on them, they all shattered. When Beauty climbed the knife ladder, she received not the slightest scratch, but when Pock Face tried to ascend, her feet were cut to the bone.

Unable to accept this, Pock Face then proposed that they each jump into a caldron of hot oil, thinking that Beauty would have to jump first, ensuring her death. When Beauty jumped, she was unharmed by the oil, but when Pock Face jumped, she did not come up again, and was boiled alive.

Beauty put the roasted bones of Pock Face into a box. Then she asked a stuttering servant to take them to the stepmother and say, "Your daughter's flesh." But the step-mother loved carp and thought he said "carp flesh." She believed that Pock Face had sent her some carp. Opening the box in great excitement, she saw the charred flesh and bones of her own daughter instead, and, letting out a piercing scream, the stepmother fell down dead.

———

Now that we've heard the whole story, let's return to the opening narrative, and then follow this with some comments.

There were two sisters. One, fine-looking, was called Beauty; the other, ugly and spoiled, was called Pock Face. Beauty's own mother had died and turned into a yellow cow that lived in the garden. Beauty was treated badly by her stepmother, who preferred her own daughter, Pock Face, to her stepdaughter. Beauty adored the yellow cow and visited her often. Pock Face got to go to the theater with her mother. Beauty, who wanted to go too, was ordered to stay home and work, straightening out the hemp.

Like Cinderella and Snow White, Beauty is denied the greater pleasures of life and must serve others as a lowly servant. A common theme in all the tales we have been discussing is the death or absence of the personal mother, who is replaced by a witch-like, negative mother figure. Another theme is the absence of the father, who is not present to rescue his daughter from such cruel treatment. Or, in some tales—Snow White, for instance—the father is indeed present but he makes no effort to help his daughter.

In many tales, stepmother figures tied to orphan children have a curious function. It is easy to hate and despise the evil stepmother, but on closer analysis, we find that even such a negative figure is important to the end result of the story. A girl who is loved too much and coddled too closely for too long by her mother will typically grow up to be overshadowed and paralyzed by such exaggerated maternal attention. If a child is ever to get away from her mother and gain a separate existence, she needs to react to something negative or irritating. If there were no evil "stepmothers" in the human psyche, then daughters would remain perpetual children or grow up as perfect clones of their mothers. Such daughters would have difficulty developing as individual women living assertive, creative, and innovative lives.

In real life we see many examples of this. I once treated a twenty-eight-year-old woman named Miranda who had a co-dependent relationship with her mother. Although Miranda held a responsible job and lived in her own apartment, she occasionally experienced severe panic attacks, shaking all over and unable to keep any food down. These

164

episodes invariably occurred whenever her mother left town on a vacation or business trip with Miranda's father. Miranda still had the habit of sharing every detail of her life with Mom and often seeking her advice. Even though Miranda was living independently as an adult, she hadn't psychologically separated from Mom. Such panic attacks are a completely normal reaction for a five-year-old child who has lost sight of her mother in a crowded shopping mall, but quite inappropriate for a mature woman. At some emotional level, Miranda was still five years old!

The stepmothers of folklore are like tough mother birds that rudely kick their little chicks out of the nest, forcing them to fend for themselves. A certain amount of tough mothering makes for tough children, who later on can meet the challenges of life with energy and confidence.

Beauty, in a fit of tears when she heard she had to straighten out the hemp, took it to her mother, the yellow cow, who devoured it and then spit it out all neatly arranged. But the next day, when Pock Face and her mother again went to the theater, Beauty was ordered to stay behind and separate the sesame seeds from the beans. Having little success, Beauty went out to the cow who said, "You stupid girl! You have to separate them with a fan." So Beauty returned and did the job quickly with a fan. Now Beauty thought the stepmother would surely let her go to the theater. But the stepmother asked Beauty, "How did you do this? Who helped you?" Beauty told her, "The cow helped me." So the stepmother went straight outside and killed the cow and used the meat for food. Unable to eat her own mother's flesh, Beauty later took the cow's bones to her room, where she hid them in an earthenware pot.

In many fairy tales, the young heroine is required to perform the task of sorting something out. Cinderella was expected to separate hundreds of peas and lentils from ashes in the kitchen hearth. The cow mother swallows the hemp and regurgitates it with all the strands neatly arranged. Beauty is required to divide sesame seeds from beans. The cow mother admonishes her to accomplish this with a fan. These tasks symbolize the threads of thought or the kernels of new possibilities that may be discerned and organized through the ruminations of the mind. Here, one slowly chews on one's ideas, partially digests them, and then brings them up again and chews some more until the job is finished. Snow White was expected to keep the little dwarves' cottage neat and clean, which is a clear analogy to the structuring process as the mind imposes order and shape onto the chaos of living. This marks the beginning of thinking for one's self rather than relying solely upon what Mom commands or orchestrates. If a girl is required to do her share of the housework, she is not being coddled. She is being encouraged to undertake mental housework!

Elsie Clews Parsons (1874-1941), the highly respected sociologist, anthropologist, and feminist who served on the faculties of Barnard College and Columbia University early in the last century, put forward the argument that women's roles as mothers and wives provide parity with the social and political roles of their male counterparts. Setting a house in order and setting a mind in order require the same kind of intelligence! Dr. Parsons contributed the last tale discussed in this book, a Pueblo story entitled "The Faithful Wife and the Woman Warrior."

Beauty's second task, that of separating the sesame seeds from the beans, proves too difficult until the cow speaks to her roughly, calling her "stupid," and suggests that she use a fan. Even the yellow cow gets irritated with her daughter's dependency and lack of resourcefulness. Such a device is well known in traditional societies as the "winnowing fan" (L. *vannus*; from *ventus* meaning "wind") employed at harvest to separate the grain from the chaff by tossing the whole mess up into the air and allowing the wind to blow away the lighter and more easily airborne husks from the heavier kernels, which fall back to the threshing floor again. Here, the strong current of air, a symbol of the discriminating spirit, the wind of the invisible god, does the actual work of separation. Such an operation represents the higher judging and refining capacity of the mind as it sifts through experience. One could also say that there is a certain whimsy associated with the winnowing fan. Just when we find our lives in a painful *cul-de-sac* or no-exit situation, just when "the nut won't crack," sometimes the best course of action is to throw the whole thing up in the air and let fate decide what we, ourselves, can't solve with our own human ingenuity. Certain challenges can't be solved by willful striving. It's a matter of the light touch or the indirect approach, less controlling and determined, that allows a situation to resolve itself more easily than if we get all heavy and serious about it. I have an outrageous clergyman friend who, at the beginning of Lent one year, indicated that he planned to give up seriousness until Easter!

Recently, I heard a writer speaking about her problems meeting a deadline set by her publisher. She had two months to complete a non-fiction work that had already gone through several revisions. As she set to work, she panicked as she struggled to revise her manuscript to the editor's satisfaction. This writer didn't see how she could make her deadline. In exasperation she threw down her pen and stormed outside to the sheep pen on her family farm. She went inside, shut the gate, and sat down. She stared at the sheep for a long time. Their gentle eyes stared back in the soft morning air as they slowly chewed their cud. She forgot all about her book. She didn't even want to think about it anymore. Time passed. Then, like a bolt of lightning from nowhere, an idea struck her. She didn't think it up. It just flashed into her head of its own accord. The idea was the scheme for organizing the difficult chapter of her book. Jumping to her feet, she rushed back to the house and set to work. By noon, the problem had been solved!

"Throwing up one's hands" is usually just a matter of avoiding responsibility, but once in a while it can be genius, if done consciously and deliberately. Such an approach is a form of the old AA adage, "Let go and let God." There are many equivalents to that writer's sheepfold experience. Sometimes it's just a matter of a walk around the block, sitting in the bathtub, or a ride on the bus—doing something else so the problem may be solved *indirectly.*

In folk tales, it is invariably the ugly child who is preferred and spoiled to death. That is also part of every mother's and every child's psychology. Spoiling is part of possession, where the preferred and coddled daughter is an extension of the mother's own life. The favored daughter remains a mere aspect of her mother, and therefore has no place of her own in the larger world. While experiencing the loss of her mother, Beauty is simultaneously freed up to psychologically develop beyond mother-boundness. Our tale reminds us that dependency and passivity and remaining the favorite are indeed "ugly" from the point of view of the emerging uniqueness of the individual. This singularity is not mere eccentricity, but a requirement of the spiritual path, especially for a Westerner. Enlightenment requires a differentiation from the standard collective "mother" culture—the usual way with the usual people with the usual ideas—the predictable course of life programmed by the social herd. So, of course, the spiritual path always involves a certain amount of pain and suffering.

In the Far East, the cow is connected to the Buddha and, therefore, to spiritual consciousness and higher wisdom. Because the cow is also associated with the Moon, it has a special feminine implication. In India, the cow stands for the feminine aspect of Brahma, the Hindu creator deity in the trinity of Brahma, Shiva, and Vishnu. The cow feeds upon the grass and herbs of the field. Symbolically, by its ruminating digestion, it is transforming the lower growths and affections of human nature into higher and more articulate feelings, represented by milk and butter, which provide rich sustenance for the evolving soul. The cow in our tale is yellow, which points to a spiritual aspect, since, in China and India, the color yellow stands for temperance, truth, and the middle way of enlightenment that bridges the opposites. In Hebrew history, the theme of milk and honey continually recurs. In the Bible, the nomadic *Habiru* folk are promised by YHWH (God) that eventually they will inherit a land filled with milk and honey after their long trek through the wilderness. Milk and honey are products of transformation in nature, from an elemental organic state into a rich source of higher nourishment. Each is related to the mother and to ancient goddess symbols: milk to the cow, and honey to the hive ruled by the queen bee. What is important here is that the embodied human psyche is also capable of such transforming activity by this special form of mental digestion, the conversion of natural instinct into the greater wisdom of human consciousness.

J. N. H. Perkins

In China and India, there are votive statues of the Buddha and other gods, such as the popular, elephant-headed deity, Ganesha (patron of new endeavors), that are portrayed with fat stomachs. The fat stomach symbolizes that wisdom has been completely digested, not having passed merely through the head. The ruminating animal stands for the processing of ideas until a transformation of the whole person has occurred. Then creative thoughts will have taken firm root in the flesh and, as a result, nourish the soul.

Still prevented from attending the theater, Beauty finally became so annoyed that she smashed everything in the house, including the earthenware pot. Suddenly, with a crackling sound, there appeared a white horse, a new dress, and a pair of embroidered shoes. Beauty pulled on the dress and the shoes, jumped on the horse, and rode out through the gate.

If the good mother, in the form of a yellow cow, had not been killed, Beauty would no doubt have continued to perform her tasks dutifully from day to day, with the help of Mama cow. She would have behaved like a good little responsible caretaker, but with no life of her own, and with no possibility of future development. She would have remained an inferior house slave.

The Swiss psychologist Carl Jung maintained that when we have to choose between two equally impossible courses of action, we are actually in a situation that can open up possibilities. We can't go left or right; neither fight nor flee; neither ascend nor descend. It is precisely at such a time that a third, as yet unrealized, possibility begins to open up. This is an advance in consciousness over the previous situation. Such a predicament characterizes the opening scene

of Dante's monumental work, *The Divine Comedy*. Caught between a mountain and a hard place and threatened by wild
animals, Dante is stuck, until an angelic messenger, Saint
Lucia, comes and tells him that the girl, Beatrice, whom he
loved from afar when he was a boy, indeed loves him even
though she is now a soul in heaven. At this point, Dante,
now filled with yearning and inspiration, is willing to travel
all the way through Hell and Purgatory and then to Heaven
in order to reach the love of his life. Here, ironically, the
gate of Hell is the third way that leads to ultimate fulfillment. As our tale unfolds, we shall see that Beauty must
experience her own version of this dark journey before she
reaches her final goal.

The good mother must die, and even her remains
must be scattered, so that her daughter's womanhood can
emerge. This is like a conversion of energy from one state
to another. Such is the job of the negative stepmother, who
acts unwittingly as a kind of goading priestess of a necessary sacrifice. Otherwise, the good mother, in one form or
another, will always be around to help. Irate, Beauty smashes everything in the house, including the earthenware jar
containing her mother's bones. Beauty is like the obedient
daughter in "The Frog King" (Grimm's No. 1). Here, the
exasperated princess finally hurls an ugly and demanding
frog against the wall with all her might! By this violent treatment ("tough love"), much like the jostling of Snow White in
her glass coffin, the princess transforms the slimy frog back
into his original human shape as a rich and kindly prince.
Similarly, Beauty has to get angry even at her good mother
before she can gain the required resources to free herself
from her mother's influence and get on with her life. Beauty has finally had it up to here with being submissive, well-
behaved, and respectful. The stepmother's repeated taunts

push Beauty over the edge toward her larger destiny. Life has an uncanny way of provoking us onto the right course.

Beauty's mother underwent three transformations. Upon her first death she becomes a yellow cow. When the stepmother and Pock Face eat the flesh of the cow after it is killed, a second transformation takes place. When Beauty shatters the earthenware pot containing the cow's bones, there is a third transformation. The mother cow's bones are converted into a horse, a dress, and shoes for Beauty. It is important to see a thread, a common substance underlying these three external physical changes.

In the case of the first, on becoming a cow, the personal characteristics disappear and the mother's parental role becomes that of a mythical Mother that stands behind the ordinary mother. Mama has turned into a Great Mama. When the stepmother and her daughter, Pock Face, devour the cow flesh, *me, myself, and I* arrogantly seizes hold of a consecrated reality. This form of conceit is commonly known as inflation or spiritual pride because a deity or some holy thing is manipulated into serving merely personal interests and egotistical demands. Such an exploitation of profound spiritual ideas and symbolic processes is widespread and is the typical cause of every ersatz ideology, where something that sounds sublime on one level is used for an entirely different purpose and reason, to produce a result unworthy of its ostensible motivation—like loving someone as a deliberate means of possessing and controlling them for our own benefit.

When Beauty smashes the pot containing her cow mother's bones, the power of the revered cow is liberated to assume new forms. In performing this sacrifice herself,

Beauty embarks on the journey toward discovering Buddha consciousness, the higher state of mind signified by the cow's rumination. In doing this, she has ceased to idolize her mother, enabling her to grow into full womanhood.

This transition demonstrates that egotistical demand must first be acknowledged so that such arrogant energies within us may be transformed, integrated, and realigned. Then they will become the healthy ingredients of our assertive motivation. Eventually, these self-centered tendencies may evolve into the higher consciousness that we call "insightful wisdom," where we may discover a great truth within ourselves. In this sense, the stepmother and her daughter, Pock Face, are shadow compensations for Beauty's childish innocence and obedience.

While Beauty was riding along, by chance one of her shoes slipped off. First a fishmonger, then a rice salesman, and finally an oil merchant each offered to retrieve her shoe if she would consent to marriage. But Beauty refused them all. However, when at last a handsome young scholar came along, Beauty asked him to get her shoe. He, too, bargained for marriage. As Beauty liked his looks, she agreed. The handsome scholar promptly returned her shoe, and they went to his house and were married.

Like Cinderella, Beauty loses her shoe! The circumstances are quite different, yet in both instances the loss and the return of the shoe are associated with gaining a desired husband. In Beauty's case it is a scholar who stands for the burgeoning mental abilities in women that we have just been discussing. The shoe episode seems to be the hinge that leads to marriage.

J. N. H. Perkins

Symbolically, our shoes insulate us from the shocks of direct experience, protecting us from some of the hard knocks of life. The right shoe protects us from the jolts of the outer conscious world and the left shields us from invasion by the inner world of the unconscious impulses and influences. With these two shoes, we may enjoy some peace of mind and reasonable stability in our lives within a sphere of stable consciousness, both outside and inside. The shoes provide purposeful limits on high-voltage experience. They are the "thick skin" for our firm standpoint in consciousness. These shoes keep us from being hypersensitive to what occurs both around us and within us.

When we lose a shoe, we lose the insulation, and as a result become more vulnerable and sensitive to an intensification of experience. The Pock Face tale doesn't say which shoe fell off, but in Cinderella, it is specifically the *left* slipper that sticks to the pitch that the Prince lays on the stairs to catch Cinderella as she rushes from the ball. By losing her left slipper, Cinderella is suddenly exposed to the interior world of the unconscious impulses, particularly to the erotic influence of male images within. Only when the shoe is regained is Cinderella ready for marriage. A marriage in a fairy tale almost always represents the achievement of wholeness in the psyche—the union of masculinity and femininity—resulting in a sympathetic alignment of our human consciousness with the archetypal world. In marriage we are meant to become one, but we are nonetheless distinct individuals. Our task in life until the day we die is to experience a marriage of the outer world with the inner world as a union of discrete partners. We must neither abandon spiritual reality for gross materialism, nor conversely, sacrifice sensuous resonance with the physical world for an ethereal, otherworldly ideal. Marriage works

174

best when the two partners have each developed as mature and carefully delineated individuals who can form a complementary union that avoids co-dependency.

Early in his marriage to his wife Sophie, George once had a startling dream:

Sophie and I are attending Wagner's great opera "Parsival." It is the final act, where the Holy Grail appears and all the knights of the Grail Castle take communion from this sacred vessel. At this very moment, it suddenly strikes me that the events on stage are no longer part of a theatrical production, but have become actual reality. At this point, Sophie shifts from her position on my left (I am on the aisle) and moves two rows directly ahead, where she takes another aisle seat with a vacant seat remaining in the row between us. As the king lifts the Holy Grail to his lips, two things occur simultaneously. Over the Cup, a vision of young lovers appears and their lips touch ever so gently. At the same time, Sophie reaches backward with her hand and I reach forward, and our fingertips just barely touch. At this second, with the music swelling in intensity, a majestic ecstasy fills everything with light and energy, and my heart melts.

Here we witness the profound mystical union in separation, the *heiros gamos* or sacred marriage, which is simultaneously a Holy Communion with God. George's dream was a great help to him in understanding and appreciating his marriage, both in an inward and in an outward manner. Sophie and George always tried hard to leave a little space between each other, so that when they were close, they could experience an ecstatic moment—a taste of romance and divinity combined. This is, of course, the central theme in the great tales of romantic love that arose during the

Gothic twelfth century, and the Grail legend is a vital example of this tradition.

Soon the couple went to Beauty's parents' house to pay their respects. Feigning hospitality, the stepmother and Pock Face asked Beauty to stay on a few days and follow her husband later. The next morning Pock Face asked Beauty to join her so they could look into the well to see who was the more beautiful. When Beauty looked over the edge, Pock Face pushed her in and Beauty drowned. When the scholar sent word asking what had detained his wife, the stepmother and Pock Face replied that Beauty had a case of small pox and needed to remain with them until she recovered from her illness. The husband sent delicate morsels of food to help nourish his wife, but Pock Face filled her own stomach with them.

Then the stepmother sent Pock Face to the husband to claim that she herself was, in fact, his wife Beauty, now recovered. It was hard for the husband to agree that this ugly girl was really his wife. But she shrieked and made such a scene that the scholar relented and, half-believing, went along with it.

Here, the well water is a variation of the stepmother queen's looking glass in the Snow White tale. If this narcissistic stage of psychological development is missed, perverted, or otherwise incomplete, then a girl will not be able to appreciate why anyone would be interested in her in the first place. Lacking a clear, positive self-image, she will feel like a nonentity. To be able to receive love and acknowledgement, she must first feel worthy of it. This requires a sufficient degree of healthy narcissism—not too much and not too little. There is even such a thing as negative narcissism—being so exaggeratingly concerned about others that we lose a healthy sense of ourselves so that our own boundaries disappear. Then we are in danger of identifying with others and thus losing sight of both the direction and the purpose of our own lives.

This narcissistic stage of reflective self-validation eventually must grow into a capacity for relationship. Here, one learns to appreciate and empathize with the feelings of others beyond *me, myself, and I,* so that there is a balanced mutuality between self and other.

Meanwhile, after Beauty died, she was transformed into a sparrow, and having flown back to her husband's house, began to call out when Pock Face was combing her hair. "Comb once, peep; comb twice, peep; comb thrice, to the spine of Pock Face," chirped the sparrow. Pock Face answered, "Comb once, comb twice, comb thrice, to the spine of Beauty." The scholar was very curious and asked the sparrow, "Why do you sing like that? Are you by any chance my wife? If you are, call three times and I will put you in a golden cage and keep you as a pet." The sparrow called three times and the scholar bought a golden cage and put the sparrow inside.

In anger, the ugly sister killed the sparrow and threw it into the garden. The dead sparrow transformed into bamboo shoots, which began to sprout in the soil. They hurt Pock Face's mouth when she ate them, but tasted delightful to the husband. Then, in anger, Pock Face had the bamboo cut down and made into a bed. But the bed pricked Pock Face in the night while the husband rested comfortably. Pock Face became cross and threw the bed onto the trash heap.

Beauty's first death changed her into a sparrow. When Pock face kills the sparrow and throws it into the garden, the dead sparrow eventually becomes a bamboo plant. First, the bamboo plant is eaten as food, and then made into a bed; finally, it is thrown out.

J. N. H. Perkins

What is the meaning of Beauty changing into a sparrow? As we said before, the bird that survives after death represents something like the *ba* soul in Egyptian mythology—the individual who has been temporarily set free by death and continues his existence in the form of a bird. In the imaginary thinking of traditional peoples, the essence or substance of a certain life is not synonymous with its outward, bodily form or local manifestation. Such a bird soul is like the concept or the innate idea of a person—at once his energizing life principle and his unique identity. Here is the power of life inside the outwardly visible body that exists in its own right and may appear in a variety of forms and figures. This does not make literal, scientific sense, but when considered from a psychological perspective, it depicts how psychic energy changes from one state into another in the personality and advances to a more integrated experience of being human. Alternatively, it can regress to a more primitive, less developed level. The sparrow in the tale demonstrates the inner or symbolic process of "reincarnation," which has nothing to do with actual past or future lives.

Beauty's soul takes the form of one bird, a sparrow. In the West the sparrow belongs to Aphrodite and in other ways stands for freedom, loyalty, and humility. The sparrow flies away to a distant place but always returns. In ancient Egypt the sparrow was associated with the stars.

The bird seems to stand for the psychic reality that cannot be permanently identified with any plain material thing. We experience this all the time in our daily lives when we lose or give away something that belongs to us. If we loan a familiar article of clothing to another person and see them wearing it, a strange feeling comes over us.

178

Emotionally, we sense that something inside of ourselves has been taken or appropriated by that other person. Grief when a loved one dies is part of the same process. Without knowing it, we live much of our lives vicariously via sympathetic projections, where we make enormous investments in people, locations and things, yet do not realize the extent of this vicarious process of displacement until the moment we are deprived. When the projection is no longer possible due to the absence of its "incarnated" object, we feel a biting sense of loss. But this can be for us a positive opportunity. We may then begin to recognize and value dimensions of our own personalities that were previously invested in another and consequently remained unknown to us. People who deeply and honestly grieve for a departed loved one often grow immeasurably.

As we have said, the spirit can also be associated with places as well as with people. Whenever I drive by houses in which I have lived in the past, I feel a tinge of nostalgia. Part of me still senses that I reside there, and even though another family now holds the deed to the property, there's a little part of me that yearns to move back. This feeling is partly a recognition of the unfinished aspects of my life that dwelt there in the past. It is the bird of my spirit that has not quite caught up with the contemporary setting of my life. The bird of my spirit still seems to haunt the old familiar house. Conversely, when a familiar situation or atmosphere starts to grow stale, then the bird is already making his departure. At that point I may need to catch up with the bird and make some creative changes. But if I don't catch the inner significance of this spirit, if it remains too much in projected form, it will lead me all over creation, tempting me to find myself anew in situation after situation, and, as the bird continually eludes me, I will never be satisfied.

This is the plague of the compulsive wanderer who can't settle down somewhere long enough to make a viable home.

When the scholar husband learns that the sparrow is indeed his wife Beauty in bird form, he buys a golden cage and entraps her as a pet. But Pock Face kills the bird and throws it out into the garden. At this point in the story, putting the sparrow in the cage is quite similar to when—in Snow White—the poisoned, unconscious princess is placed in a glass coffin with gold lettering on the outside and with three birds hovering nearby. Such is the incarceration of the feminine as a precious love object. In some respects she can be seen as a woman who is passively reactive and unable to manage her own life, since she is dead to that possibility as a conscious human being. She may only express herself via her avian soul, through a kind of "flightiness," manifested through skittish behavior or capricious moods, where an unpredictable or whimsical impulsiveness rules the day. Scarlet O'Hara's fickle character in *Gone With The Wind* is a fine example. These are psychological symptoms of her bird character. In this sense she is a lovely image of nature *for a man*, with which she is wholly identified, but incapable of a separate existence of her own. Of course, this may also occur within the inner personality of the male when he finds himself swamped by irrational moods and loses his masculine level-headedness. Men can get flighty too.

But we must remember that these women, Snow White in her glass coffin and Beauty as a bird in her cage, are transpersonal or archetypal realities that are going through monumental transformations in the psyches of us all. The coffin or cage stage is a necessary one, and in both instances the containment is a form of protection as much as it is an incarceration. It is tempting to interpret this stage as

180

narcissistic, a touch of the wicked old stepmother queen in Snow White, so that the woman in question may reflect upon herself and acknowledge the lovely desirability of her emerging womanhood. It is that stage of "I am love!" that some of us may recall from the famous off-off Broadway hit, *The Fantasticks*, where a young teenage girl, while experiencing her first romance with the boy next door, swoons and collapses on the stage from sheer emotional overload; or Maria, in Leonard Bernstein's *West Side Story*, who sings Stephen Sondheim's captivating lyrics:

> I feel pretty
> Oh so pretty
> I feel pretty and witty and gay
> And I pity
> Any girl who isn't me today.
> I feel charming
> Oh so charming
> It's alarming how charming I feel
> And so pretty
> That I hardly can believe I'm real.

In an analogous manner, a boy must get some experience of being a "he-man" and be proud of himself in this way. The problem occurs when a girl or boy gets stuck at this stage and is unable to progress any further in his or her psycho-sexual development. We see this in the inappropriate behavior of middle-aged he-men and face-lifted love-angels who never grow up emotionally.

Beauty's death as a bird and transformation into bamboo provides the necessary rootedness in Mother Earth that will allow her to mature, become stabilized, and lose her earlier flightiness. This will culminate in her reaching a special kind of strength and backbone.

Bamboo is an organic plant that has amazing engineering properties. It is very light and its hollow tubular strength-to-weight ratio is exceedingly high. In traditional south Asia it was the major construction material, and quite durable. Such a "bamboo" stage of development gives the girl a sufficient amount of toughness and resilience. In this way she exchanges her mother's bones for those of Mother Nature Herself, and makes them her own.

When the sublime value of human life regresses to animal to vegetable and then to a constructed thing (the bamboo bed), we see the regressive direction of "reincarnation." In the context of our tale, however, this regression is necessary to compensate the egotism of the stepmother and her daughter Pock Face. Beauty must retreat to the fundamental structural underpinnings of the personality before her mature womanhood can appear. When the grandiosity of *me, myself, and I* has taken such complete possession of the soul, there is no room left for human life. So first her mother, and then Beauty, loses human visibility in the conscious world and continues on in a series of hidden or disguised forms as animal or vegetable. The higher the stepmother's egotism rises, the lower descends the heroine's soul. In this setup the two will never meet. As one tries to storm heaven, the other descends to hell. So this results in increasing psychological *dissociation*, rather than *integration*. Many of our personalities are split top from bottom like this today. The spiritual and the material, the ideological and the instinctive have gone their separate ways, leading to scientific materialism with relentless self-indulgence on the one hand,

and to an ethereal and moralistic spiritualism on the other. Each by itself is dead wrong! Each is "heresy."

An old peddler woman who lived next door, a seller of money-bags, took the bed into her house and used it. Every night she had a comfortable sleep. But mysterious things occurred. Each day when she came home from selling her wares and began to arrange dinner, she discovered food already prepared and cooked. One day the old lady returned to her house earlier than usual and discovered a dark shadow washing rice. The old woman asked the shadow why she was doing this, and the shadow told the whole story of Beauty. "Please give me a rice pot for a head, a stick for a hand, a dish cloth for entrails, and fire hooks for feet, and then I can regain my former shape." As soon as the old woman provided these things, suddenly a startlingly beautiful and charming girl appeared. She gave the old woman an embroidered bag and asked her to please take it next door and sell it to her husband.

The tale says an old peddler woman who lived next door—a seller of moneybags—used the bamboo bed after it was thrown out. Pouches, bags, purses, and the like are symbols of the feminine container. Figuratively these derive from the importance of the uterus as our first home. Of course, such vessels must not be *reduced* to the idea of the womb. Just as a phallic symbol is not "really" a penis, so a moneybag is not "really" a womb. We might understand the feminine container as the atmosphere or environment *within which* something of value or importance is kept safely or allowed to function or develop. Such a container could even be a climate of thinking or a sphere of consideration in which an idea is understood and appreciated. When we say a mood envelops us, we refer to a feminine container, whether we are men or women. So often the ambience, the "weather" of our lives functions like an all-encompassing maternal atmosphere, and as Freud reminded us, our expectations, hopes and fears about life generally hark back to our original intimacy with Mama. It is *within* the domestic atmosphere of the peddler woman that Beauty is able to regain her human, flesh-and-blood incarnation. If there is a fairy godmother in this tale, it is certainly the old peddler woman.

We learn that kitchen items serve as provisional body parts in order to allow Beauty to transform again into a living human being: "A rice pot for a head, a stick for a hand, a dish cloth for entrails, and fire hooks for feet." These domestic items are, apparently, the means of restoring Beauty's former shape. They appear to be temporary, simulated body parts, serving as a provisional framework or lattice. They form a scaffold upon which the reincarnation of Beauty's spirit may occur. Ordinary domestic tools loaned by the old woman who sold moneybags become the means of Beauty's enfleshment.

I have long pondered this part of the tale and I have come to the conclusion that such a coming to one's self again, getting back into "one's own skin," particularly after some kind of crisis or major upheaval in one's life, often requires a particularly concentrated focus on *ordinariness and simple, immediate, practical materiality*, a special connection and preoccupation with familiar physical domestic tasks of life.

I once heard about a missionary priest who had lived for years in a third world country. All his commonplace domestic needs had been provided by housekeepers in the various rectories where he lived. Late in his career he suffered a nervous collapse. It was pure genius that when he entered a special treatment center back in the States, the patients were required to do their own laundry, participate in kitchen duties, and help maintain the overall household. This, in itself, helped these men return to health—to an important kind of mundane reality of which they were in great need—probably because they had become too one-sidedly "spiritual," and consequently disconnected from fundamental, hands-on living. Their personalities were being reconstituted and reintegrated or "reincarnated" by relying upon "a rice pot for a head, a stick for a hand, a dish cloth for entrails, and fire hooks for feet."

One of the well-known answers to the famous Zen koan question, "What is the Buddha?" is "go wash your bowl." Here is the wisdom stated simply. The Christian parallel to this is "How do I reach God?" to which the wise Abbe (spiritual father) of the Egyptian Desert monks replies, "Go clean your cell." It has never failed to impress me that Jesus was a carpenter, a master of hands-on work with natural materials. He did not grow up a rarified guru sitting on a silk cushion with his head in the clouds, musing on the transcendental subtleties of life.

The old woman went out and made a big noise in the lane and the husband finally came out and asked the old woman where she had gotten the bag, which he recognized as the very one he had earlier given to his wife. Then the old woman told the story of the dark shadow in her house that had turned into the beautiful girl. The old woman then repeated the whole story of Beauty's life, just as she had heard it from the lips of the girl herself. The husband put a red cloth on the ground and brought Beauty back to the house.

The red cloth on the ground reminds us that what we in the west call "the red carpet treatment" probably comes originally from Asia. In old Japan, before the time of Hirohito, the emperor was considered a god on earth. Whenever he emerged from his sacred palace, great pains were taken to keep his feet from touching the bare ground. Wherever he walked, a red carpet was spread before him. Because the Emperor's physical body was believed to be the dynamic source of power for the whole world, it was feared that if he touched the ground, this vital energy would be short-circuited and rapidly drain away, never to be recovered, and this, of course, would be the gravest catastrophe imaginable. Variations of this mythic-royal idea of insulating a king or queen can be found all over the earth in many primal cultures, from Africa to the Pacific islands. Such a meticulous respect for the royal body is reflected even to this very day in the polite court protocol for the British monarchy. If you have the good fortune to be in the immediate presence of the queen, you are prohibited from initiating any physical contact with her unless she takes the initiative, for instance, in reaching out to shake your hand. So the red cloth suggests the sublime importance and prodigious significance of Beauty as a carrier of supernormal power. In some respects, Beauty is a queen in disguise—a mask or icon of God.

Pock Face, however, grumbled that this woman was just a spirit pretending to be Beauty. Pock face wanted a trial to see who was the true wife. Beauty, who knew she was the real bride, readily agreed. They had to walk on eggs and climb a ladder of sharp knives. When Beauty trod on the eggs they remained whole, but when Pock Face stepped on them, they all shattered. When Beauty climbed the knife ladder, she received not a scratch, but when Pock Face tried to ascend, her feet were cut to the bone.

Unable to accept this, Pock Face then proposed that they each jump into a caldron of hot oil, thinking that Beauty would have to jump first, ensuring her death. When Beauty jumped, she was unharmed by the oil, but when Pock Face jumped, she did not come up again, and was boiled alive.

Beauty put the roasted bones of Pock Face into a box. Then she asked a stuttering servant to take them to the stepmother and say, "Your daughter's flesh." But the stepmother loved carp and thought he said "carp flesh." She believed that Pock Face had sent her some carp. Opening the box in great excitement, she saw the charred flesh and bones of her own daughter instead; and, letting out a piercing scream, the stepmother fell down dead.

In the episode where Beauty survives the three mortal tests, you can see the similarity to the Iron Stove tale. There, the heroine must cross the slippery glass mountain and roll over the sharp swords. In the story of Pock Face, the knives do not harm Beauty, even though she does not wear the protection of a plough wheel. But there is something new in this Chinese tale regarding stepping on eggs. To walk over the eggs without breaking them, means that we must live life with a light touch, not flat-footedly, with only heavy, literalistic and concrete thinking, so that the eggs, the nascent possibilities for the growth and development of the personality—the birth or regeneration of the bird of the spirit—are not harmed. Psychological growth must be respected as a relatively autonomous self-regulating guidance system. We can't march through life with only our conscious will and determination, holding fast to our jealously guarded opinions as we demand this or insist on that in the hard-fact world. The lightness as opposed to the heaviness points to a metaphorical and poetic type of consciousness that dances rather than walks, and sings rather than talks

J. N. H. Perkins

pedantically, for as the age-old mythic consciousness has always known, the so-called secular world is merely a veil, behind which is occurring the real transcendental drama of our existence.

5

The Princess in the Suit of Leather

The following tale, "The Princess in the Suit of Leather," another "Cinderella" variant, comes from Egypt.[24] In this tale, the heroine is active and resourceful, even more so than the princess in "The Iron Stove" and far exceeding the classic Grimm's "Cinderella", where gifts from the dead mother's grave save the day and Cinderella is relatively passive rather than dynamic. In the "Leather Suit" tale, there is no personal mother to help, although a type of unofficial godmother figure turns up at just the right moment. Neither is there a classic stepmother nor selfish stepsisters. However, there is a sort of stand-in for the stepmother, a dowager of the royal court, who callously disregards the young heroine's best interests. The heroine, functioning independently, must act in complete independence by her own wits. In the "Leather Suit," there is a very different kind of female conniving. The heroine's own strategic abilities are marked by clever subterfuge and the scheming foresight of the trickster. In this way the heroine, of marriageable age, lacks the naiveté of little seven-year-old Snow White or the child-woman, Cinderella. In the end, she can take most of the credit for her accomplishments. In "The Princess in the Suit of Leather," we see an actual protagonist, who, in her own person, encompasses much of what, in "Little Snow

White," was invested in those higher powers that seemed to be weaving the threads of fate from behind the scenes, and in "Cinderella" was represented by the gifts from her late mother's grave. This difference is a chief feature of the modern human personality, where the old gods and goddesses have now become dynamic forces roaming the unconscious landscape of the psyche.

Here's the tale in its entirety:

A king and queen, deeply in love, had a stunningly beautiful daughter. This princess was the light of her father's life, but just as she reached the flower of womanhood, her dear mother, the queen, died. The king grieved inconsolably for a year, and at last vowed to marry once again, but only to the one woman in all the land whose ankle fit exactly through his late wife's golden anklet. The whole realm was searched but the bracelet fit none of the women. Finally, it was discovered that this bangle did, in fact, conform perfectly to the leg of the most unlikely person, and this, of course, turned out to be the king's own daughter. When the king asked for advice, an old dowager of the court suggested that, under the circumstances, the king should take this fortunate opportunity and cleverly rescue his daughter from marriage to some unwanted suitor. Why not marry the princess himself?

While the maiden was being magnificently robed and adorned for her wedding to a man whose identity had been carefully hidden, at the last minute a daughter of the vizier disclosed that the princess was about to be wed to her own father! In shock and dismay, she fled the palace, and concealing herself in a tiny back street of the town, paid a leather smith and his family to quickly provide a suit of hides that would cover everything but her eyes. In this disguise, she escaped through the gate and flew away to a distant kingdom.

As the princess was arriving at the distant city, the local queen, whose attention had been drawn to the strange woman in hides, finally asked to meet this creature. The queen was touched by her feeble demeanor and amused by her curious chatter, especially by her repeated declaration, which began, "My name is Juliedah for my coat of skins. My eyes are weak; my sight is dim." The kindly queen took the poor old thing into the palace harem as a charity case and put her to work as a helper in the kitchen.

One evening, a big celebration was held in the castle, and the grand vizier invited all the women and members of the harem—even the servants. But Juliedah humbly declined and took her place on the kitchen floor, looking like an ugly pile of dirty old random hides, while the others dressed up and skipped off to the party. Late during the evening festival, a hush descended upon the room as a radiant young woman abruptly appeared. Her presence seemed to fill the whole space with light. Lovely beyond all enduring, her magnificence—as they all agreed—rivaled even that of the sun and the moon. All the women crowded around her, seeking her company, and when she had enjoyed the evening at length, though she spoke no more than polite babble, she reached into the hem of her dress and swiftly scattered a handful of sparkling gold sequins out across the ornate marble floor. As everyone gasped and scrambled to take this treasure, Juliedah slipped quietly away and resumed her leather disguise once again, taking her place on the kitchen floor.

Afterward, the queen went to the kitchen and gently poked the pile of skins with her red slipper and told Juliedah that she had missed a surprise at the party that night: a magnificent woman had appeared and mesmerized the whole harem. But the heap replied, "My eyes are weak and I cannot see."

The following morning, the queen told her son, the prince, about the beautiful woman who had appeared the night before. "Her face, neck and form were so magnificent that everyone said that she must not be the daughter of a king or even a sultan, but of someone far greater!"

The next night another great festivity was held and the same thing happened. This time, toward morning, the lovely maiden cast a handful of gleaming pearls across the floor and then slipped away.

But now the prince, who was mesmerized by the lavish descriptions he had just heard of the mysterious maiden, was hiding near the door. His intention was to delay her and inquire about her identity and origin. As she sped out, he seized her hand and began to question her, but the radiant girl abruptly pulled away, and as she wrested her fingers from his grip, his ring accidentally slipped off into her hand. Feeling it in her palm, she dashed off, crying over her shoulder, "I live in The Land of Paddles and Ladles."

The following day, the prince announced to the whole palace that shortly he would set off on a long journey in search of the beautiful maiden who lived in The Land of Paddles and Ladles. In anticipation, the kitchen staff prepared food for his journey, and old Juliedah begged to bake one of the littlest cakes being provided. In the dough of this littlest cake she hid the prince's ring.

Far along on his trek, as the prince grew hungry, he finally bit into the last small cake and was surprised when his teeth struck something hard. Reaching his fingers into his mouth and removing the object, he was dumfounded to discover his own ring! Asking who had baked the loaf, his servant replied, "It is the work of that feeble old kitchen maid whom they call Juliedah." With this, the prince immediately solved the riddle and knew that the mysterious Land of Paddles and Ladles was, in fact, the palace kitchen itself, and that the magnificent girl must somehow be connected to the old crone who worked there.

When the prince returned home, he asked that the kitchen staff prepare his dinner, with the stipulation that the tray must be delivered by Juliedah, and by none other. The first time she climbed the stairs with the dinner on top of her head, she lost her balance and the entire meal spilled down the steps. The same dinner was prepared once again, and this time two servants stood on either side to help Juliedah balance the tray properly. After the prince had dismissed the other two but commanded Juliedah to remain alone with him, he asked her to fill his goblet. As she approached, he suddenly drew his razor-sharp dagger from his belt, and, in one stroke, he slashed open Juliedah's leather suit from top to bottom. He performed this feat with such consummate skill that no harm whatsoever was done to what lay beneath the hides. As the shabby disguise collapsed in a pile on the floor, there stood before him the stellar princess his mother had described—the kind of woman who could say to the moon, "Set, so that I may reign in your place." After the proper arrangements were made, the prince and Juliedah were married and lived blissfully together.

In the beginning of our tale, shortly before the scheduled wedding ceremony, Juliedah's father had gone to his daughter's room to unveil her face and found her missing. Sometime later, he gathered his men and made a journey far and wide in search of her, wrapping in chains the old woman who had advised this incestuous marriage. By strange coincidence, he came near the very palace where Juliedah was sitting in her window. Gazing out, she immediately recognized the men of her own country and secretly asked her husband to greet them and invite them to stay. After receiving many pretexts, he convinced them to spend the night. A small feast was planned for the visitors.

Meanwhile, Juliedah begged her husband, now the sultan himself, to loan her some of his own clothes and headgear. Clad in these and thus camouflaged as a man, she attended the gathering. After dinner, Juliedah suggested that stories should be told as entertainment. When the others demurred, Juliedah, disguising her voice as well, then proceeded to tell a wondrous and intriguing tale—that of her own life, yet recited as if it were about another person—regarding a certain princess from a faraway land who had fled to escape a wrongful marriage. The old dowager, still in chains yet part of the company, politely objected several times to the young gentleman's strange tale, but Juliedah finished her story right up to the present moment, and then, abruptly tossing off her turban so that her long golden hair now cascaded over her shoulders, she looked directly into her father's eyes, identifying herself as none other than his own daughter. "You see at this moment before your eyes the very objective of your long journey. Here

I am, your child and your beloved princess, the image of my mother. I am now the sultan's wife and the queen of this vast land. It is I who have suffered the many grievous troubles that have been related to you just now, and all because of that wicked old woman—that daughter of Satan!" Utterly shocked yet immensely relieved, Juliedah's father embraced her and sang for joy.

The next morning Juliedah's father wrote a paper giving her half his kingdom, and then ordered his men to hurl the miserable old sinner off a steep cliff into the *wadi*, where she perished at the bottom of the deep chasm.

Juliedah and her husband lived happily together for the rest of their lives, until separated by death, the only power that is able divide true lovers.

———————

Now we'll look at this tale section by section with comments.

A king and queen, deeply in love, had a stunningly beautiful daughter. This princess was the light of her father's life, but just as she reached the flower of womanhood, her dear mother, the queen, died. The king grieved inconsolably for a year, and at last vowed to marry once again, but only to the one woman in all the land whose ankle fit exactly through his late wife's golden bracelet. The whole realm was searched but the bracelet fit none of the women. Finally, it was discovered that this bangle did, in fact, conform perfectly to the leg of the most unlikely person, and this, of course, turned out to be the king's own daughter. When the king asked for advice, an old dowager of the court suggested that, under the circumstances, the king should take this fortunate opportunity and cleverly rescue his daughter from marriage to some unwanted suitor. Why not marry the princess himself?

While the maiden was being magnificently robed and adorned for her wedding to a man whose identity had been carefully hidden, at the last minute a daughter of the vizier disclosed that the princess was about to be wed to her own father! In shock and dismay, she fled the palace, and concealing herself in a tiny back street of the town, paid a leather smith and his family to quickly make her a patched suit of hides that would cover everything but her eyes. In this disguise, she escaped through the gate and flew away to a distant kingdom.

All fairy tales that focus on the troublesome events that lead up to a successful royal marriage (the end result of our story) are telling us about the need to balance and relate the masculine and feminine dimensions of life. When this nuptial theme is prominent in the folklore of any culture, we can be certain that, in the *zeitgeist* at large, there is a severe imbalance, an erotic or gender-based one-sidedness that has come both to oppress the inferior side of the personality and indeed, by the same token, to limit and distort the dominant side as well. A whole life is like the perfectly engaged teardrops of the *yin* and *yang* principles that are contained in the circle of the Chinese Tao. In our western culture it is generally the feminine or *yin* side that has been suppressed to a level of inferiority or sentimentality, or has become the mere object of prurient desire. Yet it is not enough to view this need for rectification only in social, economic, or political terms in a mindset of "equal rights." Valid as these regions are for serious consideration, a narrow, social justice mentality alone lacks an appreciation of the complex depth of the individual personality, and of psychological reality in general.

The incest theme in our tale is not something about which contemporary incest survivor groups need be concerned. This symbolic and unrecognized level of father-daughter incest is pointing to the fact that if the feminine quality emerging from psychological repression *inside the human personality* subjects itself to a paternalistic mentality, then it will remain under the thumb of the conventional (super-ego), male-dominated culture and remain its slave. Feminine vitality—even within women themselves—will be held down below the level of consciousness, suppressed like the Marxist proletariat, and kept from full participation in conscious life. To appreciate the core of this, one must shift from the socio-political sphere to the psychological and the inward. The tale depicts what will happen inside you and me. If the emancipation of the feminine does occur within the depths of each of us, there will be profound ramifications in the public arena of our common life.

Father figures, especially if they are men of princely station, stand for the common cultural mindset and its values—the *zeitgeist* or the spirit of the program that rules life. From this we are taught the proper philosophy of life in the public sphere: how to live and what to believe; who we are and what we should be doing. Mother figures, analogously, seem to be the custodians of the material (matter = *mater* = mother) of our personal lives, and the biological and instinctive resources of our nature, and our sensuous appreciation of reality, as well as matters of the heart and soul, and of personal relationship. These are viewed by the masculine program as enrichments that are enjoyable, attractive, and even mesmerizing, yet they are also viewed with suspicion and not a little fear. The erotic beauty, apparent impetuosity, and wiliness of the woman, including her unpredictable intuitive imagination, are disconcerting for the man. He senses here that a soft yet powerful weapon may wrest control from him and lead him astray. All repressive, misogynous regimes are founded upon the fear of awesome feminine power. Yet the feminine world is far more than just animal impulse, sensual display, or devious subterfuge. The feminine, when recognized and dignified, brings us the wisdom and the life lessons of nature and our emotional and relational intelligence, the capacity to discriminate life from the subtler feeling side, as opposed to the more abstract, rational, and principled agenda of the male. Symbolically speaking, father rules the order of our public consciousness, whereas mother rules the sphere of our personal intimacies. Whether we are males or females, we all encompass these gender opposites within our whole personalities.

As the princess was arriving at the distant city, the local queen, whose attention had been drawn to the strange woman in hides, finally asked to meet this creature. The queen was touched by her feeble demeanor and amused by her curious chatter, especially by her repeated declaration, which began, "My name is Juliedah for my coat of skins. My eyes are weak; my sight is dim." The kindly queen took the poor old thing into the palace harem as a charity case and put her to work as a helper in the kitchen.

When the princess flees the palace, she obtains what appears to be a leather *burka* as her disguise. Because the *burka* is made of leather, it has an additional connotation. It conceals the sensuous beauty and identity of the princess behind animal hides. Her human femininity, including the status of her royal station, is hidden behind an animal exterior. In this disguise, she functions at the bottom of the social hierarchy—the lowest of the kitchen servants. She is hardly more than a beast of burden. In our tale, this lowering of her social station is not forced on her by others but freely chosen as a ploy to carry through a strategic plan. Unlike Cinderella, there are no stepmother and stepsisters to enslave her. She actually enslaves herself—on purpose—and adopts the name Juliedah, which, as my esteemed Egyptian friend, Mohsen Koly, has informed me, is the feminine diminutive of the Arabic *jeld* (Egyptian *geld*) referring to animal hide, the *'ah* suffix indicating the feminine gender.

Notice that in "The Princess and the Suit of Leather," the princess initially has no name. When later she does say who she is, it is her own invention, not a designation assigned by her parents. A name tells us who we are and what our significance is in the world. If we don't have a name, this symbolizes that our deepest reality and meaning remains a mystery to us and to others. Or, if a name changes in a story, that means that the person herself has changed. When a name is revealed somewhere in the course of a story, or perchance in a dream, an important dimension of life is being revealed and appreciated for the first time, or perhaps recalled from previous obscurity.

Juliedah is that new, intriguing, feminine quality that is making her reappearance in our tale after a long period of cultural demise. Because she invents her own name, she is a unique entity, not simply a clone of the contemporary collective culture ruled by her father the king. As we shall realize in this exposition, Juliedah is not really an ordinary human being at all, but someone "far greater," a veritable Queen of Heaven, as the tale itself later hints.

The Islamic world of the medieval Near East, at least among the upper classes (the milieu of our present tale), once had a highly sophisticated appreciation of women's capabilities. In those traditional high cultures of refined, oriental antiquity, there was a protected mystery of female dignity and wisdom. This was disguised behind the curtain of *purdah* that separated the official life of public culture from the guarded privacy of family and personal life.

Purdah protected domestic values as much as it incarcerated them. In the Muslim world, the veil traditionally worn by women in public was originally the prerogative of patrician ladies of the highest caste. It no doubt served to protect their esteemed visage from the leering common folk. Such ladies were considered too exceptional to be viewed casually by the average person. Here, the emphasis was not on the constraint of women, but on the need to carefully guard the patrician woman's privacy from the gaze of the voyeur. Much of what we witness today in terms of the restrictive political and social seclusion of women in the Middle East is the result of a long process of reactionary decay that has perverted the original significance of traditions devoted to the guarding of women's honor. Time and the changing fortunes of Islamic culture have steadily debased this protection to serve the interests of misogynist males.

The Turkish word *herem* (Arabic *haram*) refers to women's quarters, meaning literally "something forbidden or kept safe." *Herem* is like the Latin word *sacra*, which can mean either "sacred" or "accursed." This gives us an appreciation of how such terms and practices can invert and devolve into precisely the opposite meaning of their original sense. At first, women in the upper echelons were too refined or vulnerable to be seen in public. In modern times they are considered too inferior, or in some sense unworthy, to receive the public freedoms and prerogatives enjoyed by men! This is much like the sense of the term "taboo," which guards the boundaries of the sacred in the traditional ethos of more primal peoples. Later, it develops a negative connotation, the sense of "unclean," the reverse of its original meaning. In Hebrew culture as in many others, a woman's menstrual flow made her unclean during that period of her monthly cycle.[25] But it was also recognized (as in the kosher food regulations) that the blood of any animal is not fit for human consumption, not because it is bad, but precisely because blood is the very life spirit of the creature—a holy substance—belonging to God and to God alone and traditionally offered in sacrifice to the deity before the meat itself was eaten.

In ancient times, the object of male sexual desire, together with the impulse itself, much like the spirit in wine, was associated with certain eerie supernatural powers that could take complete possession of the individual. Under certain circumstances, this powerful force could produce socially disturbing effects, involving emotional instability, physical abuse, or seduction. Consequently, in many traditions, fear of and respect for the power of woman necessitated various forms of protocol and the careful managing of relations between the sexes. This was true from China to India to ancient Egypt, long before Islam emerged in the seventh century CE. The veiling of women goes back many centuries before Mohammed. To appraise the entire history of such traditions narrowly as instances of enforced female inferiority is both facile and inaccurate.

One evening, a big celebration was held in the castle, and the grand vizier invited all the women and members of the harem, even the servants. But Juliedah humbly declined and took her place on the kitchen floor, looking like an ugly pile of dirty random hides, while the others dressed up and skipped off to the party. Late during the evening festival, a hush descended upon the room as a radiant young woman abruptly appeared. Her presence seemed to fill the whole space with light. Lovely beyond all enduring, her magnificence rivaled even that of the sun and moon themselves. All the women crowded around her, seeking her company, and when she had enjoyed the evening at length, though she spoke no more than polite babble, she reached into the hem of her dress and swiftly scattered a handful of sparkling gold sequins out across the ornate marble floor. As everyone gasped and scrambled to take this treasure, Juliedah slipped quietly away and resumed her leather disguise once again, taking her place on the kitchen floor.

Afterward, the queen went to the kitchen and gently poked the pile of skins with her red slipper and told Juliedah that she had missed a surprise at the party that night: a magnificent woman had appeared and mesmerized the whole harem. But the heap replied, "My eyes are weak and I cannot see."

The following morning, the queen told her son, the prince, about the beautiful woman who had appeared the night before. "Her face, neck, and form were so magnificent that everyone said that she must not be the daughter of a king or even a sultan, but of someone far greater!"

The next night another great festivity was held and the same thing happened. This time, toward morning, the lovely maiden cast a handful of gleaming pearls across the floor and then slipped away.

Kings and queens and the other awesome figures from the story world are, of course, objective literary creations, but they can also be seen to represent that higher order of life that moves in the murky depths beneath our small, daily lives. When you encounter glittering gold, silver, and precious gems in tales, you are no longer in the ego world of plain, flat-footed reality—what Joseph Campbell humorously called the *literalistic per se*. In the prologue of his wonderful work, *The Hero With a Thousand Faces* (1949), Campbell wrote: "The latest incarnation of Oedipus, the continued romance of Beauty and the Beast, stands this afternoon on the corner of 42nd Street and Fifth Avenue, waiting for the traffic light to change." These innocent pedestrians, waiting at that famous intersection which is the location of the main branch of the New York Public Library—where magnificent stone lions, recumbent, silently guard the entrance—each contain within their souls a microcosm bursting with mythic intrigue, a vast catalogue and lexicon of demonic and angelic spirits.

In "The Princess in the Suit of Leather," the old mythic tradition of the Great Woman that preceded Islam, Judaism, and Christianity is evident. Here we see vestiges of the pre-Islamic culture, of the Bronze Age Egyptian and Minoan periods of four to five thousand years ago. Like the full veil or *burka* worn in public by traditional Islamic women, the social institution of *purdah* defended and nourished the feminine values of sensitive and discriminating feeling, refined erotic presence, and playful ingenuity. These traits were the ingredients of a free and spontaneous rapture of life, whose historic roots reached far below into the ancient rituals of the mother goddess and her dark and violent yet exhilarating rites of fertility. While *purdah* kept women from assuming a masculine role and identity in public life, it paradoxically guarded and preserved the ancient power of womanhood, a fearsome and nearly mystical authority that had existed before the advent of male dominance. When the dominant religion of a people changes, this does not always affect the lowest reaches of the psyche. Down below and still energized is the age-old system—in this case, the powerful Egyptian gods and goddesses.

In many respects, the milieu of storytelling functioned analogously to conserve the same powerful heritage of women's mysteries. Here we see Juliedah dramatically revealing the royal and stellar quality of womanhood that is concealed within the animal hide *burka*. She is not waiting for Joseph Campbell's traffic light in New York City, but with equal anonymity she is serving in the palace kitchen.

This going in and out of the animal hides has another connotation beyond the obvious. It signifies the young princess's transformation in a process of death and rebirth. When Juliedah assumes the animal skins, she is absorbed into the animal mother. As a royal princess, she dies. When she removes the *burka*, as she does when she attends the party, she is born again from the animal mother. In our modern terms, this is simply a way of saying that the princess as the mere daughter-extension of her human, cultural parents must come to an end in order to appear anew, having been regenerated by the wise powers of nature in order to attain her ultimate self. Finally, she will be a unique woman distinct from her parents. This death and rebirth happens four times in our tale. These four stages, like a quadruple baptism, encompass Juliedah's initiation rite into full womanhood. Such a transformation involves a recapturing of the most ancient image of divine femininity. The animal, we could say, is an analogy to the natural psyche, that mysterious region below the obvious surface consciousness of our lives that is the ultimate source of our energies, our intrinsic value, and our trans-personal, trans-cultural identity. Juliedah's first three transformations are connected to the animal skins. Later in the tale, the fourth and final alteration is her disappearance into, and emergence from, the garments of the male. This foreshadows the much later historical stage of our own era, where, as a brief stage in the women's liberation movement about a generation ago, women had to identify themselves with the male attitude and social posture. But presently we are coming to value a deep and profound femininity that is distinct from masculinity—one that is as strong, tenacious, and competent as it is graceful and beautiful.

As we examine the death-and-rebirth theme mentioned above, we must bear in mind that Juliedah, when out of her animal skins at each of the two evening feasts, reached into the hem of her dress and scattered sparkling gold sequins onto the marble floor the first night, and then glowing pearls the second night.

Recall what we were saying about the ancient, pre-Christian and pre-Islamic background to the culture of Egypt. In the figure of Juliedah, this surfaces as follows. The mother of the major deities of ancient Egypt—Osiris, Isis, Set, and Nepthys—was the sky goddess Nut (pronounced "Newt"), characterized in the Pyramid Texts as "the brilliant," "the Great," "The Great Protectress," "She who cannot be fertilized without putting down her arms," "She of the Hanging Breasts."[26] These are all illusions to Nut as the heavenly dome, whose toes stood on the eastern horizon and whose fingers touched the western (Fig. 1). Nut as sky goddess represented woman's love and joy.[27] Her entire body displayed the celestial waters of the upper firmament of heaven, together with the stars. Each morning she gave birth to the sun from out of her own body, while each evening she swallowed the sun as it set. As the mother of all the gods, Nut must also have given birth to the moon, in Egypt personified as the Ibis-headed Thoth, the god of computation, letters, learning, and wisdom.[28] So, nut was not only the source of light and life, but also of writing, mathematics, and intellect.

The swallowing of the sun, where the hands touch the western horizon, was the moment of impregnation (shown in Fig. 1, where the sun-disk is depicted close to her mouth). In this act, the devouring of and the coitus with her own male child were two sides of a single occurrence, because this paradoxical incestuous action was the means of re-gestating the sun god (represented by the sun disk shown near the genitals as well as the mouth) so that Horus could be born again the following day. Hathor, wearing the ram-like head-dress, was a goddess syncretic with Nut as the "Mistress of the West," welcoming the dead into the next life on the horizon where the sun finished its course every evening.

The subtle reverberations of this sky goddess-mother of the celestial sun are vast even to this very day. You can see this in the following Eastern Orthodox prayer-hymn to the Virgin Mary mother of Christ, still sung in churches and monasteries: "He hast made thy body into a throne, and thy womb more spacious than the heavens … for from you dawned the Sun of Righteousness." And then there is the poem by Sarah Williams (1837–1868), "The Old Astronomer to His Pupil," that resonates so well with this theme: "Though my soul may set in darkness, it will rise in perfect light. I have loved the stars too fondly to be fearful of the night."

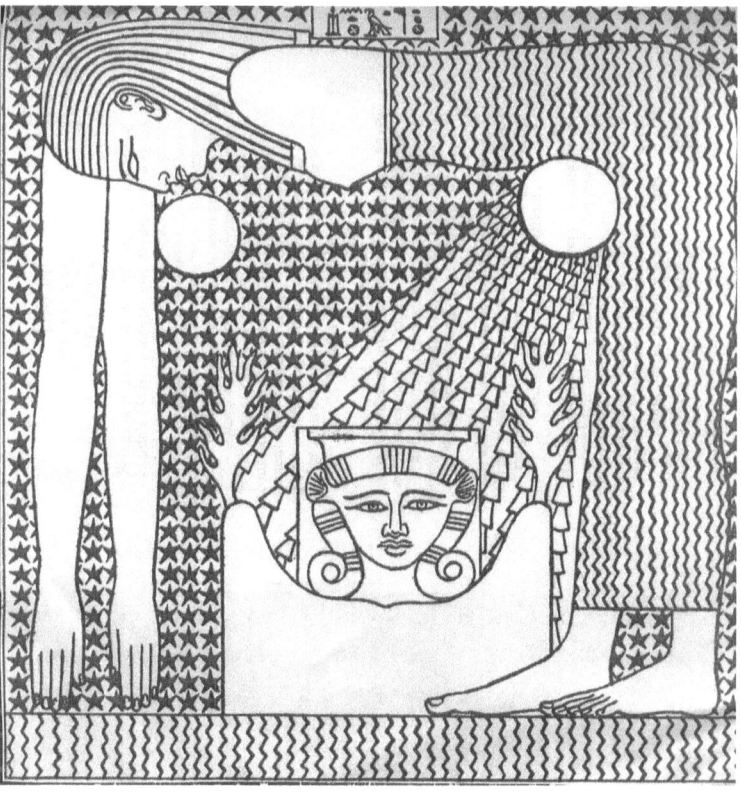

Fig. 1: Nut giving birth to the sun, the rays of which fall upon Hathor in the horizon. (From E. A. Wallis Budge, *The Gods of the Egyptians*, Vol. 2.)

J. N. H. Perkins

Fig 2: The Cow-goddess Nut. (Budge, ibid, Vol. 1)

In Fig. 2, where Nut is portrayed as a cow, notice that close to her left shoulder, the barge of the sun god Horus may be seen travelling from east to west. Nut herself, in the period previous to the Pyramid Texts, in the time of the Narner Tablets, appeared not in human form but as the cow goddess Hathor. Notice that in this figure, her belly is lined with the stars of the upper firmament. So Juliedah in her leather suit is the celestial cow goddess Hathor. Revealed in her lovely human form she is Nut, mother and bride of the sun god and origin of resourceful human consciousness.

Nut was also depicted as a cat or a lioness, the goddess of storms and terror. This should not surprise us, as Nut's own mother was Tefnut, depicted with the head of a lioness. For Juliedah to appear out of her Tefnut-Hathor animal incarnation as a marvelous woman in human form suggests that she rises from the level of the unconscious, instinctive system of prototypical nature that is narrowly aligned with the visceral energies of the body, and emerges into lucid human consciousness. This is the original liberation of the feminine, which occurred more than four thousand years ago, but which seems to have been largely forgotten, as it was gradually covered over and subdued by male dominance.

Consequently, when Juliedah scatters the sparkling gold sequins, and later the glowing pearls, she is the Egyptian goddess Nut giving birth to the sun and the moon. Here, she displays herself openly as the Queen of Heaven, predecessor of the Catholic Virgin Mother of God, and so we now understand why Juliedah is described as filling the room with light when she enters, as she becomes the mother of the sun and the moon, and the custodian of all creation.

J. N. H. Perkins

But now the prince, who was mesmerized by the lavish descriptions he had just heard of the mysterious maiden, was hiding near the door. His intention was to delay her and inquire about her identity and origin. As she sped out, he seized her hand and began to question her, but the radiant girl abruptly pulled away, and as she wrested her fingers from his grip, his ring accidentally slipped off into her hand. Feeling it in her palm, she dashed off, crying over her shoulder, "I live in The Land of Paddles and Ladles."

The following day, the prince announced to the whole palace that shortly he would set off on a long journey in search of the beautiful maiden who lived in The Land of Paddles and Ladles. In anticipation, the kitchen staff prepared food for his journey, and old Juliedah begged to bake one of the littlest cakes being provided. In the dough of this littlest cake she hid the prince's ring.

Far along on his trek, as the prince grew hungry, he finally bit into the last small cake and was surprised when his teeth struck something hard. Reaching his fingers into his mouth and removing the object, he was dumfounded to discover his own ring! Asking who had baked the loaf, his servant replied, "It is the work of that feeble old kitchen maid whom they call Juliedah." With this, the prince immediately solved the riddle and knew that the mysterious Land of Paddles and Ladles was, in fact, the palace kitchen itself, and that the magnificent girl must somehow be connected to the old crone who worked there.

When the prince returned home, he asked that the kitchen staff prepare his dinner, with the stipulation that the tray must be delivered by Juliedah, and by none other. The first time she climbed the stairs with the dinner on top of her head, she lost her balance and the entire meal spilled onto the floor. The same dinner was prepared once again and this time two servants stood on either side to help Juliedah balance the tray properly. After the prince had dis-

missed the other two but ordered Juliedah to remain alone with him, he asked her to fill his goblet. As she approached, he suddenly pulled his razor-sharp dagger from his belt, and, in one stroke, he slashed open Juliedah's leather suit from top to bottom. He performed this feat with such consummate skill that no harm whatsoever was done to what lay beneath the hides. As the shabby disguise collapsed in a pile on the floor, there stood before him the stellar princess his mother had described—the kind of woman who could say to the moon, "Set, so that I may reign in your place."

The third transformation is performed by the prince, who will eventually be Juliedah's husband. He functions as a sacrificial priest, using his sharp dagger to slit open Juliedah's outer garment of skins. In this deft action, he symbolically performs an animal sacrifice, in order to liberate and reveal the goddess lady who is concealed beneath the hides. With Juliedah's hint in her fleeting comment, "I live in The Land of Paddles and Ladles," the prince, having found the ring in his cake, has solved the riddle of Juliedah's identity and where she might be found. His sharp dagger is his obstetric blade that performs the caesarian section, delivering Juliedah from her symbolic animal incarceration. The prince's sharp, discriminating perception reveals that the chief feminine figure of life will from now on and forever be an intelligent human being, a conscious woman, enabling heaven to descend to earth, for a goddess to become a human woman, and thus enter into our actual experience of living, in flesh-and-blood form.

When the prince uses his dagger to uncover Juliedah, he is shedding light on the new feminine reality, revealing it for all to see. But it was his ring, furtively taken by Juliedah as she fled the party, which finally led him to her. A ring or other symmetrical object stands for completeness. When the prince had laid eyes upon the beautiful maiden, he was so enamored of her that she suddenly came to represent the very integrity and fullness of life itself. Without her, he himself was devoid of life. To regain the life he had lost, he had to find her, no matter what the cost. She had become his soul-sister-lover, his inner partner, the other side of his masculine life, the only one with whom he could achieve fulfillment. But as it turned out, he found this gratifying dimension, not in some mysterious faraway place, but back at home in the palace kitchen. It is the same for us all. Like Dorothy, in L. Frank Baum's *The Wizard of Oz*, we typically find ourselves journeying to distant regions where we believe we will obtain what we so desperately seek. Yet in the end, we discover that what we wanted was right there back at home from whence we first started. It was present under our very nose the whole time, but we failed to see it. This is because we generally overlook our own resources, unconsciously projecting them onto the people and things around us. The further away, and the more exotic and valuable they seem, the more we want them. The last place we are inclined to look is within ourselves.

After the proper arrangements were made, the prince and Juliedah were married and lived blissfully together.

The tale seems to say that if we wish to discover the highest value of life, we should look first into what is regarded as the lowest order of things, to uncover the prize hidden there. There is an old saying that the Pearl of Great Price will always be found in a pile of dung! This is not because the lower is better than the higher in any objective sense. It is because what is truly deemed highest often has been consigned to what is judged to be the most inferior region. There it lies hidden and destitute, because that is how it is viewed by the dominant, grandiose mindset of the culture. The psychological jargon for this worthless, useless state is *suppression* or *repression*. The economic determinism of Marx and Engels borrows the exact same mythic insight, declaring that the golden value of humanity—the hope of the future, a kind of messianic promise—lies repressed, manipulated, and tortured by the spirit of capitalism, hidden in the population of the proletarian worker class of nineteenth century European industrial society. Our tale says that there is a goddess hiding in the kitchen. She only appears to be a decrepit old scullery maid on the outside.

The inescapable conclusion is that the dominant and chauvinistic male culture *of our whole mentality* has put the celestial feminine into the lowest of regions, a region *considered* inferior. Patriarchy has made the feminine a servant and kitchen drudge inside the psyche of our common humanity. Let's face it; men have done this to actual women. But we miss the deeper significance of this sorry state of affairs if we restrict our understanding to the socio-economic level of consideration alone. This travesty is inside all of us, in the souls of both men and women. A rejection of the feminine has not been cruelly inflicted outwardly only by men. Programmed by the perennial collective culture, both sexes have agreed with, and enthusiastically participated in, such a program, barely realizing, until the past century, that a paternalistic society is dangerously one-sided. When Juliedah is finally revealed in all her glory, the kitchen and the work occurring there—for all of us—are redeemed. The kitchen is the creative center of the household personality inside us.

The psychic "kitchen," not the actual one, encompasses many things. This region of the personality, like the kitchens of the old Roman houses, lies at the very center of our existence. The kitchen, with all its symbols, functions in the soul of humanity as the temple of transformation, where our raw instinctive nature, emblemed by animal and vegetable life, is transmuted in the form of cooked and spiced food for the nourishment of our cultural consciousness. Here, instinctive animal mankind comes to a higher awareness of itself, not by transcending and escaping earthy matter, but from evolving and transforming its own intrinsic nature. Such is the deepest psychological function of all religion. The psychological or symbolic meaning of harvesting, slaughtering, and cooking is to transfigure involuntary instinct into an illumination of the mind. Consciousness is a meal that must be cooked from the ingredients of elemental nature.

Consciousness, as we observed in the Snow White tale, is the gold ore that is discovered in the earth. It requires the work of mining and smelting to transform it into its glowing metallic form. To this day, we speak of an intelligent person as "bright."

In the beginning of our tale, shortly before the scheduled wedding ceremony, Juliedah's father had gone to his daughter's room to unveil her face and found her missing. Sometime later, he gathered his men and made a journey far and wide in search of her, wrapping in chains the old woman who had advised this incestuous marriage. By strange coincidence, he came near the very palace where Juliedah was sitting in her window. Gazing out, she immediately recognized the men of her own country, and secretly asked her husband to greet them and invite them to stay. After many pretexts, he convinced them to spend the night. A small feast was planned for the visitors.

Meanwhile, Juliedah begged her husband, now the sultan himself, to loan her some of his own clothes and headgear. Clad in these, camouflaged as a man, she attended the gathering. After dinner, Juliedah suggested that stories should be told as entertainment. When the others demurred, Juliedah, disguising her voice as well, then proceeded to tell a wondrous and intriguing tale, that of her own life, yet recited as if it were about another person, a certain princess from a faraway land who had fled to escape a wrongful marriage. The old dowager, still in chains yet part of the company, politely objected several times to the young gentleman's strange tale, but Juliedah finished her story right up to the present moment, and then, abruptly tossing off her turban so that her long golden hair now cascaded over her shoulders, she looked directly into her father's eyes, identifying herself as none other than his own daughter. "You see this moment before your eyes the very object of your long journey. Here I am, your child and your beloved princess, the image of my mother. I am now the sultan's wife and the queen of this vast land. It is I who have suffered the many grievous troubles that have been related to you just now, and all because of that wicked old woman, that daughter of Satan!" Utterly shocked yet immensely relieved, Juliedah's father embraced her and sang for joy.

Juliedah's fourth and final transformation is when she disappears into, and emerges from, her male garments. She is able successfully to play a male role, then remove her male disguise at will, not confusing her intrinsic feminine self with her assumed social identity.

The next morning Juliedah's father wrote a paper giving her half his kingdom, and then ordered his men to hurl the miserable old sinner off a steep cliff into the wadi, *where she perished at the bottom of the deep chasm.*

J. N. H. Perkins

Juliedah and her husband lived happily together for the rest of their
lives, until separated by death, the only power that is able divide true lovers.

Today, it is impossible to fathom the enigma of the enclosed feminine world that lay behind the harem wall. The modern secularized Westerner finds such an arrangement unacceptable. If we view this curious pattern of sexual apartheid, however, in the interior mirror of our psyche, we might discover something very interesting. The harem is also the repressed unconscious of our own Western mentality. Indeed, we have such a harem right inside our very selves.

What we hate, condemn, or fear in other foreign cultures, what we are sure we have surpassed or corrected by our own impressive egalitarian progress, is so often what we have failed to acknowledge, value, and nourish in ourselves!

The conscious illumination that we so desperately require cannot be gained through rationalistic progress alone, by marching confidently ahead into the future as we re-invent life according to some popular *ism*. It cannot be achieved by rising above the instinctive mother-ground of feminine organic life in a flight of spiritual or intellectual detachment that breaks aggressively with the past. The longed-for wisdom and the true opening of the eyes only begin when we finally discover and value what had flowered in peak moments during the vast years before, but which has been long forgotten and devalued. All we need do is respectfully descend to it within ourselves through the vertical time-column of the psyche, recognize it, embrace it, and thus awaken it in our present hour of need.

6

Vasilisa the Beautiful

Now to Russia and a visit to one of its most popular tales, "Vasilisa the Beautiful,"[29] about a beautiful young maiden and her encounter with the infamous *Baba* (literally "country woman") *Yaga* (unknown meaning), a human-eating witch who lives in a hut resting on chicken feet and surrounded by a fence of human skulls. This story is another Cinderella type of tale but with some interesting and startling features. The name *Vasilisa* originates from the Greek man's name *Basileus* (Russian: Vasilii), meaning "king." For this reason, Vasilisa has some masculine overtones, yet appears in the feminine gender indicating "queen." Vasilisa is an old Russian name not so often encountered in modern times. The Russians are said to believe that Vasilisa is a folk symbol for Wisdom, otherwise known as *Sophia*, the Biblical feminine presence mentioned repeatedly in the book of Ecclesiastes, who, according to scripture, was with God even before the beginning of the world, and who continues to inspire icon writers (artists).[30]

Compared to the "Fatherland" of Germany, whose national icon is the invincible eagle of the sky god *Odin* (analogous to the Greek *Zeus* and the Roman *Jupiter*),

J. N. H. Perkins

Russia has a stronger feminine dimension within its deep, earthy soul. A folk of potent imagination and a thirst for the tragically mysterious and the darkly mystical, the Russians call their country not the fatherland but "Mother Russia." The brown bear, first cousin of our American grizzly—forest symbol of the awesome moon-goddess Artemis—is Russia's national emblem. The present tale displays the formidable and sometimes frightening capacities of this rich feminine disposition, which is also, of course, fierce nature herself!

First, let's read through the entire tale from beginning to end, then take it section by section with commentary regarding the significance of the characters and circumstances. The beginning is quite typical:

A merchant and his wife, after twelve years, finally had a beautiful daughter named Vasilisa. But when the child was eight years old, her mother became seriously ill. Sensing the coming of death, she blessed her little girl and entrusted a magic doll to her, warning Vasilisa that she must take great care to hide the doll and keep it a secret. Whenever Vasilisa needed help or advice, she was to feed the doll and then ask it questions. Before long, the mother passed to the next world.

The merchant father grieved, but in time he took another wife with daughters slightly older than Vasilisa. The new wife envied Vasilisa because she was so much more beautiful than her plain, thin stepsisters, so the new wife gave Vasilisa most of the housework to do. She accepted it all in good humor, and as time passed, even with her long hard hours and exposure to the wind and sun in the fields, Vasilisa grew prettier, more robust and buxom each day,

218

and finally reached marriageable age. Soon all the young men of the village were courting her. Meanwhile, the stepmother and her daughters became even paler and thinner, and none of the men showed any interest in them. So the stepmother let it be known to all that Vasilisa could not be given in marriage until after her stepsisters were both married.

From then on, the mean stepmother thought up even more work for her comely stepdaughter, while the stepsisters sat idly with folded hands. At last, Vasilisa, exhausted from her labors, decided to ask her doll for advice. Late one night, after saving most of her meal and hiding it in her room, she gave it to her doll. When the doll had finished her supper, Vasilisa poured out her misery, telling the doll how, despite living in her father's house, she was miserable because of her terrible stepmother. She asked the doll, "How should I live my life, and what should I do?" The doll comforted her and said not to worry. From then on, although Vasilisa seemed to be doing the work each day, it was really the doll who accomplished nearly everything swiftly and perfectly, allowing Vasilisa to rest and grow ever more beautiful. The doll was particularly adept at all the garden work, while Vasilisa enjoyed picking and smelling the beautiful flowers. The doll even found Vasilisa an herb that would protect her from sunburn.

Vasilisa's father had to embark on a very long journey, and while he was gone, his wife moved to another cottage, located on the edge of a vast and dark forest. In a glade deep in this wood was the hut of the Baba Yaga. Yaga's little house stood on chicken feet, and this witch ate any people who came near her, as if they were chickens instead of humans. No one had ever visited her hut and returned home to tell about it. As a ruse to get rid of beautiful Vasilisa, the stepmother repeatedly sent her on errands in the forest, encouraging her to go deeper and deeper. On these treks, the doll always advised Vasilisa to walk in a different direction from where the Baba Yaga lived. So, every day Vasilisa returned safely to the stepmother's cottage, looking healthy and strong.

One winter evening, the stepmother ordered the three girls to engage in some handiwork that was to be finished the same night. While the stepdaughters made lace and stockings, Vasilisa was required to spin. Only one short candle was permitted to burn in the room. Before the women were finished, the elder stepsister trimmed the candle, extinguishing it as if by accident; but actually, she did it on purpose. Next, the stepsisters sent Vasilisa into the forest to get some fire from the Baba Yaga.

Vasilisa, shaking with fear, went to her room, shut the door, fed her doll, and then asked for advice. The doll assured Vasilisa that, if she put the doll in her pocket and kept her there at all times, the doll would protect her. So Vasilisa entered the dark forest and walked all night and on into the evening of the following day. From time to time during her long trek, a horseman flew by, first one all in white, then one all in red. Late in the afternoon, Vasilisa arrived at Baba Yaga's hut. Yaga's house was surrounded by a fence capped with human skulls. Suddenly, a third black horseman riding a black horse shot past, and it was night once again. Now the human skulls atop the fence gleamed with the bright fires inside of each. There were so many bright skulls that the dark night was as light and white as day! Then a sudden gust of wind shook the trees, and the leaves rustled and quivered eerily, and the fierce Baba Yaga arrived home, gliding along in her mortar, paddling with its pestle, and sweeping away her tracks with a broom.

"I smell a Russian!" growled Baba Yaga. "What do you want here, before I eat you up?" "Gra, Gra, Grandma," Vasilisa replied, stuttering as she bowed very low. "I ha-have been sent here by my-my sisters to get fire." "I know who they are, of course," growled Baba Yaga. "Well, you'll have to stay with me for awhile. Now you just get in there and cook my dinner. Make everything perfect or I'll eat you for dessert, my pretty!"

So Vasilisa, still trembling, lit a torch from the bright lantern skulls and entered the dark house. As she explored the kitchen, she found the ingredients for dinner, enough for a dozen people, and a copious supply for future meals as well, and a rich store of all kinds of wine and beer and mead in the cellar, waiting to be drunk. After Vasilisa prepared the dinner, Baba Yaga sat down in her big chair and ate everything. She drank up all the bottles, and then, before going to sleep, she gave Vasilisa a long list of household chores to do the following day, and the next, and the day after that, and still more. One job was to sort out the bins of wheat and the storehouses of poppy seeds, clean the dust off each individual grain, and do it all before nightfall. This chore was to be done in addition to other assigned housework. Vasilisa went to bed, gave most of her own dinner to the doll, and then broke into floods of tears. Sobbing, she begged the little doll to tell her what to do. The doll's eyes flashed like bright candles as she replied, "Just keep me in your pocket, and I will take care of everything. Eat your supper, say your prayers, and rest easily. The morning is far wiser than the evening." So, during the following days

221

the doll completed the allotted work in short order, and Baba Yaga could never find anything in the girl's work to criticize.

Out of respect for her mistress, Vasilisa never spoke to Baba Yaga as she followed each order precisely. One evening, as Vasilisa stood silently by while Baba ate her dinner, the witch gruffly asked the girl why she never spoke. "Well, Grandmother, I was afraid to say anything. B-but I do have one question, if you will permit me to ask." "Speak up, child," snarled the witch. Then Vasilisa inquired about the three horsemen that flew past her in the forest—the white, the red, and the black. "Oh, that is easy," replied Yaga. "The white rider is my bright day. The red rider is my red sun. And the black rider is my dark night. These are all my trusted servants who do my will."

Then, warming to the conversation, Baba Yaga cackled to Vasilisa, "Now it's my turn. How do you manage so quickly to do all the work I set out for you?" Vasilisa replied, "I am helped by the blessings of my dear mother that remain with me always." "So that's how you do it, eh?" replied Baba Yaga. "Well, be gone with you! I want no saintly ones in this place!" Immediately, Baba Yaga dragged Vasilisa out the door and gave her one of the lantern skulls from her fence. Then, pushing her roughly through the gate, she cried, "Take it; that's what your sisters wanted!"

Vasilisa, with the skull brightly lighting the way, finally reached home, and she was about to throw the skull away, when the bony lantern itself murmured, "Don't get rid of me. Bring me to your stepmother." Entering the dark house, Vasilisa met her stepmother and stepsisters, who now treated her with respect, saying that since her departure, they were unable to make any light at all in their house, no matter how hard they tried. Even if they brought fire from the outside, it immediately extinguished itself. Then Vasilisa showed them the skull. It stared at them with its intense flaming eyes, and it stared and stared so long and so brightly and so hotly that in no time the stepmother and stepsisters were completely incinerated, burned to a crisp with only a dry pile of ashes remaining.

Vasilisa buried the skull in the ground and went to live with a kind, old, childless woman until her father should return. Feeling restless for handiwork, Vasilisa asked the old woman to buy her some flax, and sitting at the wheel, she spun like the wind, rapidly making the finest and the thinnest linen yarn ever seen. Then she asked for a loom to weave the cloth, but none that were available were excellent enough for the job. Vasilisa asked her doll what to do, and the doll told her to get an old comb, an old shuttle, and the long, shaggy mane of a horse. Vasilisa got these and gave them to her doll. She slept soundly that night, and in the morning, when she entered the parlor, she was surprised to see standing before her a fine new loom of exceptional quality and strength, with a delicately tuned mechanism. When Vasilisa sat down at her new loom, the shuttle flew back and forth, and rich and delicate linen fabric came pouring out, yard after yard, almost as if it were weaving itself. In no time at all, the material was finished, and Vasilisa asked the old woman to go out and sell the fine linen. The old lady, believing this linen to be fit only for a king, took it straight to the czar's palace, where, because of the exceptional quality of the material, she was finally shown in to see the king himself. The czar, inspecting the cloth carefully, was extremely impressed by its quality. He asked about the price, but the woman replied that the material was not for sale, and instead, she offered it freely as a gift.

The czar gave the woman some presents of his own and then ordered his tailors to make a dozen shirts from the linen, but no one on the palace staff was able to sew finely enough to stitch the elegant pieces together. So the czar sent for the woman again, and, giving her the material, asked her to perform the fine stitching. "But I myself neither spun nor wove, nor shall I be able to sew this material," she replied, "for this is all the expert work of the young maiden whom I have protected in my house." "Then I command that she do it," replied the czar. So the woman took the linen back, and Vasilisa admitted that she already knew she would have to sew the linen herself. Immediately, she set to work, and when she had finished making the shirts, the woman delivered them to the czar.

The following day, Vasilisa carefully bathed, anointed herself, and brushed her hair a thousand strokes, dressed in her finest clothes, and then sat in the window looking out, wondering what would happen next. Before long, a messenger from the czar appeared, and announcing himself, declared that the czar himself wished to see the very person who did the amazing stitching.

When Vasilisa arrived at the palace and appeared before the czar, he gazed upon her and could not take his eyes away. Within minutes, he fell helplessly and passionately in love. The young czar proposed, Vasilisa accepted, and they were married immediately in a grand and elegant ceremony. Before long, Vasilisa's father came to live with them, as well as the kindly old woman who had given refuge to Vasilisa. Together they all lived in joy and contentment for the rest of their lives.

———————

Now let's take the story section by section.

A merchant and his wife, after twelve years, finally had a beautiful daughter named Vasilisa. But when the child was eight years old, her mother became seriously ill. Sensing the coming of death, she blessed her little girl and entrusted a magic doll to her, warning Vasilisa that she must take great care to hide the doll and keep it a secret. Whenever Vasilisa needed help or advice, she was to feed the doll and then ask it questions. Before long, the mother passed to the next world.

The merchant father grieved, but in time he took another wife with daughters slightly older than Vasilisa. The new wife envied Vasilisa because she was so much more beautiful than her plain, thin stepsisters, so the new wife gave Vasilisa most of the housework to do. She accepted it all in good humor, and as time passed, even with her long hard hours and exposure to the wind and sun in the fields, Vasilisa grew prettier, more robust, and more buxom each day, and finally reached marriageable age. Soon all the young men of the village were courting her. Meanwhile, the stepmother and her daughters became even paler and thinner, and none of the men showed any interest in them. So the stepmother let it be known to all that Vasilisa could not be given in marriage until after her stepsisters were both married.

From then on, the mean stepmother thought up even more work for her comely stepdaughter, while the stepsisters sat idly with folded hands. At last Vasilisa, exhausted from her labors, decided to ask her doll for advice. Late one night, after saving most of her

225

J. N. H. Perkins

meal and hiding it in her room, she gave it to her doll. When the doll had finished her supper, Vasilisa poured out her misery, telling the doll how, despite living in her father's house, she was miserable because of her terrible stepmother. She asked the doll, "How should I live my life, and what should I do?" The doll comforted her and said not to worry. From then on, although Vasilisa seemed to be doing the work each day, it was really the doll who accomplished nearly everything swiftly and perfectly, allowing Vasilisa to rest and grow ever more beautiful. The doll was particularly adept at all the garden work, while Vasilisa enjoyed picking and smelling the beautiful flowers. The doll even found Vasilisa an herb that would protect her from sunburn.

In the Vasilisa tale, the magical doll is a unique entity we have not seen in the other tales so far discussed. She is not only wise, but performs all the work, and her presence is a safeguard against every harm. We modern folk think of dolls as nothing more than children's toys or as aesthetic ornaments. Since the 18th century Enlightenment, we have been taught to leave such superstitious foolishness behind in the nursery.

In a previous chapter, we spoke of the *homunculus*, or little person who is simultaneously the great person. The tiny, seed-like *Atman* soul of Hindu Indian mysticism, the interior equivalent of the great cosmic *Self*, is a close parallel to the doll in our present tale. When children play with dolls or other doll-like toys, including trucks, trains, bulldozers, and the like, they are engaging in what psychologists call projection: a transference of family and self onto an ambient set of external objects. By this means, children form a relation to their deeper personalities and are able to experiment safely with developing feelings and ideas in relation to the environment. The focal point of a child psychiatrist's consulting room is not a chair, couch, or desk, but a doll house, and often a miniature construction site, where a youngster may express imaginatively all that is churning within its soul.

I remember the time when my office suite-mate, Naomi, a child psychiatrist, allowed me to observe such a session. It was one of the most refreshing experiences of my life! Naomi sat down on the floor in the play area and asked the youngster a few questions now and then about what was happening inside the doll house, and the child told her everything she needed to know about the home atmosphere, the child's view of parental rapport, the chemistry between the child and the parents, and the tenor of sibling bonds within the household.

Dolls, then, become vessels for experiencing something very real. The child's own personality and its perception of the surrounding world are actualized and expressed through play. Consequently, ideas and feelings become very tangible! All of the good and evil occurrences in our world stem directly from such imaginations that flow from the unconscious. In the same manner, all symbols, if they are true *symbols* (windows on the ineffable) and not merely *signs* (contrived denotations of known objects), connect us to a larger and deeper reality that we are incapable of knowing with the rational mind alone. Signs rationally *denote* while symbols irrationally *connote*. It is the *connotational*, iconic, or metaphorical power of the symbolic imagination that opens up the vast horizons of our lives.

Vasilisa's mother gave her a special doll before dying, leaving the girl behind to cope with what rapidly became a very hostile world. In a sense, we could say that the doll is a symbol of Vasilisa's larger self, the greater and stronger personality and competence dwelling within her, of which she is so far quite ignorant. This realization comes to her slowly and indirectly. Here the doll is a psychic mirror, connecting her imagination to the next stage of development. In this manner, Vasilisa is put in touch with her wise and competent abilities. The totality of Vasilisa includes herself and her doll companion. Together they make one whole person in depth.

Earlier we said that the housework in these Cinderella-type stories represents not just domestic chores per se, but keeping one's thoughts straight, putting the household of one's mind in order.

The doll does most of the labor in the tale and possesses all the energy and wisdom, but there is another detail that is important. Vasilisa gives most of her food each day to the doll, yet she grows ever more robust and buxom. In this way, Vasilisa denies herself on one level, in order to feed a higher principle within herself that continually rewards her. Interpreted psychologically, while Vasilisa's ego is humble, her inner self, represented by the doll, is a veritable wonder-worker of cleverness and vitality. We might understand this circumstance as "putting the talents or the gifts of your greater self to work for you."

Vasilisa's father had to embark on a very long journey, and while he was gone, his wife moved to another cottage, located on the edge of a vast and dark forest. In a glade deep in this wood was the hut of the Baba Yaga. Yaga's little house stood on chicken feet, and this witch ate any people who came near her, as if they were chickens instead of humans. No one had ever visited her hut and returned home to tell about it. As a ruse to get rid of beautiful Vasilisa, the stepmother repeatedly sent her on errands in the forest, encouraging her to go deeper and deeper. On these treks, the doll always advised Vasilisa to walk in a different direction from where the Baba Yaga lived. So, every day Vasilisa returned safely to the stepmother's cottage, looking healthy and strong.

Baba Yaga is not alone in the history of the world's religions and myths. She is a local variant of those mother goddesses from time immemorial, who, paradoxically, comprehend extremes of bliss and happiness on the one hand, and darkest fear, dismemberment, and death on the other. The mother goddess is the compost heap of life. The end and the beginning of all things meet in her prolific tomb-womb, which is at once both hell and heaven. The difference depends upon the attitude of the approaching mind. If negative and rejecting, then she is hell. If positive and accepting, then she is heaven. Those whose dispositions are restricted to *me, myself, and I* get caught up in the negative mother goddess.

We spoke before about how the ancient mother-goddess principle expresses the violent aggression, killing, dismemberment, and engorgement inherent in the hierarchical food chain of nature. Life lives upon life in a continuously streaming bloodbath. On the plane of nature, the larger and the stronger feed voraciously upon the smaller and the weaker. This, according to ancient Hindu and pre-patriarchal teaching, is *the* disturbing yet sublime truth about life, the fundamental conundrum of our existence. We contemporary, First World Westerners simply don't wish to think about this repulsive ordeal—this carnage that surrounds us on all sides, and that is the very principle and function of the human digestive system. We know perfectly well what goes on in the slaughterhouse long before the

229

supermarket butcher prepares those neat little pink morsels wrapped in plastic for our refrigerators at home. We
know that bloody traffic accidents attract the leering gaze
of us rubberneckers as we travel up and down the highway.
Intellectually, we know what transpires on the battlefield.
But the mutilated bodies of our young soldiers, dead or
barely alive minus arms or legs that are shipped back from
the war zones of the world, are carefully hidden from view.
If we were allowed to see these disfigured bodies up close,
we would linger transfixed, filled with morbid fascination.
Something in our deep and primal nature has an insatiable
appetite for this repelling dimension of existence.

We moderns are ambivalent about the Baba Yaga side
of life. Our official philosophy strives for peace, healing,
and warm, deferential relationship. But our penchant for
sadomasochistic sex and violence in films, on television,
and over the internet proves that we have an addictive craving for these brutal matters that extends beyond all bounds.
Such scenes give us an emotional thrill far beyond our willingness to admit it. They are as spellbinding as they are
repellant.

*One winter evening, the stepmother ordered the three girls to
engage in some handiwork that was to be finished the same night.
While the stepdaughters made lace and stockings, Vasilisa was required to spin. Only one short candle was permitted to burn in the
room. Before the women were finished, the elder stepsister trimmed
the candle, extinguishing it as if by accident. Next, the stepsisters
sent Vasilisa into the forest to get some fire from the Baba Yaga.*

*Vasilisa, shaking with fear, went to her room, shut the door,
fed her doll, and then asked for advice. The doll assured Vasilisa
that, if she put the doll in her pocket and kept her there at all times,*

the doll would protect her. So Vasilisa entered the dark forest and walked all night and on into the evening of the following day. From time to time during her long trek, a horseman flew by, first one all in white, then one all in red. Late in the afternoon, Vasilisa arrived at Baba Yaga's hut. Yaga's house was surrounded by a fence capped with human skulls. Suddenly, a third black horseman riding a black horse shot past and it was night once again. Now the human skulls atop the fence gleamed with the bright fires inside of each. There were so many bright skulls that the dark night was as light and white as day! Then a sudden gust of wind shook the trees, and the leaves rustled and quivered eerily and the fierce Baba Yaga arrived home, gliding along in her mortar, paddling with its pestle, and sweeping away her tracks with a broom.

"I smell a Russian!" growled Baba Yaga. "What do you want here, before I eat you up?" "Gra, Gra, Grandma," Vasilisa stuttered, as she bowed very low. "I ha-have been sent here by my-my sisters to get fire." "I know who they are, of course," growled Baba Yaga. "Well, you'll have to stay with me for a while. You just get in there and cook my dinner. Make everything perfect or I'll eat you for dessert!" So Vasilisa, still trembling, lit a torch from the bright lantern skulls and entered the dark house. As she explored the kitchen, she found the ingredients for dinner, enough for a dozen people, and an endless supply for future meals as well, and a rich store of all kinds of wine and beer and mead in the cellar, waiting to be drunk. After Vasilisa prepared the dinner, Baba Yaga sat down in her big chair and ate everything. She drank up all the bottles, and then, before going to sleep, she gave Vasilisa a long list of household chores to do the following day, and the next, and the day after that, and still more. One job was to sort out the bins of wheat and the storehouses of poppy seeds, clean the dust off each individual grain, and do it all before nightfall. This chore was to be done in addition to other assigned housework. Vasilisa went to bed, gave most of her own dinner to the doll, and then broke into floods of tears. Sobbing,

she begged the little doll to tell her what to do. The doll's eyes flashed like bright candles as she replied, "Just keep me in your pocket, and I will take care of everything. Eat your supper, say your prayers, and rest easily. The morning is far wiser than the evening." So, during the following days, the doll completed the allotted work in short order, and Baba Yaga could never find anything in the girl's work to criticize.

Out of respect for her mistress, Vasilisa never spoke to Baba Yaga as she followed each order precisely. One evening, as Vasilisa stood silently by while Baba ate her dinner, the witch gruffly asked the girl why she never spoke. "Well, Grandmother, I was afraid to say anything. B-But I do have one question, if you will permit me to ask." "Speak up, child," snarled the witch. Then Vasilisa inquired about the three horsemen that flew past her in the forest—the white, the red, and the black. "Oh, that is easy," replied Yaga. "The white rider is my bright day. The red rider is my red sun. And the black rider is my dark night. These are all my trusted servants who do my will."

Then, warming to the conversation, Baba Yaga cackled to Vasilisa, "Now it's my turn. How do you manage so quickly to do all the work I set out for you?" Vasilisa replied, "I am helped by the blessings of my dear mother that remain with me always." "So that's how you do it, eh?" replied Baba Yaga. "Well, be gone with you! I want no saintly ones in this place!" Immediately, Baba Yaga dragged Vasilisa out the door and gave her one of the lantern skulls from her fence. Then, pushing her roughly through the gate, she cried, "Take it; that's what your sisters wanted!"

For eons, human sacrifice was practiced openly in most parts of the Near East, Africa, and in the southeastern Asian and Pacific island cultures. In India, gory immolations continued right up until 1835 when they were prohibited by the newly arrived British colonial power. After that, however, such essential practices were piously maintained for years *sub rosa* whenever and wherever possible. As a rule, children were sacrificed on a weekly basis to the great Mother, *Durga*, "she who is difficult of approach," the consort of the dancing Shiva, otherwise known as Chandika or Kali, for whom the city of Calcutta is named. Typically, firstborn sons were offered by families as precious gifts to the gods.

We have a remnant of this ancient practice in the Biblical account of Abraham's sacrifice of Isaac.[31] In the Genesis story, God asked Abraham to make a burnt offering of his son Isaac, his only child, by first slaying the boy with a sacrificial knife and then immolating the corpse in a fire built for that purpose. At the last second, once Abraham had clearly proved his willingness to commit this dreadful act in obedience to God's command, an angelic messenger instructed Abraham to substitute a ram for Isaac, and so the boy was saved from death. This is typical of the patriarchal stage, where actual human sacrifice now becomes symbolized through the use of an animal substitute—in this case, the zodiacal sign of Ares, signified by the Ram emblem.

Baba Yaga's mythic cousin, Kali, is the great goddess of India. An elemental and highly ambivalent Mother Nature figure, Kali is the female partner to Shiva, "the destroyer," who dances in the circle of flames while the universe dissolves. Shiva is the bright promise available to those who appreciate the sublime meaning of sacrifice as the way to blissful renewal. Kali's images generally depict her with four arms, naked, with black skin, and with fierce, wildly intense eyes, a long protruding tongue, lips smeared with blood, and necklaces of human skulls adorning her breast. She is usually seen standing on a corpse, laughing in triumph, revealing her dreadful teeth.[32] Sometimes she holds a human skull in one hand and a sacrificial saber in the other. Kali's stomach is an abyss that can never be filled. Her lust for blood can never be satiated, even by the rivers of scarlet that flow continuously from the beheaded offerings presented at her temple altars.

In earlier days, the festivals to Kali were generally cruel and orgiastic.[33] Her time of day was midnight, symbolizing the moment when the power of destruction rules absolutely.[34] Such destruction is not, however, catastrophic annihilation as we Westerners understand it, but the psychological dismemberment that is necessary for the reconstitution and renewal of our mentality. The closest Western analogy to this experience would be the mystical "Dark Night of the Soul" of St. John of the Cross. Here, our outlook shifts to a heightened level of comprehension, where we may glimpse that greater, transcendental reality that lies beyond the literal realm of mere worldly appearance. Kali stands for naked eternity, a primary reality veiled behind and beyond secondary time/existence. Kali *as* time dissociates all things, but because Kali herself is *beyond* time, those who are devoted to her and realize her significance awaken to the principle that is behind temporal time: ultimate bliss, wisdom, and peace.

Like Baba Yaga, Kali is the supreme night (in Hebrew *lailah*, Delilah) that swallows all that exists. Her four arms are the pillars of the world and the four directions of space. The severed corpse head she proudly displays in one hand proclaims, "This is what you must expect!"[35]

In the temple of Shiva at Tanjore, a male child was sacrificed every Friday evening, purchased for that very purpose. At the famous shrine Dantesvari in Bastar, in 1830, twenty-five men were immolated on the altar by the local king. In the sixteenth century, Nar Narayan, the Koch king, sacrificed one hundred and fifty men in a single ceremony. The decapitated heads were then piled up before the image of the goddess. Most often, the candidacy for such a high privilege was entirely voluntary, and in no sense was the rite considered an unjust form of cruelty or a denial of human rights.[36]

Today in the modern West, of course, such practices are considered horrific—insane and wanton squanderings of healthy humanity for no good purpose whatsoever. Consequently, it is particularly difficult for people of our own squeamish sensitivity to appreciate the deep meaning and the weighty significance of such ancient, sanguine rites, and the supreme importance of the dark goddess of death and destruction, as a comprehensive philosophy of life, not just in the public life of a culture, but also within the soul-psyche of humanity.

The archaic Greek version of Baba Yaga-Kali-Shiva is Dionysus, the god of intoxicating wine, who dances through the world to the sharp rhythms of the wailing flutes. Here boundaries are erased, scruples annihilated, and instinct is given free reign, as the god himself takes entire possession of one's faculties. In this orgy of rampant zeal, all separations are erased, and all become one in the utterly joyful enthusiasm of the celebration. The women participants, or *maenads* (wild or mad women), who were the chief ministrants, roamed the mountains at night, slaughtering wild animals with their bare hands and tearing them to pieces. As the blood flowed, the joy and the intoxication increased beyond all bounds. In the background of all this is the great

Kali, the violent Earth Mother, *Magna Mater*, Baba Yaga, surrounded by her burning, dismembered heads that light the way in the dark night of our delusions.

But Vasilisa herself is somehow more than all this. She is a classic hero who disappears into the dark forest. Vasilisa enters the unknown mystery of our lives, the primordial unconscious mind, the terrible and frightening side of our instinctive humanity, where the awesome mother goddess still functions within our subliminal psychology. Here, she succeeds in her own version of the dark night of the soul and safely returns to our realm of conscious time and space with a boon or a greater truth, represented by the fiery skull— the vital spiritual energy of the living soul that shines radiantly through the death experience. That prize, which will transform into benevolent feminine strength, courage, and wisdom, allows the progression of this story, as well as the story of our lives, to flow toward its bright conclusion. Following the incineration of her wicked stepmother and stepsisters, when Vasilisa later buries the gleaming skull, we know that she has finally integrated with her conscious disposition the fierce volatile strength of primeval womanhood.

In acquiring the light from Baba Yaga, Vasilisa is a type of the Greek Titan, Prometheus, who stole fire from the gods in order to enlighten mankind, who until then had lived in darkness. Accordingly, Vasilisa seems to move the Kali consciousness a step further forward, beyond the gruesome and bloody rites toward a more reflective, humane awareness. Much like the Hebrew prophets and the bloodless sacrifice of the Catholic Mass, Vasilisa transforms the orgy of sensual death and destruction into a reflective moral insight within the mind and heart of humanity.

Lady Life allows herself to be fathomed and understood up to a point, but no further. She always remains veiled in relative shadow, to be experienced safely and accurately only by reflected, indirect light, through a mentality capable of nuanced connotation. And that is precisely the significance of the herb that Vasilisa's doll finds in the garden near the beginning of the tale, a medicinal plant that will shield Vasilisa from sunburn. There is something in nature that resents exhaustive decoding and voyeuristic exposition. One has only to think of the mythic scene where Actaeon accidentally discovers Diana bathing naked in a mountain pool with her nymphs. It is the last thing he sees as a human being, for when she discovers his leering gaze, Diana playfully flicks water at him, transforming Actaeon into a dumb stag, later to be hunted down and ripped to pieces by his own dogs. That seems to be the fate of the masculine rationalistic mind when it begins to wander too far into the jealously guarded secrets of feminine nature.

As my friend, Joyce Oates, once reminded me, we can try to analyze the experience of living life, but our scrutiny is often illusive, and we experience instead an atmosphere, a sensation, not unlike the feeling evoked by music: you can know it, appreciate it in a way, but you certainly can't decode or explain it. That's the limitation of consciousness. Some people think the word "awareness" is a better and more elastic term than "consciousness." But on closer inspection, the word "consciousness" comprises the very genius of paradox: *con* = to be with, to accompany, to be in relation; and *scious* = to know. To remain immersed in, and in touch with, the mystery of life, and at the same time to know it with some objectivity, is the miracle of all miracles. This is the art and the poetry of living. I like to imagine it as a person standing in the deep shadow of a tree, protected from the glare of the sun, yet able to gaze out onto the illuminated landscape. One must hide a little on the softer fringes of intellect, in the penumbra where the lighting is indirect, to get the right view of things. Otherwise our bright consciousness is a bull in a china shop, and very little survives after the sun god has finished crashing around all day.

Increasing consciousness always destroys a sense of the mystery, wonder, and security of life, and produces anxiety, like an innocent and happy child who suddenly discovers the cruelty and complexity of the larger "real" adult world. The stages of life are threefold and can be interpreted as a journey from the naiveté of childhood to enlightened understanding: 1. Living innocently within the mystery with no consciousness, remaining in childlike, blissful ignorance, yet completely merged with dynamic life; 2. Achieving rational consciousness but losing the mystery and the enchantment of living and falling victim to anxiety and unattainable desire; 3. Marrying the mystery and the awareness to form a unified wholeness of being and knowledge. In the third stage, the dark inscrutability and the sharp consciousness interpenetrate each other creatively. Sometimes this three-stage scenario is described as unconscious wholeness, consciousness lacking wholeness, and consciousness with simultaneous wholeness—or the three stages of enchantment, disenchantment, and re-enchantment. Life, like a dream, is so mysterious.

Men, who tend to feel confident in their bright *yang* sunshine, are at the same time often blind to the darker shadow regions of life. They can experience these regions, but more unconsciously as vague and uncontrolled emotion. By contrast, women seem to have a higher degree of emotional intelligence than men, and their feeling values are in some respects more trustworthy tools for navigating these subtler regions of life.

Here is one more observation before we proceed further: the three horsemen who fly by Vasilisa in the forest, standing for white day, red sun, and black night, comprise the same colors as Snow White. These colors, which are often encountered in folk literature, seem to represent the three basic periodic rhythms of our mentality: the early light of the first diffuse awareness; the brilliant, highly focused rationality of sunrise to late afternoon; and the pitch-black oblivion of unconscious night—birth, life and death as the three psychological stages of our existence, occurring repeatedly during each successive phase of our lives. For an integrated humanity, one must be able to encounter and accommodate each stage of transition along the path toward wholeness.

Vasilisa, with the skull brightly lighting the way, finally reached home, and was about to throw the skull away, when the bony lantern itself murmured, "Don't get rid of me. Bring me to your stepmother." Entering the dark house, Vasilisa met her stepmother and sisters, who now treated her with respect, saying that since her departure, they were unable to make any light at all in their house, no matter how hard they tried. Even if they brought fire from the outside, it immediately extinguished itself. Then Vasilisa showed them the skull. It stared at them with its intense flaming eyes, and it stared and stared so long and so brightly and so hotly that in no time the stepmother and stepsisters were completely incinerated, burned to a crisp with only a dry pile of ashes remaining.

While Vasilisa is away getting light from the Baba Yaga, the stepmother and stepsisters are unable to illuminate their house, no matter how hard they try. Fire simply won't burn there without Vasilisa. Her Promethean act is a successful gaining of the fire of human consciousness from the gods, which will illuminate the mind of humanity. As we learn, its brilliance is so powerful and burning that it completely destroys the spiteful stepmother and her daughters. Their ruse of sending Vasilisa to get fire from Baba Yaga backfired, resulting in their own destruction.

What precisely does the skull destroy? The flaming head demolishes unbridled ambition, possessiveness, and envy, the "small-mindedness" of the shallow, egoistic personality, the chief characteristic of *me, myself, and I*. The tale says the stepmother and her daughters grow increasingly pale and thin, reflecting their bloodless, unhealthy, insubstantial natures.

Fire is not only a fundamental source of light and warmth. Fire is also passion, erotic desire, inspiration, and motivation. Fire is the purgatorial cleansing flame that burns away all the perversions of true health, tempering and strengthening our mettle and determination for living. What remains is good, strong, whole, and healthy. In this way, fire as spirit is the great transformer and purifier. Fire is also intelligence, illumination of the mind, and spiritual enlightenment. These tendencies are all opposite to those of the stepmother and stepsisters, who are blind, stupid, and ignorant by comparison.

The fire is in the skull that Baba Yaga gives to Vasilisa. The skeleton heads that line the fence around the witch's house are apparently the bony remains of those whom Baba Yaga has previously eaten. The burning flames within are the living souls, the life forces that survive after the demise of the body, but which hover about the corpses in their graves. The jack-o-lantern is the emblem of these spirit presences on All Hallows' Eve, the night preceding All Saints Day. Baba Yaga is not simply an evil person, or even an evil side of the human personality. Quite to the contrary, she is a figure or symbol of the fact of death that, sooner or later, comes to every living creature without exception. But on another plane, Baba Yaga, as the mother of death, is also the darker side of psychological transformation from one stage of life to the next. To acknowledge her is to admit that nothing may last except through change and renewal—that many of our jealously held attitudes and values must die repeatedly in order for our lives to be full and complete.

We learn an important lesson from this episode of the tale: the best awareness is gained from looking *into* the darkness, by immersing ourselves in the mystery of life while keeping our eyes wide open in vigilance, rather than attempting to rise above the darkness to form a superior, ethereal consciousness. The mystery of life is not simply a superstition. Rather, it is the mother of all true realization. The illumination we seek is a light that shines *in* the darkness, not *above* it. A rational consciousness that believes that it has conquered superstition through a higher progressive awakening is a Luciferian light, an evil, repressive, and fragmenting consciousness, the bogus opposite of a divine revelation.

Some years ago, our friends, Jill Knapp and her husband Jim Gunn, both astrophysicists at Princeton, invited me to visit the lab where they were building a complex digital camera for the new Sloan Survey telescope in New Mexico. I gazed endlessly at magnificent color photographs of deep outer space, depicting dazzling star formations millions and millions of light years away, showing our universe much nearer the time of its origin. When we relaxed over coffee afterward, I exclaimed, "Jill, it's all so mysterious … so terribly mysterious!" to which she replied with characteristic irony, "Yes, it certainly is … and we don't even know if we are asking the right questions."

Vasilisa buried the skull in the ground and went to live with a kind, old, childless woman until her father should return. Feeling restless for handiwork, Vasilisa asked the old woman to buy her some flax, and sitting at the wheel, she spun like the wind, rapidly making the finest and the thinnest linen yarn ever seen. Then she asked for a loom to weave the cloth, but none that were available were excellent enough for the job. Vasilisa asked her doll what to do, and the doll told her to get an old comb, an old shuttle, and the long shaggy mane of a horse. Vasilisa got these and gave them to her doll. She slept soundly that night, and in the morning, when she entered the parlor, she was surprised to see standing before her a fine new loom of exceptional quality and strength, with a delicately tuned mechanism. When Vasilisa sat down at her new loom, the shuttle flew back and forth, and rich and delicate linen fabric came pouring out, yard after yard, almost as if it were weaving itself. In no time at all the material was finished, and Vasilisa asked the old woman to go out and sell the fine linen. The old lady, believing this linen to be fit only for a king, took it straight to the czar's palace where, because of the exceptional quality of the material, she was finally shown in to see the king. The czar, inspecting the cloth carefully, was extremely impressed by its quality. He asked about the price, but the woman replied that the material was not for sale, and instead, she offered it freely as a gift.

The czar gave the woman some presents of his own and then ordered his tailors to make a dozen shirts from the linen, but no one in the palace staff was able to sew finely enough to stitch the elegant pieces together. So the czar sent for the woman again and, giving her the material, asked her to perform the fine stitching. "But I myself neither spun nor wove, nor shall I be able to sew this material," she replied, "for this is all the expert work of the young maiden whom I have protected in my house." "Then I command that she do it," replied the czar. So the woman took the linen back, and Vasilisa admitted that she already knew she would have to sew the linen herself. Immediately, she set to work, and when she had finished making the shirts, the woman delivered them to the czar.

The following day, Vasilisa carefully bathed, anointed herself, and brushed her hair a thousand strokes, dressed in her finest clothes, and then sat in the window looking out, wondering what would happen next. Before long, a messenger from the czar appeared, and announcing himself, declared that the czar himself wished to see the very person who did the amazing stitching.

When Vasilisa arrived at the palace and appeared before the czar, he gazed upon her and could not take his eyes away. Within minutes, he fell helplessly and passionately in love. The young czar proposed, Vasilisa accepted, and they were married immediately in a grand and elegant ceremony. Before long, Vasilisa's father came to live with them, as well as the kindly old woman who had given refuge to Vasilisa. Together they all lived in joy and contentment for the rest of their lives.

The Vasilisa tale culminates with a section on spinning, weaving, and sewing. The original flax ends up becoming fine linen shirts for the czar himself. Then the happy royal marriage is the immediate result. As we discuss this marriage, keep in mind that Vasilisa and the czar represent the feminine and masculine polarities that we have just been discussing in terms of consciousness and the mystery of life—polarities that come to join each other creatively and reciprocally in blissful matrimony. These opposites are not specifically about men and women per se.

Common flax (L. *Linum usitatissimum*) was one of the first crops domesticated by man. Its use is far older than cotton. Flax is thought to have originated in the Mediterranean region of Europe. The Swiss Lake Dweller People of the Neolithic (New Stone) Age apparently produced flax utilizing the fiber as well as the seed. In Africa, linen cloth made from flax was used to wrap the mummies in the early Egyptian tombs. The thread that Ariadne gave to Theseus to guide him out of the Cretan labyrinth was of linen yarn.

All of the stages of spinning, weaving, and sewing represent transforming evolutions of raw nature, like cooking and metallurgy. The distaff stick for holding the flax, and the spindle used for twisting the threads, are age-old symbols for feminine creativity, and they are iconic emblems of the *Magna Mater* from whose fruitful loom-womb all life emerges. Spinning is a metaphysical myth of the origins of temporal life, of the mysterious mechanisms of the womb of the goddess, not merely an allusion to ordinary domestic activity. Thoughts, ideas, and new attitudes are cleverly spun by the creative mind, as well as actual organic material like flax, wool, or cotton. The skeins of material produced from the spinning wheel are considered the children of the Great Lady—the fruit of her womb.

Spinning, weaving, and sewing synthesize the material of life, binding together the various strands of our existence. They are associated with the feminine symbolism of the moon, earth, and vegetation—the polar opposite of analysis, abstraction, and categorization. These major constituents of rational activity are symbolized by the bright sunshine that, with its sharply focused light, reveals the fine distinctions of our experience, often analyzing them to death. When the "shadier" potentialities of the feminine disposition work together with the more obvious rationality of the masculine—and when this occurs with mutual respect—living becomes a supple art and a revealing science at the same time. Then rational understanding augments and enriches our embedded nature, rather than extinguishing the haunting and mysterious rapture of life in the glare of the noonday sun.

The big task is to understand and appreciate our emotional experience of life without annihilating it in the process. When psychoanalysis was the rage in the 1930s among certain creative artists, they often hesitated, saying, "Yes, therapy may very well cure my demons. But unfortunately, it might cure my angels too!" The mythological discussion of this need for balance is often expressed in the folkloristic theme of the animal or bird woman who one day comes into a relation with a human man. He falls in love with her and sometimes, by stealing and hiding her animal skins or feathers, he keeps her in her human manifestation—at least for a while. Or in other instances, she agrees to marriage, but there is a condition that he must not ask too many questions about her life or attempt to see where she goes on certain occasions, for if he does, she will disappear forever into the vast realm of nature. In this way, the connection between the man and the lovely and mysterious woman maintains a certain tenuous character. The male is required to demur and respect the female's privacy and her autonomy within certain established limits. If he tries to dominate and possess her, he will surely lose her. The same is true regarding our relationship to the ineffable mystery of life. We just

245

can't package it and keep it safely in our cerebral pocket, or bottle this water of life and sell it as a commodity.

Years ago, we hired an Irish *au pair* to look after our two boys when they were young. One Christmas, Breege flew back to Ireland to spend the holiday with her family in Mayo. Before she left, I asked her if she would bring me a rock from her father's farm. After the holidays, Breege returned, opened her suitcase, and handed me a package. Undoing the wrapper, I found a crystalline rock that fit very nicely in the palm of my hand.

"Now, Breege, just where on your farm did you find this rock?"

"From the fairy ground in the field behind the house," she replied.

In answer to my questions, she described this "fairy ground" as a wee bit of wild nature in the middle of a farmer's field, a little copse where bushes and trees and undisturbed nature were allowed to thrive freely. Breege told me that her father had thought of clearing it out and ploughing it like the rest of the pasture, but that his friends down at the pub one evening had warned him that doing so would certainly bring bad luck, so the little thicket of trees and bushes remained, and does to this day.

I still have this rock and proudly display it on my desk. It is a constant reminder that a little wildness and untamed imagination must be reserved and protected from the intrusion of our modern rational mentality, for that is where the excitement and the mystery of our lives are kept safe from the prying eyes of our high-powered, spotlight consciousness. And I know, too, that I have, within my own soul, such a fairy ground, and I have determined that nothing shall ever violate it!

Vasilisa appears in a number of Russian fairy tales where she assumes various roles. Sometimes, as in the present tale, she is an innocent young girl passing through adolescence. In "The Sea King and Vasilisa the Wise," she is a spoonbill ibis who is caught bathing in her human form while her bird costume is lying on the shore. Because a prince who has found her clothing consents to return her feathers to her, she blesses him with her wise and powerful assistance, subsequently performing impossible tasks in order to rescue the prince from the threat of death by the evil Sea King. In "The Sea King," Vasilisa herself performs the miraculous deeds assumed by the doll in our present tale. In "The Sea King," she is a sort of goddess figure of superhuman talents—actions far greater than the little doll's prodigious domestic abilities. This Vasilisa, or one much like her, plainly lives in that little fairy ground that rests in the shadow of Mt. Nephan, near Crossmolina, Mayo, Ireland.

In "Vasilisa, the Priest's Daughter," she is an inveterate tomboy dressed in men's clothing (like Juliedah toward the end of the "Leather Suit" tale), calling herself Vasili, who succeeds in outwitting a certain king Barkhat who tries relentlessly to discover whether or not Vasili is really a woman concealed in male raiment. His last ploy is to ask Vasili to bathe nude with him. Vasilisa bathes first alone, dresses again, and is gone before the king enters the bathhouse. So he fails to determine if Vasili is a woman, but we suspect that if he had, he would have tried to seduce and possess her! She tricks and frustrates his every attempt, and in the end, the narrator says, "And so King Barkhat got nothing for all his trouble; Vasilisa Vasilyevna was a clever girl, and very pretty too!"

As one reads "Vasilisa, the Priest's Daughter," one senses that there is an upbeat and very self-possessed woman under the male disguise. This is certainly not a female who wishes she had been born a man! It is her clever assumption of the male role that makes the tale interesting. I think this demonstrates that women may very well gain something from playing male roles and playing them expertly, but that underneath it all they are definitely women who are aware of what they are doing. They are not in the least confused about their gender identity or their female sexuality. One could say that these tales augur the stage of feminine liberation in which women must come to assume a male posture as preparation for the final stage, when a strong, new, and transformed feminine presence may safely reveal itself.

Of course, in "The Priest's Daughter," the reason Vasilisa remains disguised inside man's clothing is that she is shielding herself from undue exposure to the powerful gaze of the sun king. It is the leering and intrusive erotic stare of masculine consciousness that she resists, not so much actual men, but masculine consciousness itself in both sexes. The men's clothing serves the same purpose as the sun-resistant herb in "Vasilisa the Beautiful" and in some degree the leather burka in the Juliedah story. We must learn to appreciate these veilings, not as repressive political incarcerations, but as vital mythic protections. There is a need for a psychological sanctuary where the feminine side within us all may enjoy self-determination. The feminine requires its own sphere of influence, without being relentlessly exploited by masculine motives and interests, particularly by a wrongly used rational intellect and a misdirected sexual aggressiveness that inflicts itself upon life. We all require a curtain of *purdah* inside ourselves behind which we may practice the noble art of living and loving.

Moonlight has been a celestial symbol of feminine awareness, because *Luna* sheds a gentler, reflected light on earth during nighttime, when the masculine sun has gone to his grave in the west. To our distant ancestors, the dew, which we now know is caused by condensation as the atmosphere cools after sunset, was thought to come directly from the moon. In very hot, dry, cloudless climates, where the temperature falls dramatically in the evening, the dew is quite heavy, and so its dampness assuages the dryness of the scorching day, symbolized by the fiery countenance of the *toro/taurus*, the hot-tempered bull, the Mithraic emblem of the summer sun. One has only to recall the Egyptian cosmology of Nut birthing and devouring the sun to realize the necessary sacrifice of solar consciousness in order to renew and refresh and safeguard our appreciation of feminine organic existence in the rich nature of our lives.

7

The Faithful Wife and the Woman Warrior

The following tale is from the Native American tradition. It is a Pueblo story with Apache characters and was reported first hand in 1940 by the highly respected anthropologist and feminist, Elsie Clews Parsons (1875-1941). Dr. Parsons, who taught at Barnard and Columbia Colleges, was the first woman president of the American Anthropological Society and a founder of the New School for Social Research in New York. Her book, *Pueblo Indian Religion* (1939), is now a classic. I have slightly condensed and paraphrased parts of it. It is called "The Faithful Wife and the Woman Warrior."[37]

First, let's read the whole tale through, and then take it section by section as we did in the previous chapters.

There were two warrior friends, Blue Hawk, who was married to the Apache chief's daughter, and his friend Red Hawk, who was unmarried. One time they went off to fight against another hostile tribe to get some scalps. When they camped at night, Red Hawk said to Blue Hawk, "What do you suppose your wife is doing tonight while you are away? Like most women, don't you think she's sleeping with another man? "That's what you think," replied Blue Hawk, "but I would never get such an idea in my head. My wife is faithful to me."

"I'll bet I could go back tonight and sleep with your wife," said Red Hawk. "She would never accept you," replied Blue Hawk. "I'll bet you anything she would!" teased Red Hawk.

So they each bet everything they had—pack horses, food, weapons, all their possessions at home—everything! Red Hawk went back to the village and hung around Blue Hawk's wife's teepee. He looked at her, he smiled at her, he tried to be friendly and get her attention in every way he could, but Blue Hawk's wife totally ignored him. "Maybe she really is as true as Blue Hawk said," thought Red Hawk.

By now, Red Hawk knew he would probably lose the bet, so he decided to play a trick—a serious and mean trick—on his friend Blue Hawk. He went to a certain old woman of the village and told her everything—all about the bet and how shamed he felt because Blue Hawk's wife paid no attention to him at all. "Is there any way I can see her naked?" Red Hawk asked the old woman, "or at least find out in some other way what she looks like without her clothes on? I will pay you for this favor." "Yes, grandson, I will find out for you," said the woman.

Then, leaning on her cane in the hot sun, she shuffled slowly past the wife's teepee. Blue Hawk's wife saw her, felt compassion, and invited the old woman into the tent to rest awhile. The woman stayed for a long time and seemed to fall asleep, but during the night, she was really awake as she secretly peeped through a hole in the blanket to see what Blue Hawk's wife looked like when she undressed for bed.

Blue Hawk's wife had a very long golden braid of hair growing from the center of her abdomen, which she unwrapped, combed out, and re-braided, winding it around her body five times. The old woman also noticed that Blue Hawk's wife had a black mark on her backbone.

The following morning, when the old woman excused herself and returned home to feed her turkeys, Red Hawk was waiting and asked her what she had seen, and the woman reported everything. Red Hawk rode back to where Blue Hawk was preparing for battle and told him of how his wife looked without any clothes, and all about the long braid and the black mark. "There, now do you still believe that your wife is faithful to you?" Blue Hawk was silent. His head drooped. "A promise is a promise," teased Red Hawk.

So Blue Hawk gave Red Hawk everything he had with him, and when they got back to the village, all the rest of his belongings. Blue Hawk's wife was alarmed by her husband's strange behavior and asked him why he was giving everything away, like people do when they are making funeral offerings. But Blue Hawk made no reply and went to work in silence, constructing a large rawhide trunk, in which he put money, food, and cooking gear. Finally, Blue Hawk spoke to his wife, saying, "We are going on a long trek to the great water. I have made this trunk for you to ride in so you will be protected from the sun." Blue Hawk asked his wife to put on her finest clothes and then he put her in the trunk.

Blue Hawk put the trunk on a cart, hitched the cart to his horses, and set forth. When they got to the first big river, Blue Hawk took the trunk and threw it into the deep water. Then he went back to his village, but said nothing, even when people asked him where his wife was. But the chief, father of Blue Hawk's wife, was suspicious. So he dug a deep hole down into the underworld and arranged for his son-in-law to fall down into that hole.

Meanwhile, a fisherman on the river hooked something heavy with his line and thought he had caught a huge fish. Drawing in his line, he was amazed to see the trunk, and pulled it out. When he opened it, he saw a very pretty girl, all dressed up, lying inside. He invited her to his camp, but before she agreed, she insisted that he switch clothes with her. When they got back to the fisherman's camp, his people were preparing for war. Blue Hawk's wife, now dressed as a warrior, joined the fighting men. On their journey, the other warriors noticed that their new young comrade had eyes like a woman and moved his body like a woman. One of them said, "Tonight I will be friendly and try to discover if he is really a man or a woman."

Blue Hawk's wife had told the men that she was a medicine man, a shaman, and she requested that she stay in a teepee set apart from the rest of the band. She said her medicine was the sun, which explained why she carried a white eagle feather. The young man who wanted to make friends came over and asked to sleep in her tent. In the night, the boy stayed awake and tried to get close to Blue Hawk's wife, but she remained awake the whole time, and when he reached out to touch her she said, "Don't do that!" Later he tried again, and she said abruptly, "Why don't you go to sleep!"

Death and the Maiden

For the next few nights each warrior, one after another, asked to sleep in her tent and tried to get close to her,
but with the same result as the first, so that none of them
succeeded in learning her secret. Finally, the warriors arrived in the enemy's land. Again Blue Hawk's wife had her
tent pitched separately from the others. She told them to
stay inside their tents and be quiet, as it was time for her
to perform some powerful rituals. When all was still, Blue
Hawk's wife spat great sun medicine in the direction of
the enemy's camp. The result was that she single-handedly
killed the whole enemy war party in one stroke. Then she
came out of her tent and gave a war whoop, and all the rest
of the men came out of their tents gave their war whoops.
Still disguised as the medicine man, she announced to the
whole gathering, "I just fought a big battle and killed all of
the enemy braves myself. Now I will find the dead and cut
off their ears and scalps and take their shields, their bows
and arrows, and their war clubs."

When Blue Hawk's wife, the medicine man, returned
with the scalps and ears and weapons, the grateful chief
of the fisherman's tribe offered to have a young brave accompany her home to her own people. But she refused and
insisted on going alone.

After she arrived at her own village where her father
was chief, she took off her men's clothes, and there she
stood, a very pretty young woman, the faithful wife of Blue
Hawk, whom he had thrown into the river. "I alone, and
single-handedly, killed all of your enemy," she announced
to the entire village. "Here are their scalps, ears, and weapons. They are yours!" Looking at her father, she said, "You
shut up my husband in a dark pit because of the trick that

Red Hawk played on him. He is innocent of any wrongdoing. Now bring him to me!"

Blue Hawk was brought up from the pit and stood before his faithful wife. His eyes were cast down, he was bent over, and he wore a painful expression on his thin and pale face. "You were beaten in the contest with Red Hawk because he made you think that he knew my body, but he deceived you. You know that I love you completely and honestly and truly! Now go and get Red Hawk and that conniving old woman!"

Soon Blue Hawk and some of the braves returned with the two culprits, and brought them before the chief in the center of the gathering. Now the girl said to her father, "Have the men get the wildest ponies we have and bring them here." Then she ordered them to tie Red Hawk's ankles to the tail of one pony and those of the old woman to the tail of the other one. After this was done, the ponies were set lose and whipped. Off they dashed across the countryside, kicking and leaping and jumping wildly here and there, up and down the hills, and careering over stones and rocks, so that Red Hawk and the old woman were torn to pieces far away from the camp, and nothing was left of them.

Now let's look at this tale section by section.

There were two warrior friends, Blue Hawk, who was married to the Apache chief's daughter, and his friend Red Hawk, who was unmarried. One time they went off to fight against another hostile tribe to get some scalps. When they camped at night, Red

Hawk said to Blue Hawk, "What do you suppose your wife is doing tonight while you are away? Like most women, don't you think she's sleeping with another man? "That's what you think," replied Blue Hawk, "but I would never get such an idea in my head. My wife is faithful to me."

"I'll bet I could go back tonight and sleep with your wife," said Red Hawk. "She would never accept you," replied Blue Hawk. "I'll bet you anything she would!" teased Red Hawk.

So they each bet everything they had—pack horses, food, weapons, all their possessions at home—everything!

Traditional native stories from the Americas and Africa are filled with a character known as a "trickster." Coyote in Native American stories and Br'er Rabbit in the Afro-American stories are typical examples, as is Anansi, the freeloading spider, in popular African and Caribbean folklore. Usually, these indolent rascals fail in the end, so such stories are moral lessons in honesty and integrity. Yet they also convey a lesson on how cleverness and a certain amount of scheming and one-upmanship can be important in meeting the challenges of life. Trying to keep these trickster tendencies under control and pointed in a constructive direction seems to be the purpose of many of these traditional con-artist stories.

Folk tales, like individual dreams, depict a cross-section of the human personality. Here, Blue Hawk and Red Hawk stand for the two typical attitudes that reside in the average human person. One side is trusting, the other skeptical. Blue Hawk is content and secure; Red Hawk is a lazy bamboozler who will take outrageous risks to satisfy his extravagant desires. He uses his clever wits to keep from exerting himself. Such freeloader sociopaths have an enormous sense of narcissistic entitlement. They feel they deserve what they desire, and have no moral compunctions about how they get what they want.

Blue Hawk knows for certain that his wife is faithful, but the Red Hawk inside him says, "Just you wait! She's not what you think." One could see it either way: as Blue Hawk contending with his "rascal red" aspect, or Red Hawk competing with his "true blue" tendencies.

Red Hawk went back to the village and hung around Blue Hawk's wife's teepee. He looked at her, he smiled at her, he tried to be friendly and get her attention in every way he could, but Blue Hawk's wife totally ignored him. "Maybe she really is as true as Blue Hawk said," thought Red Hawk.

By now, Red Hawk knew he would probably lose the bet, so he decided to play a trick—a serious and mean trick—on his friend Blue Hawk. He went to a certain old woman of the village and told her everything—all about the bet and how shamed he felt because Blue Hawk's wife paid no attention to him at all. "Is there any way I can see her naked?" Red Hawk asked the old woman, "or at least find out in some other way what she looks like without her clothes on? I will pay you for this favor." "Yes, grandson, I will find out for you," said the woman.

Then, leaning on her cane in the hot sun, she shuffled slowly past the wife's teepee. Blue Hawk's wife saw her, felt compassion, and invited the old woman into the tent to rest awhile. The woman stayed for a long time and seemed to fall asleep, but during the night, she was really awake as she secretly peeped through a hole in the blanket to see what Blue Hawk's wife looked like when she undressed for bed.

Blue Hawk's wife had a very long golden braid of hair grow-ing from the center of her abdomen, which she unwrapped, combed out, and re-braided, winding it around her body five times. The old woman also noticed that Blue Hawk's wife had a black mark on her backbone.

The old woman in our tale is a ubiquitous type in folk literature. She is a Pandora figure, a curious, snoopy fe-male, who customarily precipitates a monumental crisis. In-variably, however, this crisis is merely the initial episode in a long series of painful adventures that end, finally, with bliss-ful fulfillment and a much larger scope of living. Viewed from the end perspective and looking back, the original crisis can be seen as a *felix culpa*, a happy fault, that in the long run produces a joyful denouement. The old grand-mother is like the disobedient First Eve who ironically pre-figured the much later Second Eve, mother of the Savior.

The masculine side of life says, "I know what I'm talk-ing about. Believe me. Trust me." But the feminine side, like a cat, says, "Well, maybe … but, uh … I think I'll go see for myself first." Children have plenty of primitive tricksters inside them. Before they are old enough to know better, they can lie, cheat, tell stories, and take foolish risks. This perfectly normal behavior should be gently corrected but not squelched, because these very tendencies, when trans-formed later in adulthood, are the resources for courage, originality, and invention.

The old woman learns that Blue Hawk's wife has a very strange bodily feature. A thick braid of blond hair grows from the very middle of her abdomen. When she undresses at night, she combs it out carefully, re-braids it, and wraps it around her body exactly five times.

J. N. H. Perkins

The combing and braiding of hair is familiar to us from the previous stories we have encountered. Combing hair, sorting seeds, keeping a house in order, spinning and weaving, are symbols for organizing the mind, getting one's thoughts straight, focusing one's attention, and synthesizing ideas. Recall that the German word for "fair" is *fegen*, to sweep, clean, or straighten up. While Snow White, "the fairest of all," was keeping the household in order, the dwarves were mining gold from the mountain. This gold came from within Mother Earth, just as the golden braid emerges from the innards of Blue Hawk's wife. That makes this Native American woman a version of the Mountain Mother, as in *Sierra Madre*. In "Snow White," the little dwarf *cabiri* were the midwives, assisting with the birth of the sun god in his metallic and elemental form from the womb of the underworld. As we have seen in a previous chapter, the underworld and the over world (night ocean and day sky) of ancient Egypt were united in the single image of the goddess Nut, the container of the cycles of life, who gave birth to the sun each morning and devoured him in the evening.

In the nineteen sixties, the writer Ken Kesey remarked, "It is not by getting *out* of the world that we become enlightened, but by getting *into* the world." With the combing of the abdominal hair, an intrinsic or earthy intelligence is being affirmed: the bowels of our human nature are producing something enlightening, as opposed to an *extrinsic* intelligence associated with the higher brain. This gold, in braid or metallic form, is born from the organic feminine realm, from the mystery of life. Here we notice a parallel to the appearance of the Christ, "the Sun of Righteousness," who, it is believed, was conceived within a mortal woman's uterus and then born from her body in a cave with farm animals (theme of earthy origins associated with instincts).

He did not appear in the world as a supernaturalistic spirit or as a disembodied intellectual concept for the purpose of leading people *out* of the world. These examples point to a holistic, organic sense of living intelligently at home within our visceral emotions and impulses, rather than according to an abstract or airy ideal. In a televised interview with Bill Moyers, Joseph Campbell was asked about the significance of the Virgin Birth (more accurately the Virgin *Conception*) in the history of the beliefs and folklore of all traditions. Campbell replied, "It is the birth of a spiritual life of consciousness from out of the body of animal mankind."

The lesson here is that our mind and our spiritual outlook, whatever its ultimate origin, has its proximate source within our physical nature, within our mortal bodies, including our sensuous relation to the people, things, and environment of our terrestrial world. Far too many people today are mentally dissociated and isolated, in the sense that they live on an abstract plane of principles and ideologies. In this way, they lose touch with visceral feeling and emotion, as well as with their capacity for intimacy. When that occurs, the body goes one way and the mind another and the two do not meet. Figuratively speaking, such idealistic people are attempting to get *out* of the world, not *into* it! Ultimately, we belong here, feet on the ground, not somewhere else.

The location specified for the gold braid is at the level of the *solar plexus*. This is roughly associated with what we lay people call the "pit of the stomach." Anatomically, it consists of a dense region of interconnecting blood vessels and a thick interlaced network of nerve ganglia composing the autonomic or involuntary nervous system. Traditional nomenclature refers to this region as "solar," alluding to the celestial sun, because the pattern of this web of nerve fibers appears to radiate out from a common center like the rays of the sun. The word *plexus* literally means "braid" and is the source of our word "complex," meaning "braided with," and the verb "to plait," meaning "to weave or interlace." The word "braid" comes down to us from the Middle English word *breyden*—"snatch" or "plait"—and the Middle High German word *brettan*—"to draw, as with a sword"—which is behind our expression "to upbraid," to criticize severely. So it is obvious that this *plexus* is associated with sharply aggressive and judging tendencies in the human personality. Here is a solar capacity for bright discrimination and assertion that resides in the very center of our being; a kind of instinctive or innate intelligence; something that emerges from the very bowels of our human nature.

Because this braid of hair is blond—quite uncommon among Native Americans, whose hair is typically jet black—we must assume that this young woman is most unusual in the native culture. Later, we learn that she is a female shaman or medicine woman, whose spiritual power, or at least the evidence of it, which she has kept secret under her clothing, is linked directly to the sun. We are in intriguing territory as we realize such amazing similarities between Native American folklore and ancient medical and religious traditions on the opposite side of the world. Is this due primarily to the global migration of ideas, or does it also, in part, result from a mysterious tendency of the human nervous system to produce parallel mythic images, what Plato, Gregory of Nyssa, Irenaeus, Augustine, Philo of Alexandria, Sir Francis Bacon, Descartes, and Locke, and later the psychologist Jung, called "archetypal" motifs? This subject is controversial among anthropologists. No one has finally resolved the question of why the Ziggurat temples of

3000 BCE in Mesopotamia (Iraq) and the Mayan stepped pyramids of Guatemala and the Yucatan that date from 500 CE are so remarkably similar.

Blue Hawk's wife winds the braid five times around her body. The number five stands for quintessence, the ancient fifth and highest essence, the purest and most concentrated essence of anything, called *ether*, following the first four: fire, earth, air, and water. It was believed that this ethereal element permeated all of nature, in consequence giving material reality its spiritual significance. The archaic symbol for this five-fold scheme is the pyramid, resting upon four corners at the foundation with a single peak at the top uniting the four triangular sides with the base. In ancient Egypt, the pyramid was a symbol of the sun, expressing the power of its resurrection from the underworld, under whose aegis the divine pharaohs, as sun kings, were buried until their anticipated resurrection. The pyramid denotes the solar power emerging in the morning from the subterranean ocean world of the sun god's night-sea journey below the earth. An obelisk, like the Washington Monument, a symbol called an "earth phallus," is a variation on the pyramid symbolism and stands for the fertilizing power of the sun's dagger-like rays, the penetrating spirit of the Great Father in heaven that breaks out of the womb of the underworld each morning. Hence, every obelisk symbolizes a sunrise. The reverse side of our one dollar currency note displays this pyramid, depicting a radiating eye at the peak, standing for the falcon (a family of birds of which the hawk is a sub-group) eye of the Egyptian sun god Horus as he rules the world. Furthermore, there is a possible correspondence between the four base corners of the pyramid and the four limbs of the sky goddess Nut, whose hands and feet designate the four cardinal directions of terrestrial space.

J. N. H. Perkins

In the Kundalini Yoga symbolism of India, the level of conscious development or *chakra* associated with the solar plexus is called *Manipura*, which means "City of the Shining Jewel." This is the third of seven levels of ascent toward enlightenment. These seven chakras are located at a point mid-way between the anus and the genitals, the genitals, solar-plexus, heart, larynx, mid-forehead and top of the scull. *Manipura* emits fiery heat and light. It is displayed as a downward pointing triangle (one inverted face of a pyramid) colored red-orange, outlined in yellow, and expressing the power of the rising sun. This chakra stands for the supreme strength that may consume and master the world. Its energy is violent, the chakra of pure aggression and brilliant mastery. Achievement, conquest, and self-assurance are its attributes.

But there is a previous stage of development that comes before this third chakra, *Manipura*. That is *Svadhisththana*, the second charka, located at the level of the genitals. Insofar as Blue Hawk's wife is associated with the power chakra *Manipura*, she represents an advance over this prior stage of psycho-sexual development, which is the level at which Red Hawk is stuck. He is preoccupied with sex and sexual conquest. For him, everything revolves around getting into bed with a woman. There are many men today whose aspirations are limited to this particular focus. Sigmund Freud himself was very much preoccupied with this stage of development and viewed all the psychological transitions of human life in terms of sex. His associate, Alfred Adler, who later departed from the Freudian circle and formed his own school of psychology, moved up a notch and made *Manipura*, or power, the key to all human behavior. However it is very doubtful that either of these great thinkers had any awareness of Asian-Indian yogic symbols.

In our story, the volatile solar energy of *Manipura* appears from out of Blue Hawk's wife's abdomen! Blue Hawk's wife carries the significance of the sky goddess, who has the power to produce the violent energy of the sun from within herself, for this, we are told, is the source of the shamanic ability she displays later in the story. Here we have a most remarkable woman! In the manner in which we have explained above, she has the internal power of the sun, an inner resource that she may use for the well-being of her people.

Manipura is also the chakra of aggressive devouring—of conquering the world and turning it into one's own substance. In this way, Manipura is related to the symbolism of hunting, cooking, and eating. Many of our dreams that focus on cooking and eating are dealing with the psychological process of incorporation of what was first experienced as a projection onto external reality. All sacramental symbols in the world's religions that center on sacrificial and ceremonial eating stand for the incorporation into one's psyche of divine or transpersonal realities. This has the effect of enlarging and deepening the scope of the human personality, so that the higher powers are able to inspire us from *within the heart and the soul* rather than remaining outside simply as concrete external forces. On a higher, more insightful level, it is the all-consuming energy of the solar-plexus chakra *Manipura* that fuels this stage of self-collection and consolidation within the personality.

The following morning, when the old woman excused herself and returned home to feed her turkeys, Red Hawk was waiting and asked her what she had seen, and the woman reported everything. Red Hawk rode back to where Blue Hawk was preparing for battle and told him of how his wife looked without any clothes, and all

J. N. H. Perkins

about the long braid and the black mark. "There, now do you still believe that your wife is faithful to you?" Blue Hawk was silent. His head drooped. "A promise is a promise," teased Red Hawk.

Blue Hawk should have trusted his wife's good faith, no matter what evidence was provided. The question lingers, "But why didn't he?" That, I believe, is crucial to understanding this intriguing tale.

Blue Hawk didn't because he couldn't even *imagine* that his wife would cheat on him! If we can't even *imagine* something, then it means that we have no knowledge of those same tendencies within ourselves. The woman who is shocked to learn that her husband has been having an affair for years and insists that she never suspected anything was amiss, must have had her head in the sand. In the reverse situation, if a man can't possibly fathom his wife's erotic yearnings, then he probably isn't emotionally aware of her in the first place. In both instances, what is missing is the imagination of the trickster.

In our western symbolical tradition, the color blue is associated with heavenly purity and innocence, and red with earthiness, fire, and passion. We need to experience both sides of this spectrum, heaven and earth united into one, to live whole and fulfilling lives. In the region where this tale circulated, the American Southwest, the earth is quite red. The relatively cloudless sky typically is a vast expanse of radiant azure. The same polarities must have held true for these Native Americans. An individual needs to have a firm basis in earthy instinct in order to achieve a convincing and realistic spirituality. We are all composed of night and day, of the dark and enchanting mystery of physical emotion and impulse as well as the bright and clear light of reason.

In ancient Greece these capacities fell under the aegis of the gods Dionysus and Apollo respectively. We need to let go and to satisfy the itchy yearnings of life, yet at the same time set limits, make intelligent choices, exercise discipline, and keep our desires in order. Somewhere deep inside us, these conflicting energies meet in one point, and this is the paradoxical center of wholeness and holiness within the completely integrated human personality.

Red Hawk displays an impressive tactical ability that we imagine could be put to more productive use under other circumstances, and with a different attitude. Red Hawk is a little like an incorrigible computer hacker who is invading various internet sites so that valuable systems and databases are either compromised or destroyed. On this level he must be stopped. But think how much he could accomplish if employed as an innovator in a software design company! In the same way, a criminal has the potential to make an excellent detective, while an investigator with no criminal intuition is bound to fail. It strikes me that Blue Hawk is too naïve and innocent. He lacks the devilish cunning represented by Red Hawk. He is like the naive detective who has no criminal imagination. Such a cop will never crack a case. The successful cop can think like a criminal, and a successful criminal can think like a policeman. We must acknowledge both the good and the bad in ourselves if we are to reach health. It is not good to be only good!

Conventional behavior programmed by social conditioning is naïve and stupid. It is anything but moral. Behavior is only ethically commendable when an individual has the knowledge and the capability of committing a moral transgression. If one has no acquaintance with the impulse of dishonesty, thievery, trickery, or sexual licentiousness in

J. N. H. Perkins

oneself, or even the capacity to commit murder, then one's outward behavior is merely conventional, not moral. The desire, the means, and the opportunity to commit an infraction, but the conscious wisdom and self-control not to actually do it, are the chief hallmarks of true morality. We need not express everything literally to achieve wholeness, but we must know the good and the bad motives within ourselves. In this way, bad people must learn to be good, and good people must learn to be bad! The secret here is to understand the difference between conscious *being* and unconscious *behaving*, so that the dark side may be integrated rather than being acted out impulsively.

Red Hawk quickly discovers that Blue Hawk's wife is no easy prey. In native cultures there was more fidelity than we commonly believe, although polygamy was often practiced, with a man marrying his wife's sisters as well. Apache girls, for instance, were chaste before marriage. When children had finished puberty, they were usually married in a family arrangement that had important economic and social ramifications in the local tribe.[38] For example, arranged marriages allowed clan affiliations to remain intact. In many traditional cultures, carefully designated degrees of consanguinity defined eligible marriage candidates, i.e., one might marry a second or third cousin on the mother's side but not marry beyond a fourth within that bloodline. These highly ritualized social arrangements in a finely tuned network of structured kin relationships belie the modern assumption that primal peoples were blatantly promiscuous. Rather, their social structures and their rules of behavior reveal a high degree of cultural sophistication and practicality, devoted to the well-being and internal relations of the larger community. The supposed indiscriminate sexual
268

behavior of primal peoples is simply a racist projection of the white European man's repressed unconscious.

So Blue Hawk gave Red Hawk everything he had with him, and when they got back to the village, all the rest of his belongings. Blue Hawk's wife was alarmed by her husband's strange behavior and asked him why he was giving everything away, like people do when they are making funeral offerings. But Blue Hawk made no reply and went to work in silence, constructing a large rawhide trunk, in which he put money, food, and cooking gear. Finally, Blue Hawk spoke to his wife, saying, "We are going on a long trek to the great water. I have made this trunk for you to ride in so you will be protected from the sun." Blue Hawk asked his wife to put on her finest clothes and then he put her in the trunk.

Blue Hawk put the trunk on a cart, hitched the cart to his horses, and set forth. When they got to the first big river, Blue Hawk took the trunk out and threw it into the deep water. Then he went back to his village, but said nothing, even when people asked him where his wife was. But the chief, father of Blue Hawk's wife, was suspicious. So he dug a deep hole down into the underworld and arranged for his son-in-law to fall down into that hole.

On the surface, tossing the trunk containing his wife into the river might suggest a violent repression of Blue Hawk's feminine side. The fact that he put her in a trunk in her finest clothes together with food and cooking utensils suggests that he was preparing her for a traditional burial. His wife was aghast at his giving everything away, and likened this action to the rituals associated with a funeral. At this point, however, it is helpful to remember that all shamans, from Siberia to Alaska and throughout the Americas, practiced a ritualistic death and rebirth, a symbolic spiritual journey, often entering deep water to encounter

269

the "mother of the sea beasts"—an initiation rite for access to full spiritual empowerment.[39] Accordingly, one could say that Blue Hawk is his wife's unwitting shamanistic helper or enabler, as he sends her on her journey, fully equipped with food and cooking utensils. And, because she is carried in the rawhide trunk, contained and protected by animal skins (like Juliedah), her journey through the underworld is ensured. Identification with animal instinct is apparently helpful when powerful spirits are encountered, offering protection from the danger of psychological dissociation. The animal skins ground the wife in earthy nature so she is able to survive the tremendous ordeal.

There are a great many myths and fairy tale themes of the hero or heroine being put into a trunk or box that is then tossed into a large body of water. Chief among these is the Greek story of Perseus, whose mother Danae had been locked in a bronze prison by her father, King Akrisios, because it had been prophesied that she would give birth to a child who would kill his grandfather and seize the power of the realm. Through an open window, the god Zeus saw Danae and loved her, so in a golden shower (sunshine symbolism) he poured in and impregnated Danae, and she gave birth to the great Perseus, slayer of the Gorgon. When Akrisios learned of this, he had mother and grandchild put into a chest, which was then dumped into the sea. But instead of sinking, it drifted to another shore. There, mother and child were rescued, enabling the heroic adventures of Perseus to begin. In addition, there is the Biblical tale of the infant Moses, who was protected from hostile forces by being placed in a floating basket and hidden in the bulrushes along the Nile River. These are all completely standard hero themes.

We have already referred to the child of good fortune in the tale "The Devil's Three Golden Hairs." In that tale, before the episode with the robbers, the king placed the child in a box and threw him into the river, where he was finally caught in the weir (fish trap) of a mill and rescued by the miller and his wife. The child of good fortune eventually got the three golden hairs from the head of the sundevil and won the hand of the king's daughter. So, Blue Hawk, like the selfish king, is the unwitting helper of his wife's heroic success, and his wife bears interesting similarities to the Child of Good Fortune tale from the European folklore tradition.

These abandoned-in-a-box motifs are related to the renewal of the sun, in the cycle of the eternal return through the night-sea journey of the underworld. When a new transformative version of consciousness is in the wings, nothing can stop it from emerging, as it is destined to become the truth of a new age, both for the individual and for a major cultural epoch. The new life is like a fish that navigates easily in the spiritual regions surrounding our terrestrial consciousness—in the sky as the constellation Pisces—or in the nether regions as Leviathan, where the highest star formations sink below the earth each night before rising into the heavenly realm of brilliant day. Here the highest becomes the lowest and the lowest the highest in an eternally revolving cycle. Any individual or society who can acknowledge the paradoxical irony of this turning knows the secret of the mythic cosmos and is energized by it. Claiming and possessing the grandeur of the heights—as do the proud and paranoid kings of myth and folk tale—is inevitably a delusion, which is sure to founder as the cosmos revolves in its ever-recurring phases. The proud characters of myth and story, who reach for the sun without first walking through the underworld, are versions of the fall of Lucifer, who, after achieving the glorious heights, plummets catastrophically into the Sheol, the deep abyss of the dead below.

It is the same lesson over and over, repeated redundantly in all the tales of the world: One must pass through the shadow of death before one may rightly achieve enlightenment. In our own lives, we do this by not shying away from depression, alienation, and failure, as if something cosmic has gone wrong, but by acknowledging our darker moods and learning from them. Everything that happens to us in the journey of life, the good and the bad, the fair and the unfair, the successes and the failures, are there for an inscrutable reason, and each contributes to our integrity as human beings.

Meanwhile, a fisherman on the river hooked something heavy with his line and thought he had caught a huge fish. Drawing in his line, he was amazed to see the trunk, and pulled it out. When he opened it, he saw a very pretty girl, all dressed up, lying inside. He invited her to his camp, but before she agreed, she insisted that he switch clothes with her (Juliedah again). *When they got back to the fisherman's camp, his people were preparing for war. Blue Hawk's wife, now dressed as a warrior, joined the fighting men. On their journey, the other warriors noticed that their new young comrade had eyes like a woman and moved his body like a woman. One of them said, "Tonight I will be friendly and try to discover if he is really a man or a woman."*

Blue Hawk's wife had told the men that she was a medicine man, a shaman, and she requested that she be allowed to stay in a teepee set apart from the rest of the band. She said her medicine was the sun, which explained why she carried a white eagle feather. The young man who wanted to make friends came over and asked to sleep in her tent. In the night, the boy stayed awake and tried to get close to the medicine man, but she remained awake the whole time, and when he reached out to touch her, she said, "Don't do that!" Later he tried again, and she said abruptly, "Why don't you go to sleep!"

For the next few nights, each warrior, one after another, asked to sleep in her tent and tried to get close to her, but with the same result as the first, so that none of them succeeded in learning her secret. ("Vasilisa, the Priest's Daughter" again!) Finally, the warriors arrived in the enemy's land. Again, Blue Hawk's wife had her tent pitched separately from the others. She ordered them to stay inside their tents and be quiet, as it was time for her to perform a powerful medicine ritual. When all was still, Blue Hawk's wife spat great sun medicine in the direction of the enemy's camp. The result was that she single-handedly killed the whole enemy war party in one stroke. Then she came out of her tent and gave a war whoop, and all the rest of the men came out of their tents and gave their war whoops. Still disguised as the medicine man, she announced to the whole gathering, "I just fought a big battle and killed all of the enemy braves myself. Now I will find the dead and cut off their ears and scalps and take their shields, their bows and arrows, and their war clubs."

When Blue Hawk's wife returned with the scalps and ears and weapons, the grateful chief of the fisherman's tribe offered to have a young brave accompany her home to her own people. But she refused and insisted on going alone.

After she arrived at her own village where her father was chief, she took off her men's clothes, and there she stood, a very pretty young woman, the faithful wife of Blue Hawk, whom he had thrown into the river. "I alone, and single-handedly, killed all of your enemy," she announced to the entire village. "Here are their

273

scalps, ears, and weapons. They are yours!" Looking at her father, she said, "You shut up my husband in a dark pit because of the trick that Red Hawk played on him. He is innocent of any wrongdoing. Now bring him to me!"

Blue Hawk was brought up from the pit and stood before his faithful wife. His eyes were cast down, he was bent over, and he wore a painful expression on his thin and pale face. "You were beaten in the contest with Red Hawk because he made you think that he knew my body, but he deceived you. You know that I love you honestly and truly! Now go and get Red Hawk and that conniving old woman!"

Soon Blue Hawk and some of the braves returned with the two culprits, and brought them before the chief in the center of the gathering. Now the girl said to her father, "Have the men get the wildest ponies we have and bring them here." When the ponies arrived, she ordered them to tie Red Hawk's ankles to the tail of one pony and those of the old woman to the tail of the other one. Then the ponies were set lose and whipped. Off they dashed across the countryside, kicking and leaping and jumping wildly here and there, up and down the hills and careering over stones and rocks, so that Red Hawk and the old woman were torn to pieces far away from the camp, and nothing was left of them.

This tragi-comic tale ends with a remarkable display of cosmic strength and marital devotion on the part of Blue Hawk's wife, who is revealed to be the original American "Wonder Woman." By her presence and powers, the enemy tribe is beaten. None of the men lifted a finger!

Apparently, this shamanic ability is inherent in Mrs. Blue Hawk's nature, as evidenced by the peculiar braid of blond hair that emerges from the middle of her body. But she has kept this a secret, hidden beneath her clothing. Only the intrusion of the old woman has made it necessary for her to use this power, although even then, she performs her medicine magic while disguised as a man. Besides Blue Hawk, only the old woman and Red Hawk ever know of this strange blond braid. When they die under the heels of the wild ponies, their knowledge perishes with them, and Blue Hawk's wife's secret remains safe.

Secrets are very important psychologically. It is usually prudent to reveal painful or shameful secrets at an appropriate time to the right person in order not to suffer inordinate isolation. But there are many important secrets that we would do best to keep to ourselves, since they give us authenticity and individuality. Secrets are what belong to us and differentiate us from the common herd. Motormouths who gush all their secrets indiscriminately forfeit their souls. When something is secret, we know that it is powerfully important—too important and too precious to be dragged through the streets of commonplace conversation and gossip. There are certain things of which one may not speak, not out of embarrassment or guilt, but because the secret is too sublime to share with just anyone. A certain degree of privacy is the chastity or the *purdah* of the soul.

There are many Native American tales that involve a significant woman who has a name. Here, however, the name of Blue Hawk's wife is never mentioned. She performs her impressive medicine incognito, and while she is disguised in male clothing, no one knows who she is, with the exception of one man, namely the brave who pulled her trunk from the river with his fishing line. He clearly witnessed that she was a woman, agreed to switch clothing with her, and apparently took care not to reveal her sex to his comrades when they returned together to his encampment. This is a small detail but an important one.

Why didn't Blue Hawk's wife declare openly her shamanic role instead of disguising herself as a man? Because she sensed that, as a woman, her abilities would not be respected? This is doubtful as Native Americans were accustomed to medicine women, shamanesses, or female magicians of one sort or another, and valued their powers for the well-being of the larger community. It is important not to project backwards the bias of our own social milieu onto primal peoples whose lives and values are vastly different from our own. The Native American Indian did not operate from the perspective of European patriarchy, and resented the White Man's intrusion into his communal life and sacred traditions. Considering Blue Hawk's wife's previous experience of Red Hawk's trickery, which her shamanistic awareness had apparently already fathomed, her task was temporarily to shield herself from all erotic male influence. Adopting the male clothing has nothing directly to do with the intrinsic power of her medicine magic. We might think of the period when she dresses like a man as a period of insured chastity, an introverted form of sexual containment required for her deep meditation as she focuses her solar energy on the hostile tribe. One imagines that at the instant of her powerful medicine, Blue Hawk's wife is like the virgin mother-bride of the sun, incarnating and focusing this enormous cosmic power in order to defend her people. At this peak moment, she is partner to no earthly man, but is consorting with the heavenly powers as she becomes a converging lens for directing their colossal energy.

Now you might wonder, "All modern women certainly can't be Native American shamanesses or mothers of famous Greek heroes, so what possibly could be the relevance of this story nowadays?" The point we are making here is that women, and the feminine side of men, are powerful resources, serving as channels for the appearance in our world of a great new consciousness that is not the run-of-the-mill mentality typical of the standard patriarchal culture, but a creative awareness that can revolutionize the way we live our lives.

Helen, a very bright woman in her mid-fifties with seven children, was the daughter of an MIT research scientist. Once a student at Radcliffe, she left college to be married. Helen had recently lost her husband. She had the following dream:

I am in a house (not like my actual one) with a ground floor that is slightly recessed into the earth. It is nighttime and I check to see if all the windows and doors are locked. I feel that there is something ominous lurking outside, perhaps a wild animal. Just as I realize that I forgot to check the front door, I look up and am surprised to see it swing open, and then a huge lion comes walking slowly into the hallway. I retreat into the living room and the lion ambles in after me. He walks slowly over into a corner, lies down, and makes himself comfortable. I stand across the room looking at him. As his eyes meet mine, I start to realize that he is a friendly lion and will do me no harm.

Here is the sun-power in his animal incarnation as Leo the Lion, whose huge shaggy mane stands for the rays of light that stream from heaven. He comes to visit Helen in a peaceful manner because her feminine awareness is securely anchored in Mother Earth, i.e. the house of her consciousness is slightly below ground level. Leo arrives in the evening because that is the time of day when the great goddess has fully contained the volatile sun god and nurtures him in her tomb-womb. The lesson here for Helen, and for all of us, is that great brilliance, the intelligence that can really make a difference in the world, will appear in and through the feminine side of our lives if we are connected to down-to-earth instinct. With her nature so imbedded, Helen is able to benefit safely from, and wisely use, her powerful intellect without becoming intellectualistic or pedantic. The greater the intellectual or spiritual gift, the greater the humility (*humus*–earth) required! Albert Einstein, who once lived a few doors around the corner from our house here in Princeton, was once asked what sort of town this was. He replied, "A pleasant country village, populated, however, by far too many demagogues on stilts."

Psychologically, every partnered man or woman has one hidden dimension of himself or herself that refuses to be constrained by the bonds of marriage. This serves to protect and foster a creative erotic freedom that is limited neither by cultural norms nor by the spouse's "rights." Such an interiorized love that plumbs the imaginative depths of the soul is the foundation of every contemplative calling. Every one of us has this sense of vocation somewhere within the depths of our soul as part of our genius for living, even if we are not mystical hermits or spiritual recluses. The shamanic woman's inner and hidden dimension is her gold braid. Her relation to the power of the sun forms her inner cosmic marriage—her nuptial partnership to the vast energies of life. Such a woman—and this dimension lies within every woman and every man—must not be tampered with, for on this level she or he must remain a virgin even while outwardly partnered. Such a "virginity," however, is not anti-sex, but a continuing openness to a fresh, spirited experience of life within the soul. Once it arises here, it may then emerge to change the world.

In all traditional societies, this level of mystical encounter, sometimes referred to as the marriage of the soul with God, was and is the main focus of contemplative life. In a more poetic key, the phenomenon is wonderfully demonstrated in *A Portrait of the Artist as a Young Man,* by James Joyce, when, on Dublin's Sandymount Strand one afternoon, young Stephen Dedalus spied a shy girl alone on the beach and was completely transfixed: "A wild angel had appeared to him, the angel of mortal youth and beauty, an envoy from the fair courts of life." With the vision of that seabird maiden, skirts hiked up to her underpants as she waded innocently in the tidal rivulet, Stephen passed from death to life, and new creative energy surged powerfully in his veins. Because "she suffered his gaze without shame or wantonness," her arresting image passed directly into his soul, and he was able to leave her to herself, and at the same time to find *himself,* together with his life-long vocation as a creative artist.[40] Somewhere inside all of us we have such a wild angel—mortal and immortal at the same time—that may inspire us to amazing and unusual efforts. Joyce did not write this encounter merely as his own private memoir, but as the biography of everybody! "Here Comes Everybody" are the passwords to all his creative works, just as "Here Comes Everybody" is the key to all traditional stories about the human situation.

The predicament of Blue Hawk and his wife gives insight into how we can embrace wholeness, descending into the dark (our own private hell!) and then uniting it with the light, joining the lowest with the highest, our voracious,

J. N. H. Perkins

down-in-the-mud, earthy nature with the bright lucidity of spirit, thereby releasing fresh energy that will transform us, and by association, the greater society in which we live.

Endnotes

1   This retelling is based upon the original translation from the German by Margaret Hunt, as revised, corrected, and completed by James Stern, appearing in *The Complete Grimm's Fairy Tales* (New York: Pantheon Books, 1944; Random House, 1972). Introduction by Padraic Colum, Folkloristic commentary by Joseph Campbell, with 212 illustrations by Josef Scharl. This is tale number 53 of the total 210 tales. Of necessity, the text has been slightly modified to avoid copyright infringement, but nothing of vital importance has been changed, discarded, or bowdlerized.

2   ween, i.e. believe, hope; from Venus: love, charm.

3.   "And with the morn [morning] those angel faces smile, which I have loved long since and lost awhile." J. H. Newman, "The Pillar of the Cloud."

4.   ween, i.e. believe, hope; from Venus: love, charm.

5.   C. G. Jung to his students, passed down by word of mouth.

6.   The earliest kings were the bull-Moon-god *Nanna* incarnate, while their queen consorts were cow-Venus-goddesses. Courtly music was played on a magnificent, richly decorated lyre. A state-of-the-art instrument at the time, having been introduced in the late fourth

millennium BCE, this lyre was capped by the figure of a golden bull's head, from whose chin descended a blue lapis lazuli beard. The forehead sprouted lapis hair and, on either side, crescent shaped lapis-tipped gold horns representing the first and last phases of the moon cycle. While from the lady court minstrel's lyre flowed the celestial music of the spheres, we speculate that the royal couple reposed, resplendently, surrounded by an adoring noble court personifying the other planets and major stars. These celestial aristocrats were not considered to be human beings at all in the modern secular meaning of the term, but veritable gods on earth, vaguely like movie "stars" are adulated today, only infinitely more so. Their lives were considered eternal, extending beyond the finality of earthly death. A number of these artifacts from Sir Leonard Wooley's excavations may be viewed in the collections of the University of Pennsylvania's Museum of Archeology and Anthropology.

7. Joseph Campbell, *The Masks of God: Oriental Mythology* (New York: Viking Press, 1962) p. 44.

8. Luke 17:21 KJ.

9. John 1:5; 9.

10. Referring to the poem by T. S. Eliot.

11. Franz Werfel, *The Song of Bernadette* (New York: Viking Penguin, 1942) p. 146.

12. William Butler Yeats', "The Second Coming."

13. The gypsy coquette in Georges Bizet's opera *Carmen.*

14. Sir James Frazer, *The Golden Bough: Adonis, Attis, Osiris Vol. II* (New York: Macmillan/St. Martin's Press, 1966) pp. 6-8.

15. Frazer, V. p. 26.

16. Rainer Maria Rilke, "Orpheus, Euridyce, Hermes" in *Possibility of Being: A Selection of Poems by Rainer Maria Rilke*, tr. by J. B. Leishman (New Directions, 1977) p. 47.

17. Emily Bronte, *Wuthering Heights* (NY: Bantam Classic Edition, 1981) p. 153.

18. We see a variant of the imprisoned sun god in the Biblical tale about Samson and Delilah, recorded in the Book of Judges. The old Hebrew name for the sun is "shemesh," rendered in Phoenician or Aramaic as *Shimshon*, i.e. "man of the sun"–Samson. The Hebrew word for night, darkness, or evening is *lailah*, i.e. Delilah–"[One who] weakened, or uprooted, or impoverished." So within the Hebrew folktale of Samson and Delilah, we find hidden the same myth of the devouring of the masculine sun by the feminine powers of night.

19. A. K. Ramanujan, *Folktales From India* in the series *Pantheon Fairy Tale and Folklore Library* (NY: Pantheon Books, 1994).

20. Mk 10:31.

21. Eph 4:22-24.

22. Joseph Campbell, *The Mythic Image* (Princeton: Princeton University Press, 1974) p. 118.

23. Wolfram Eberhard, ed., *Folktales of China* (Chicago: U. of Chicago Press, 1965) p.156-161; note on tale #66: p. 235.

24. Inea Bushnaq, *Arab Folktales* (New York: Pantheon Books, 1986) pp. 193-200; Carter, Angela, *The Old Wives Fairy Tale Book* (New York: Pantheon Books, 1994) p. 39 ff.; Tatar, Maria, *The Classic Fairy Tales* (New York: Norton & Company, 1999) p. 131 ff.

25. For this ritual regulation, see the Bible, Leviticus, Ch. 15.

26. Joseph Campbell, *Oriental Mythology*, p. 111 ff.

27. James Henry Breasted, *A History of Egypt*, p. 59.

28. Ibid.

29. Aleksandr Afanas'ev, coll., *Russian Fairy Tales.* (NY: Pantheon Books, 1945; Random House, 1973) pp. 439-446.

30. Evgenii Trubetskoi, "Inoe Tsarstvo," *Literaturnaia Ucheba*, #2, 1990, pp. 114-117. Originally pub. 1923.

31. Genesis 22:1-14.

32. Alain Danielou, *Hindu Polytheism* (New York: Bollingen Series LXXIII, Pantheon Books, 1964) p. 271.

33. Ibid. p. 264.

34. Ibid. p. 268-9.

35. Ibid. p. 272.

36. E. A. Gait, "Human Sacrifice (Indian)" in James Hastings' *Encyclopaedia of Religion and Ethics*, Vol. VI, pp. 849-853.

37. Richard Erdoes and Alfonso Ortiz, eds., *American Indian Myths and Legends* (New York: Pantheon Books, 1984) pp. 315-318. Franz Boas characterized Elsie Clews Parsons's books on Pueblo religion as a collection of "all we know" about the subject. Before retiring to do private research, Dr. Parsons taught at Barnard College and Columbia University.

38. Hastings, Vol. 1, p. 601.

39. Mircea Iliade, *Shamanism*. (New York: Pantheon Books, Bollingen Series LXXVI, 1964) pp. 288 ff.

40. Joyce, *Portrait of the Artist as a Young Man*, pp. 169-172.

www.ingramcontent.com/pod-product-compliance
Lightning Source LLC
Chambersburg PA
CBHW030251290526
45785CB00001B/48

9781480042452